Reviews for

This fascinating and delightful ac
of a distinguished British diploma
Middle East and Africa, it involves a ñost of
prominent international personalities, as well as Cold War spies and
the Gulf War of 1991 where Munro exposes the diplomatic
management of war. And all this with a light humour while giving a
perceptive analysis of British policy in a post-imperial world. Never
imagine a diplomat's life to be dull and just partying.

Keep The Flag Flying is a compulsive read indeed - with added
humour, drama and deft political judgment.

– General Peter de la Billière

It's been half a century since Lawrence Durrell entertained us with
Esprit de Corps and his humorous vignettes of diplomatic life. Now
Keep the Flag Flying joins the elite band of Foreign Office memoirs
that illuminate the world while making you laugh out loud. Alan
Munro is funny, but warm and compassionate as well. He has written
a fluent, limpid and thoroughly engaging account of a career – of an
entire world, indeed – that is packed with wisdom and humanity,
along with its share of folly and sadness. Keep the Flag Flying is the
perfect companion for every traveller – and especially for those who
like to travel in the comfort of their own armchair.

– Robert Lacey

This refreshingly down-to-earth and often funny volume… manages
the rare feat of also being very insightful… These memoirs, mostly
focused on the Middle East, will also appeal to those with a general
interest in British foreign policy… .a warm and engaging read."

– Royal United Services Institute Journal

KEEP THE
FLAG
FLYING

Luetka

KEEP THE FLAG FLYING

A DIPLOMATIC MEMOIR

Alan Munro

G

GILGAMESH
PUBLISHING LTD

Keep the Flag Flying

Published by Gilgamesh Publishing in 2012
Email: info@gilgamesh-publishing.co.uk
www.gilgamesh-publishing.co.uk

ISBN 978-1-908531-15-5

2 4 6 8 0 9 7 5 3

CIP Data: A catalogue for this book is
available from the British Library

*Dedicated with respect and affection to
le Corps Diplomatique*

Books by the same author:

Arab Storm:
Politics and Diplomacy Behind The Gulf War

An Arabian Affair:
Gulf War from Saudi Arabia

TABLE OF CONTENTS

Author's Acknowledgements

A walk along memory's long lane cannot be undertaken alone. There need to be companions to help refresh the ineluctable distortions in recollections of events and scenery encountered along the way. Among the many who come to mind here I am particularly grateful for the contributions in the shape of anecdotes and prompts from Dick Beeston, Patrick Wright, John Graham, Peter and Liz Davies, Derek Plumbly, Prince Abdullah bin Faisal bin Turki, Teymour Ali Reza, George Asseily, Mark Scrase-Dickens, Keith Middlemas, Rosemary Foxcroft, Malcolm Davidson, David Sulzberger, Clive and Ann Smith, Kenneth Pridham, Marcus Beresford, Peter and Felicity Wakefield, and Nick Cocking. Numerous friends and colleagues across the Arab world and further afield also have their welcome part in the story.

I am grateful to Tessa Blackburn for permission to quote a passage from the poem 'Medina' by her husband, Raymond Blackburn MP, as well as to Terry Griffiths for his helpful advice on jacket design, and to Keith Levett of the Savile Row tailors, Henry Poole, for having come up with an ambassadorial dress hat complete with ostrich plumes. Max Scott and Charles Powell of Gilgamesh deserve warm thanks for their efficient, and flexible, role in bringing the book to publication.

My own family have been a constant source of enlightenment and encouragement. My deepest fund of gratitude goes to Grania without whose lively recollections of the adventures and adversities we have shared along diplomacy's eventful trail this memoir would never have surfaced.

Alan Munro

Introduction

A system of indoor relief for the aristocracy

Jeremy Bentham

The profession of diplomacy has an uneven image in the public eye; frequently caricatured as stuffy individuals, mannered and sybaritic in their lifestyle, steeped in etiquette and devious with words, an anachronism in the contemporary world of integrated global intercourse and instant communication. Here is a meretricious myth of long standing, readily preserved to the benefit of a frivolous media and entertainment industry. The Carlton-Browne image does an injustice to a highly motivated Service. It is however too deeply entrenched to dispel.

Yet without a sensitive interface and dialogue between states, and skilled negotiators to engage with the points where national interests conflict and work for agreement on crucial areas involving security, law and trade, even war and peace, our world would become a more brutish place. With a new century, new issues of global concern – environment, resource distribution, migration and regional inequalities, to say nothing of the menace of international terrorism – are calling for the attention of diplomacy. Styles are changing and the apparatus of protocol too, while advances in technology have accelerated the process of communication. But the challenges to international cooperation and harmony are as acute as ever; diplomacy has certainly not had its day.

Four centuries of international engagement have endowed the United Kingdom with a major role in world events and a sense of responsibility for their consequences which goes well beyond this country's size or strength. For all Britain's retreat from empire its embers continue to absorb

9

her into a network of influence and interests, combined with an inherited sense of moral purpose. The sometimes turbulent disbandment of a global colonial system has yielded a Commonwealth family with a strong heritage of political, cultural and economic association for which Britain serves as the hub, and which continues to imbue our diplomacy with an ongoing involvement. In particular regions such as the Middle East and Africa, both of which feature prominently in the present narrative, the legacies of imperial history, together with the dynamics of nearly fifty antagonistic, though now concluded, years of Cold War competition, have continued to frustrate periodic attempts by this country to draw in its horns and withdraw from intractable disputes that confound the international horizon.

Moreover this prominent role on the world's stage is widely accepted, indeed encouraged; many states within the world community continue to look to Britain to "box above her weight", whether it be in the intricate pursuit of conflict resolution and international development through the United Nations and other political and economic institutions, or over proliferating challenges to global security and to the environment. This is particularly so in the present era of uneasy adjustment to a world in which the impact of American power predominates, and is often resented. The skill and the experience of Britain's diplomats are essential assets in underpinning this precious eminence.

A diplomatic career is a demanding one, both for officials and their families, as they migrate between foreign postings – some congenial, others arduous and occasionally dangerous. The constant attempt to reconcile the national interest with principle requires objectivity to be tempered by versatility, and calls for stamina too, particularly under the relentless pressures of policy formulation, interaction with political masters, parliamentary business and periodic crisis management within the Whitehall bear pit. E-mail and the personal computer may have displaced the clatter of encrypted Morse telegrams and the hissing of Lamson tubes as the vehicles of swift communication, but shoe leather is still worn out in navigating the labyrinth of corridors within the Foreign Office's elegant pile. Despite a national employment environment of ever-widening opportunity and where priority tends to be given to financial reward in place of public service, the career continues to hold an attraction for those whose perspectives extend beyond their national frontiers.

In the decades following the Second World War it could be said that the Diplomatic Service had an undue proportion of national talent locked up within it. There was force in this argument; a stable of racehorses some of which are pulling milk floats, as one member put it. The situation, in part the consequence of bulk intakes to an overstaffed service in the immediate post-war years, led to frustration over promotion blockages and an excess of bureaucracy as reports and recommendations were passed along a chain where each link sought to adjust an emphasis here or embellish a point of syntax there. It was moreover a period of national impoverishment in which a sparkling theatrical company found itself endeavouring to play its long-established roles with threadbare props and costumes, until the 1980s saw decline checked with a welcome recovery of national self-assurance and a new wardrobe. Yet the final product could be sure to set a high standard in both substance and style, an advantage which today's much slimmed down Service cannot always guarantee.

Among the most distinctive, and also rewarding, features of the diplomatic profession are variety and comradeship. It affords an incomparable opportunity to gain insights into, and often affection for, other countries and to interact with fellow beings of all shapes and shades. Itinerancy is blended with a generous array of roles and responsibilities – political, commercial, consular, managerial, cultural, humanitarian, thespian, even the occasional foray into espionage – the list is infinite. Advocacy has to combine with analysis, engagement with detachment. In traditional British fashion specialisation is leavened with respect for all-round experience. Out of all this medley however comes also a store of adventures, some quaint, some tender, others more grave, bizarre or plain absurd; and this is where a sense of humour comes in handy.

The narrative is set within a half-century of post-imperial adjustment in Britain's foreign policy – a time during which her diplomatic outreach would no longer be buttressed by garrisons and gunboats, nor her manufacturers and trading houses be household names around the markets of the world. The nation's security would henceforward need to be pursued through multilateral organisations and alliances and her economic prosperity through multinational enterprises as an imperial identity was reset upon a European axis. Yet this withdrawal from a global role was complicated by an overriding concern, shared with western partners, to counter the extension – political and economic as well as military – of Soviet Marxist ascendancy across a fractious post-colonial world.

This book is intended to convey something of the flavour – and the frivolities – of escapades and encounters which have come the way of my wife and me in the course of thirty-five years in diplomacy, in the Middle East, Africa and South America, and at home too. It is no purpose of mine to denigrate or burlesque any individuals who appear in its pages. My hope is to entertain and so bring out the human side, as well as the value, of a profession in which "life's rich tapestry" plays an uncommonly prominent part.

Shemlan, Lebanon
1958-1960

The Arabs are always young; it is the only race that never withers

Benjamin Disraeli, *Tancred*

T he Viscount of British European Airways hops its way across Europe as far as Beirut. My first taste of the Arab world is the brilliant October sunlight of a Lebanese autumn, on a narrow coastal strip lined with a spectacular backdrop of a towering mountain range, the Levant's awesome barrier to the desert lands beyond. It is in this Arcadian scene that I shall be spending the next fifteen months in an intensive effort to master the complexities of the Arabic language.

Yet the airport is full of military transport planes, American at that, embarking troops in full battle gear. From now on, American and British boots on the ground are to be an inescapable accompaniment to my Middle East career. A palpable tension prevails behind Lebanon's traditional façade of enterprise and entertainment. The US marines who greet my arrival had landed across Beirut's delectable beaches in the heat of high summer to shore up the pro-western yet discredited government of President Camille Chamoun as the country goes through another of its periodic bouts of Muslim-Christian intercommunal strife. This is a reflection of the infectious wave of pan-Arab nationalism inspired by the army-led revolutions of the charismatic Gamal Abdel Nasser in Egypt, and followed this very summer by an army coup headed by the regicide Abdul Karim Qasim in Iraq. In the event Beirut's seaborne "invasion" had turned into a glorious anticlimax as bikini-clad bathers leapt into the waves to help the burdened troops ashore.

13

British paratroops were meanwhile being called on to undertake a similar stabilising role in next door Jordan.

I am quickly on my way up the mountain face by a tortuous road to the village of Shemlan, a Maronite Christian community set some three thousand feet high in the imposing mountains of the Shuf amid terraced apple orchards and other villages, some Sunni or Shi'a Muslim, others with members of the schismatic Druze sect; a cross-section of Lebanon's sectarian chequerboard. This is the location of the Middle East Centre for Arabic Studies, or MECAS as it is known, the Arabic language school run by the Foreign Office and regularly attacked in Egypt's hostile broadcasts as the "school for spies". Hastily evacuated during the sectarian crossfire of the summer's troubles, its interrupted studies have just resumed. The setting is idyllic, if primitive, with only the occasional raucous bray of a working donkey to breach the torpid murmur of village life. Apples and olives are cultivated along narrow terraces that cling precariously to the rocky hillsides. A new custom-built academy is nearing completion up above the village; meanwhile we live and study in what had been a 19th-century silkworm factory. The early dusk means deciphering fine Arabic print by the glare of a mantled Tilley lamp for lack of reliable electric power, hot water involves lighting an ancient wood-burning boiler, the frosts and occasional mountain snows of winter are held at bay with smoky paraffin heaters, and the climb up the lane to the centre of the village and its Cliff House café for a stiff glass of arak and a hubble bubble pipe involves a steep gradient of at least 60 degrees. There is ample compensation however in the buildings' graceful arches and balconies from which to enjoy the soft mountain air of the summer months, the night-time panorama of Beirut's seductive and sinful lights that beckon far below, and the beauty of Lebanon's natural and historic treasures, classical and Islamic, cedars, caverns and castles, plus a gourmet's cuisine, all within a spectacular drive. It is tempting to put aside the interminable vocabulary lists and the Rev. Thatcher's classic grammar with its arcane explanations of the "broken plural" and the nine ascending forms of Arabic verbs. But we are kept hard at the grindstone. It all comes as a shock after the gentle routine and the diversions of study in Cambridge.

That it is time to be off is, however, brought home sharply a few days before my departure. Returning from a farewell visit to my grandmother I manage to run into the back of another car on a wet country road. Someone has reported the accident and a police car soon appears. Taking one look at me in the gathering dusk, the young patrolman says, "You were at Clare College, Cambridge." "How on earth do you know that?" "Well," he goes on, understandably enjoying my astonishment, "I was playing cricket in Cambridge last summer for the Sussex Police. After the game we were taken on a tour round some of the colleges. We were just passing the gate of what we were told was Clare when you came through it." "But have I the look of a felon, officer, that you recall me so clearly now that we meet miles away on a Sussex lane?" "Not at all. But I never forget a face!" Bravo the Sussex Constabulary; England is clearly getting too hot for me.

* * * * *

My despatch to Lebanon has been preceded by a rapid and bewildering introduction to the Foreign Office in Whitehall. Having succeeded at a second attempt to pass the entry competition for the Diplomatic Service (a mental inability to do basic arithmetic scuppered the first go), I have joined later than the year's main intake, commissioned into the humble rank of Third Secretary and on a none too bounteous salary of £700 a year. There had been one false start already. In early summer I had received out of the blue an invitation on Foreign Office paper to come for an interview. I duly turned up at an anonymous address in Carlton House Terrace where an equally anonymous personage probed me on my approach to life and offered me a trainee position. Surprised by this short cut it occurred to me that we might be at cross purposes. And so it turned out. Finding that I was already going through the standard recruitment process my interviewer excused the confusion and explained that he represented the "other side" of the diplomatic apparatus. When I enquired out of curiosity how their "cloak and dagger" talent spotters had found me he replied with a conspiratorial air that my name had been mentioned "on the platform at Balcombe railway station" – goodness knows why. Ever since then each time I take the Brighton line I look out as the train whirls through Balcombe, deep in the Sussex Weald, for two figures in dark overcoats and bowler hats pointing in my direction.

Most new entrants are required to undertake study in a "hard" language, Asian, African or East European. I have had my eye on Russian studies with a view to specialising in relations with a combative Soviet Union, seeking to extend a global hegemony from behind the Iron Curtain that has divided post-war Europe. But this is not to be. Language places have already been allocated – Slavic, Chinese, Japanese, Finnish, Farsi, Thai, Burmese, Amharic – you name it. One of the largest quotas is reserved for Arabic, in order to staff the priority which relations with the Arab world continue to be accorded in the scheme of British diplomacy. So it is that I find myself drafted into the "Camel Corps". Foreign Office lore has it that Arabic is bound to ensure a posting to Iceland, but as things turn out I have had no reason for regret; the pattern of history which continues to link Britain so closely with the turbulent Middle East has ensured an absorbing engagement with this region, its politics, peoples and their cultures to an extent that would not have been the case had I been set to chipping away at the apparently impregnable armour of the Soviet bloc.

A whirlwind couple of days within the rambling and grimy edifice which houses the Foreign Office and old India Office are all that can be spared to acquaint me with its highly geared systems. There are fleeting recollections of the elegant but dilapidated Durbar Court and Locarno Room, today the setting for splendid receptions but then filled with wartime huts and cubicles where countless fingers and pencils encrypted and decrypted cipher messages in what must have been soul-destroying monotony, of the locksmiths up in their tower who seek to explain the intricacies of manifoil combinations – "Wouldn't fit it on a rabbit hutch, squire" – and the Divisions deep in the capacious attics where young clerks supply the operating departments below with docketed papers – no compendious files then. As for an introduction to the transaction of diplomatic business itself there appears to be no time for that before I am off to Beirut. It will all have to be absorbed by trial and error later on.

* * * * *

The mysteries of protocol bulk large in the new entrant's induction. These are illuminated in a formidable booklet with the awesome title of "Guidance on foreign usages and ceremony, and other matters, for a Member of His Majesty's Foreign Service on his first appointment to a Post Abroad", the work of Sir Marcus Cheke, a former ambassador to the Vatican and Vice-Marshal of the Diplomatic Corps in London, and one of the last remnants of the "old school".

Written in the era of exclusively male officers it contains an intimidating and archaic litany of the do's and don'ts of diplomatic etiquette, ranging from the deferential through the condescending to the plain priggish. The narrative is set in a fictitious British embassy under the leadership of Sir Henry Sealingwax to which the new recruit, Mr John Bull, with his young wife, has been appointed as Third Secretary, the most humble of ranks and now suddenly a person of standing; the author compares this transformation to Hilaire Belloc's Lord Lucky who "rose in half an hour to riches, dignity and power". Among its gems are instructions on how to address your ambassador and his lady, how to observe the right pecking order within the local corps, the significance of presenting your visiting card with the correct corner turned down, how to introduce your wife in company, the intricacies of *placement* at your dinner table, how to avoid the inevitable bores in the local British "colony", whom to cultivate in local society, even when to tip your hat in a lift…. For some reason Sir Marcus is particularly disdainful of the ceremonious etiquette of Latins and Swedes. Back in those days of formal courtesies we feel compelled to read and mark these arcane injunctions, albeit with a subversive health warning that "one Cheke is stupid enough; if there were two Chekes we'd have a complete arse."

* * * * *

Meanwhile high on Mount Lebanon our heads are kept well down to the mastering of the art of writing from right to left and in a new alphabet. Considerable time is spent in front of the mirror attempting to articulate the unique Arabic consonant *'ain*, which is said to derive from the groan of a camel in distress and involves awkward constriction of the throat muscles, often in mid-word. Gradually the richness of the language with its logical edifice of word development from basic verbal roots begins to unravel its own mystery; decryption of the sophisticated grammar is not helped by the absence of vowels, though it is some relief to find a tongue in which no rule is ever broken. Variations in regional dialects stretching from Morocco to Iraq will come later; for now the standard literary form has to be absorbed. This remarkable *lingua franca*, a legacy of some fifteen centuries of political and religious history and still familiar alongside the vernacular of any bazaar, provides the Arab peoples with an invaluable foundation for their powerful sense of shared identity – rather as Latin served to bind educated circles across mediaeval Europe.

There is time however to explore Lebanon's fascinating byways, and across the border in Syria too where an uneasy political union with the revolutionary Egypt of Gamal Abdel Nasser has recently been forged. With a friend from Cambridge days, Julian Lush, who is on the language course, we make visits to the towering Roman ruins of Baalbek in the high Beqaa valley beyond the Lebanon range, to magnificent Crusader and Saracen castles and handsome oriental palaces, sometimes finding ourselves as we drive seduced by the rhetoric, delivered in hauntingly rhythmic Arabic, of Gamal Abdel Nasser's polemical radio broadcasts to his bewitched Arab audience. There are forays as far as Damascus with its great mosque and labyrinth of souks, Hama on the Orontes with its creaking waterwheels, north into Turkish Antioch and south through Jordan to a spiritually evocative yet, after three millennia of bloodstained history, still poisonously divided Jerusalem, and on through the desert to Petra, its rediscovered splendours immortalised in the verse of John William Burgon a century earlier:

> Match me such marvel save in eastern clime,
> A rose-red city, half as old as time.

With the local village carpenter I go on pigeon shooting forays in the fertile Beqaa valley behind the high Lebanon range, though his bag turns out to consist mainly of sparrows, a Lebanese delicacy; it is an idyllic spot hemmed in by snow-crested mountains to either side and where terrapins lie in the spring sunlight along the banks of rippling streams. There is good wine to be tasted in the Beqaa vineyards and grilled fowl with arak to follow at Zahle, and weekend skiing high up at the famous cedars of Becharreh, crucible of the mystical poetry of Khalil Gibran. Yet as ever in Lebanon mishaps are a part of life, even on the ski slopes. On one crowded weekend two mountain clans take it into their heads to pursue an ancient feud with a shoot out and choose the beginners' hill for their *battue*. Some luckless tyros, having not yet learnt how to stop, sail on into a hail of crossfire...

Above all there is the distracting allure of Beirut with its welter of elegance and squalor, of Christian and Muslim cultures rubbing along together in a haphazard dialect of French and Arabic, of cafes, nightclubs and rattling trams. It is a bit of a honeypot for us students as we find ways to make our funds stretch around the city's attractions. A stylish restaurant on the seafront, Lucullus, offers a marvellous version of the traditional

Lebanese *mezze* hors d'oeuvre, so ample that it will carry us through the next week of isolation in Shemlan. We tuck in to the array of dishes and then are mysteriously called away from the table before taking the rest of the menu. A shared taxi service runs up and down the mountain to the city, far more rapid than the antiquated mountain railway built in Ottoman times with its optimistic name of the Damas, Homs et Prolongements. We squeeze into the battered Mercedes between grave Druze elders, white cloths wound around their red tarboosh hats. Once discovered to be British they set to nudging us while rubbing their two index fingers together in conspiratorial fashion with a refrain of "very good – eighteen-sixty". This cabalistic date turns out to refer to a major sectarian conflict in Lebanon, when, in the face of a massacre of Maronite Christians by the Druzes, France intervened to protect the former. This prompted Lord Palmerston to send a British fleet to see off the French, whereupon the grateful Druzes resumed their pogrom. This dubious debt to Britain is still being acknowledged by our fellow taxi riders. Indeed the ancestral hall of their chiefs, the Jumblatt dynasty, at Mukhtara deep in the mountains is bordered with a painted fresco of the reputed engagement when the Royal Navy chased away the French from Lebanon's coast.

* * * * *

With the Christmas of 1958 bringing a short break from study, a fellow student, Bill Norton, suggests a visit to Turkey. Bill has already had an adventurous experience during the previous summer when in the midst of Lebanon's political upheaval he chose to go birdwatching in the northern hills near Syria's meandering border. Inevitably he strayed across the frontier and fell into the hands of villagers who, understandably suspicious at finding an Englishman armed with binoculars, were about to apply their own summary justice when a posse of Lebanese came by and rescued him from a probable lynching. On reflection it was a madcap idea of ours to head for the freezing Anatolian plateau in midwinter. In the event fate takes a hand; the Turkish Airlines flight to Adana fails to materialise for several days, during which I go down with an attack of what turns out to be jaundice. My initial encounter with the Shemlan doctor is however less than encouraging, consisting of a summary consultation in my beginner's Arabic and a prescription for quantities of sweet fizzy Seven-Up. On leaving his clinic I notice that the framed certificate, proudly displayed on his wall for the edification of patients, is a diploma, issued by some American academy, for proficiency in playing the mandolin. Turning more unwell and yellow by the day a Greek doctor down in Beirut finally hits on hepatitis and packs me off for a prolonged stay in the hospital attached to the renowned American University of Beirut.

I start off in a ward with five Lebanese men, each with some brand of infectious illness. Here is a real immersion into local Arab society such as our isolated situation up at the school struggles to provide. Come evening, one of them tells me, in a precise English, that he is accustomed to telling the others a story each night. Tonight he will relate Sir Walter Scott's *Ivanhoe,* with which he hopes I am sufficiently familiar to follow his account in Arabic. I try to recapture a sketchy recollection of a romantic plot involving Crusader knights and an exotic Jewess in the days of King Richard Coeur de Lion, possibly a controversial tale to choose when local opinion is roused over the current fate of Palestine. Once on our way I soon find myself lost, while his audience listens with rapt attention. For here is an example of the great storytelling tradition that has flourished for centuries across the Arab world until supplanted by the visual narrative of the cinema. Three hours later we reach a drowsy midnight and the story still unfolds while the narrator shows no sign of flagging. It is a *tour de force* which would have earned the admiration of Sir Walter. Fortunately for me however I am moved the next day into private isolation and thus spared the full chronicle of the Waverley novels.

* * * * *

With the rudiments of literary Arabic after eight months of intensive study more or less etched into the brain, May is set aside for a month of travel in order to acquire facility with the spoken tongue. I opt to try my luck in Jordan where the youthful King Hussein has succeeded in stabilising his authority in the face of Egyptian-initiated attempts at nationalist subversion. The country still shows considerable British influence, not least in its army, the Arab Legion, until recently commanded by General Glubb Pasha. I duly fall on my feet when the British Defence Attaché, Col. Nigel Bromage, himself a former Legion officer and subsequently an influential figure in Saudi Arabia's National Guard, suggests that I undertake a survey in the southern desert of bedouin groups of the Howeitat tribe who are victims of a serious winter drought and should be beneficiaries of a proposed food relief programme. I can base myself on the town of Ma'an in the vicinity of Petra. This is an opportunity not to be missed. Armed with a pile of military maps of the desert area and an Arab Legion Land Rover plus driver, Mohammed, I set off for the deserts and mountains of the far south.

Ma'an is a poor place of mud-brick houses with bedouin encamped around. Its most imposing building is the station, a lone outpost of the old Hejaz railway, constructed in the last days of Ottoman Turkish rule before the First World War by German engineers to transport pilgrims southwards from Damascus to Medina and Mecca, as well as to facilitate the garrisoning of Turkey's fragile authority over western Arabia. This is the line of rail that was to gain wide fame through the sabotage exploits of Col. T.E.Lawrence of Arabia and his colleagues, when they joined the tribal army formed with British encouragement by the Hashemite Sharif of Mecca in 1917 to drive the Turks out of Arabia right up to Damascus, the beginning of the "Arab Revolt". Beside the station stands the dilapidated Petra Hotel, another relic of Ottoman times, with a handful of dust-filled rooms, one porous bathroom and an inedible menu. Its proprietor too is a former soldier of Jemal Pasha's Turkish army; all in all an ineffable time warp. From my window in the early morning I see the daily train, hauled by a huge steam locomotive, rumble off on its slow eight-hour run to Amman.

Mohammed and I are soon off into the scrubby wilderness in search of bedouin encampments. Mercifully he knows the lie of this land, as my map-reading skills, learnt on the north German plain during military service, are little use in this featureless environment. There follows a period of memorable experiences, with nights under goat-hair tents with a hospitable, yet ill-affordable for our hosts, feast of rice and young kid (eyes and certain other organs reserved for the guests) while the old men relate tales of raids and excursions led by their warrior sheikh, Auda Abu Tayyi, and of Lawrence too. In the bedouin tradition a young man is deputed to serve as my companion. When, no doubt by design, I end up for the night lying against the cloth partition that divides the women from the men in the large tent, I wake from time to time to find curious fingers prodding me through the screen to the accompaniment of stifled feminine giggles. Perforce my spoken Arabic improves by the day, though the guttural bedouin accent is a handicap.

At one point we are marooned in an encampment for a couple of days by a ferocious sandstorm, the stinging grains of which make it impossible to see landmarks. Another time a shock absorber breaks on the Land Rover with a loud crack as we negotiate a dry and rocky stream bed in the middle of nowhere. What to do? Mohammed is unperturbed. "We go to *warsha*," he says, using an Arabic word that I am quite unable to find in my pocket dictionary. Still he seems to know what he is doing. We bump along for a stifling hour until, approaching a small hill, there are the traces of a track and then whitewashed stones along its verges. "*Warsha, warsha!*" Mohammed exclaims, and lo and behold we turn a corner to find a wooden arch and a brightly painted sign saying "Command Workshop, Electrical and Mechanical Engineers". A mirage surely... but no. A smart sergeant meets us at the gate and on hearing our problem invites me to take tea with the officers in their mess while the shock absorber is replaced. After an agreeable hour comparing notes on military life with the Jordanian officers the sergeant reappears to say that car and driver await. With warm salutations Mohammed and I return to the desert. "*Warsha*," says Mohammed with calm satisfaction, and then the penny drops. The magic word is not Arabic at all, but a corruption of the British army word for a REME workshop. And what a miracle to find it in that wilderness.

A couple of nights are spent in the isolated police fort on the desert floor of the Wadi Rum, a spectacular valley enclosed on each side by high outcrops of deep red sandstone. It will soon afterwards become a memorable location for the film *Lawrence of Arabia*, but back in 1959 it has yet to feature on the tourist trail. Water is drawn from the fort's well by a ragged and intimidating figure with long dreadlocks; the police sergeant reassures me with the news that he is serving out a sentence for murder. We accompany the morning camel patrol to visit a group of Howeitat bedouin camped further down the *wadi*. Their food stocks are almost exhausted.

Back in Ma'an the food convoy has arrived with precious sacks of flour and rice. It is organised by a dedicated group of young American and Palestinian volunteers, members of the ultra-Protestant Mennonite sect, who appear to be strictly vegetarian to the point where they even foreswear the use of bone buttons on their garments. We put together a scheme for distribution through police posts across the region I have been surveying. Some jostling occurs as the tribespeople assemble; at one point I am summoned before the governor of Ma'an province in a dispute over distribution. But there is nothing like a strong trestle table and chair for the assertion of authority in a clamorous situation (a tip I would be giving to our daughter Joanna forty years on when she is to run a relief operation for Care International in war-torn Sierra Leone). I also have to learn not to express too much admiration for any object, lest it be promptly offloaded onto me in accord with the bedouin code of etiquette. At one point I am presented with a handsome Arab stallion which I had taken for a ride. It is no easy task to return the beast without causing loss of face to its over-generous bedouin owner.

It is time however to return to school in Lebanon. One last drama arises on the eve of my departure on the train for Amman. The ancient hotel proprietor comes in a perturbed state and waving a telegram. It is in English, sent from Thomas Cook's agency in Frankfurt, to inform the Petra Hotel at Ma'an that the Graf and Gräfin von Windisch-Grätz wish to reserve a room for a couple of nights in order to visit Petra in the course of their honeymoon. They will be arriving by ship at Aqaba, Jordan's Red Sea port, and request that a "motor" be sent to meet them. This is indeed something from another era. The high days when Thomas Cook first introduced his overland tours to Petra are way in the past. It is hard to imagine how such scions of the former Austro-Hungarian nobility could survive even one night in the primitive conditions of the Petra Hotel. The Turkish proprietor is of the same uneasy mind, so we draft a polite reply regretting that the hotel has no rooms to spare on the nights in question. I depart on the desert train for Amman next day with a clear conscience.

* * * * *

The bedouin experience has done good things for my Arabic, but there are still eight tough months of study ahead to pass the interpretership examinations. There is time however to enjoy Lebanese friendships along with Beirut's bright lights, though a romantic attachment has started to distract me from study, resulting in my being brought up short by our well-respected headmaster, Donald Maitland. The affair is destined to meet a painful ending. One unwelcome legacy of my bedouin hosts' cuisine will stay with me for months ahead, involving treatment with quantities of kaolin powder and an eventual sojourn in London's renowned Hospital for Tropical Diseases. A particularly tedious consequence of the medication occurs on returning from a trip to northern Syria when a customs official at a remote Lebanese border post in the Beqaa valley happens on the emergency packet of white powder in the car and proceeds to remove the seats and wheels in the hope of uncovering a major narcotics run. Disappointed at drawing a blank and only then persuaded of the real purpose of the substance, he kindly leaves me to reassemble the vehicle. It is not until well into the night that I make it back over the high Lebanon range to Shemlan.

London
1960

The Foreign Office is there to look after foreigners
Whitehall jibe

Having emerged from Shemlan's Arabic hothouse as a qualified interpreter, I find myself despatched back to London for incarceration throughout a gloomy February in the Hospital for Tropical Diseases in deepest St Pancras. My bedouin sojourn the previous spring appears to have exacted its price. The large ward is shared with an oddly assorted mixture of Sri Lankan tea planters and Jamaican railway porters, all with very un-British afflictions. Released at last, I turn up at the Foreign Office's Personnel Department to discover how I am to be employed until cleared to return to the Middle East.

The department occupies a fine house in Carlton House Terrace, adjacent to the Duke of York's Steps. I am intrigued to find the operating instructions in the antiquated lift are in German. Of course – this used to be the German embassy up until the outbreak of war in 1939, the base from which Adolf Hitler's arrogant ambassador, Joachim von Ribbentrop, sought to ingratiate his way into the confidence of members of the British political establishment, including King Edward VIII and Wallis Simpson. Moreover a small headstone behind the front railings marks the grave of his favourite dog, Giro, *"ein treuer Begleiter"*.

The personnel officer tells me I am to start in a temporary post in the Western Department, pursuing residual claims by British individuals against the German government, including compensation for incarcerations in the course of the war. This will be my delayed indoctrination into the bureaucracy of diplomacy. But before we go further there is a small matter that needs to be cleared up. My contact address in Britain is registered as the Cabaret Club, London. This has apparently raised some eyebrows, not least on the security side – hardly an appropriate base for a budding diplomat… It turns out to be a clerical corruption of the Cavalry Club in Piccadilly, where I had perched myself when joining the Service 18 months earlier. His relief is evident.

* * * * *

1960 sees the Foreign Office on the eve of a decade of major change in its organisation and systems to speed up the transaction of business in the face of a proliferation of specialised international bodies and of newly independent states. There remain however lingering shadows of the severe knock to the Service's sense of Britain's diplomatic prestige and overseas mission resulting from the débacle of the abortive Anglo-French invasion of the Suez Canal only four years earlier, and the subsequent shock from having been caught unawares by the bloody revolution which overthrew the Hashemite monarchy in her close Arab ally, Iraq, two years ago. Moreover Selwyn Lloyd, who as Foreign Secretary had played a significant part in the run-up to the Suez disaster, is still sitting in the imposing office at the top of the grand staircase.

The Office's splendid neoclassical edifice, shared with the Home Office and the Commonwealth Relations Office, is drab with its coating of wartime grime. One arrives from the Underground at the Downing Street archway each morning in starched collar and dark suit or even pinstripe trousers, complete with bowler hat and umbrella, to find an old man with a venerable beard, kneeling before the door of No. 10 for a half hour's earnest prayer with the aid of a rosary. The policeman on duty forbears to disturb his orisons. One morning on crossing Downing Street to enter the Office, I find myself hailed by the duty constable. He turns out to be an acquaintance from Cambridge who, complete with a law degree, has joined the force, only to find himself assigned to watch the door of No. 10 – perhaps to be on hand should the Prime Minister suddenly require advice on a finer point of law.

Physical security is still agreeably relaxed; there is no requirement at the door to show one's pass, which with its large red triangle looks not unlike the label on a bottle of Bass beer. A cheerful Express Dairy milkman daily drifts through the maze of corridors dropping off pint bottles in every department. Saturday morning working has only recently come to an end. Pigeons copulate contentedly on each window ledge, while frock-coated messengers, under the watchful eye of the building's Housekeeper, Mr Maynard, wheel trolley loads of dockets bundled up in the indispensable red tape, wads of telegrams from overseas posts and maroon boxes of highly classified papers up and down the long passages, pausing occasionally to answer summons by bell to replenish scuttles with coal for the open fires that keep off the chill in the offices. We lock up our sensitive papers each night in wooden presses secured by padlock and hasp – no manifoil combinations to remember. There is even a man who does a regular round to rewind the elegant mantel clocks. The ancient lift by the main door, operated by a one-armed attendant, is agonisingly slow; it is said that an American ambassador, being conveyed up to make his first call on the Foreign Secretary, commented, "Back home trees grow faster." An uninspiring lunch is available in the canteen of the adjacent Ministry of Housing and Local Government, to be followed by a brisk walk around the lake in St James' Park; the Foreign Office is far too grand to have its own canteen.

Internal business is still conducted through formal procedures laid down in the Order Book, our bureaucratic Bible. Opinions on issues of policy are exchanged through written minutes, "white", "blue", "ideal" or "ephemeral", or with elegantly constructed submissions and drafts of correspondence. There is an old world formality to communications with other ministries; "Sir, I am directed by the Secretary of State, etc., etc.", or the slightly less stiff "demi-official letter", and occasionally a more personal style, though rarely on Christian name terms. Clarity of exposition is paramount, and correct syntax; one's superiors, almost without exception male and many with distinguished war service behind them, demand high standards here. One also acquires the obfuscatory art of drafting uninformative replies to questions on sensitive matters of policy raised by Members of Parliament. The telephone, running through an internal exchange attended by an army of obliging ladies who seem to know every person's extension by heart, is regarded with suspicion, and meetings, which might have speeded up the discussion of policy, are infrequent. And yet the system, for all its top heaviness and demand for manual support, works well enough.

* * * *

Ensconced in the Western Department and deep into a catalogue of unsettled war reparations claims on behalf of British citizens seeking redress for ill treatment at the hands of the Nazi regime, including victims of concentration camps, my main contact is with Herr Dr Schmidt of the German Embassy. In due course he invites me to join him for lunch, my first diplomatic social engagement. He suggests we meet at one o'clock at the Rembrandt Hotel, opposite the Victoria and Albert Museum. On the morning of our encounter I realise that I have no idea what he looks like. In response to an appeal for help in identification my mentor in our "third room", Kenneth Pridham, volunteers after careful (and mischievous) reflection that Dr Schmidt reminds him of a U-boat commander. As it happens I have never met one of this tough breed, having been mercifully spared such an encounter when crossing the Atlantic with my mother and brother, Neil, in a well-protected convoy back in 1942 to join our father at the High Commission in Ottawa. I therefore set off with a Hollywood-inspired image of Trevor Howard, grim and gaunt, eyes glued to the periscope and with cheeks adorned with the scars of sword cuts; not one's preconception of the typical diplomat, even a German one.

A survey of the plush lobby of the hotel fails to reveal anyone who might have just steered out into the North Sea from Kiel. I wait as the minutes pass – half an hour and more. Shortly before two the concierge comes up to ask if by any chance I am awaiting Dr Schmidt, who turns out to be the mild-looking, bespectacled man who has been sitting next to me all this time, referring frequently to his watch. In some confusion we introduce ourselves; "You do not look old enough," says Dr Schmidt, which I am uncertain whether to take as a compliment. I can hardly respond that he in no way resembles a U-boat commander. Conversation over an abbreviated lunch is not helped by my enquiring whether he has visited England before. Yes, he has spent several years in the north. In what capacity? "Lend a hand on ze land," Dr Schmidt rejoins sharply. So, a prisoner of war set to work on a farm, yet he claims to have appreciated the experience. Perhaps his appointment to undertake war compensation work is an inspired move on the part of the Auswärtiges Amt; he has always been most cooperative in our common task.

* * * * *

Our budding relationship has not much longer to run however, as I am shortly transferred to the Permanent Under-Secretary's Department, which behind its cryptic title has responsibility for intelligence coordination and planning in the event of international crises or even war. For this is still a time of British global engagement with a genuine shadow of potential hostilities with a militant Soviet Union. Berlin, still under allied occupation, looks a likely flashpoint for conflict. My colleagues set a high professional and intellectual standard, and the work of analysing the political background to possible trouble spots is stimulating. One of the objects of our attention even then is Afghanistan, a traditional monarchy where deep tribal divisions are seen as a target for Soviet encroachment – the Great Game still being played out. Indeed Lord Curzon had forecast at a dinner of the Royal Asian Society way back in 1908 that one hundred years on Afghanistan would be "as important and vital a subject as it is now"; a prescient observation indeed.

One major preoccupation for Britain's foreign and defence policy makers is the long-running Cod War with Iceland over fishing rights. Brief skirmishes involving trawlers and naval protection vessels occur almost daily in the cold waters of the North Atlantic. The gentle Scot with whom I share an office is married to an Icelander. Each reported encounter produces a prompt telephone call in which her national indignation is audibly vented on her luckless husband in shrill Icelandic. It is all most entertaining. Inevitably he soon finds himself posted out of this frying pan to head the British Embassy in Reykjavik!

As for me I am cleared to return to Arab shores. It turns out to be Beirut, the seductive intersection of all the currents and intrigues that bedevil the Middle East's turbulent scene, and with warm personal connections to retrieve, among which however one jilted fiancée.

Lebanon
1960-1962

A diplomat has to think twice before saying nothing

Anon

Beirut's vibrant atmosphere affords a warm and familiar welcome. The towering mountain backdrop that divides the Mediterranean shore from the deep Syrian desert offers a cool refuge from the limp summer heat. For the present Lebanon has managed to stabilise her acute sectarian and political divisions in a self-indulgent pursuit of business, laced with pleasure. Cairo's antagonistic mood of nationalism under Gamal Abdel Nasser has seen its international community – investors, media and agencies, plus a few sybarites – migrate *en masse* to Beirut's more tolerant surroundings. The British Embassy has in consequence seen its size swollen to serve as a principal listening post for the securing of Britain's still extensive interests amongst the turbulent currents of nationalist Arab politics and the legion of hapless Palestinian refugees who have become pawns in an immobilised Arab-Israeli confrontation.

I am fortunate to fall on my feet with the offer by Desmond Cochrane, an Irish baronet married into Beirut's wealthy Sursock dynasty, of a flat in the former coach house of the family's spun sugar palace in the elegant Greek Orthodox Achrafiyeh quarter. Behind the palm-filled garden lies the Aero Club, home of all that is smartest in Beirut's Christian establishment and presided over by "le Président" Gabriel Trad, never without a fragrant gardenia in his buttonhole. The ornate 19th-century villas that adorn the neighbourhood would form a graceful set for a Glyndebourne opera, in contrast with the turbulent Basta quarter, the "manor" of the city's Sunni Muslim ascendancy. The dominant Maronite Christian community, together with the Druze clans, tend to keep to their mountain fiefs, while the subordinated Shi'as lead a peasant existence in the further corners of the Beqaa Valley. All this makes for an unstable intercommunal brew, created when France carved a Greater Lebanon out of Turkey's Syrian province after the First World War. (Britain would leave similarly volatile legacies through Arab/Jewish tensions in mandated Palestine, and mixing Sunni and Shi'a Arabs with Kurds in a new Iraqi kingdom.)

Achrafiyeh's narrow streets resound to the morning cries of tradesmen calling out their wares, and mingling with the chimes of the bells from the Greek Orthodox archbishopric and the Papal Order of the Knights of Malta. It makes for an idyllic scene, sadly not to survive intact the bitterly destructive civil war into which Lebanon would be plunged a few years on. The ground floor is the office of the Irish Consulate-General, Desmond having secured that honorary and duty-free perk for himself; I believe he holds the reciprocal appointment when back at home in the Irish Republic. Anyway he and Yvonne are always stylish hosts. It is somehow in character to find that the large map of Ireland on the consulate wall predates the 1921 Treaty and partition.

* * * * *

Initially I take over from Patrick Wright as the embassy's junior press attaché, moving across a year later to the political section of the chancery, after a five month attachment in Kuwait. The press work, by no means onerous, involves encouraging a favourable understanding through the partisan local French and Arabic media of British policies in this tense region, to counter insidious and hostile propaganda emanating from a revolutionary Egypt and Iraq with Soviet support. The bitter legacy of what is seen as Britain's betrayal of the Arab population of Palestine with the creation of Israel only twelve years earlier, and the visible presence of destitute Palestinian refugees camped about, make for uphill work. Yet this is still a post-imperial era in which Britain sees a global role for herself and her finger in every Middle Eastern pie.

There is a swollen British press corps to be handled. They benefit from Beirut's good air network to chase each other's tails around the Middle East arena, or even write their copy vicariously from the comfort of St Georges Hotel's celebrated bar. They constitute a distinguished roll-call, marking the priority accorded to the Arab world by foreign editors; Gerald Priestland of the BBC, Jerome Caminada of *The Times*, the veteran Ian Colvin of the *Telegraph*, Michael Adams of *The Guardian* – a champion of the Palestinians' plight, Dick Beeston of the *News Chronicle*, the monocled Colonel Slade-Baker of *The Sunday Times*, Ralph Izzard of the *Daily Mail*, Patrick Seale and lesser fry. Dick Beeston's wife, Moyra, has been producing a daily programme in English for Lebanese radio. It ends in tears and recrimination when the Central Office of Information in London contrives to mix the radio tapes destined for Lebanon and Israel, with the result that Lebanese listeners are treated to an account of the success of an Israeli family who migrate to Canada. This is inflammatory stuff in the present tense circumstances; the English hour is summarily terminated.

Notable among the press gallery is Kim Philby, writing for the *Economist* and *Observer*. A former member of the Secret Intelligence Service he will two years later be dramatically unmasked as the third member of the notorious diplomatic spy ring involving Guy Burgess and Donald MacLean, who had fled from Britain to the Soviet Union ten years ago. Faced with exposure he will make his own sudden night flit to Moscow on board a Russian freighter sailing from Beirut harbour while guests wait impatiently for him to turn up at a dinner party in the apartment of a colleague, Glen Balfour-Paul. Kim and his American wife, Eleanor, keep a hospitable establishment in the Rue Kantara and are rarely to be found sober. The strain of dissimulation is beginning to tell; yet curiously he still appears to arouse loyalty among former MI6 colleagues, headed by his old comrade-in-arms Nicholas Elliott, who assure me Kim is to be trusted with sensitive information*. There are intriguing academic figures around too, some, like Christopher Scaife, characters straight out of Lawrence Durrell's fashionable *Alexandria Quartet*. Expelled from Egypt in the wake of the Suez affair, they have found a refuge in Beirut's renowned American University. Another intriguing character is Theo Larsen, a member of the Swedish clan that owns the old American Colony Hotel in Arab Jerusalem; with a stylish English wife, admired for having been one of the *belle monde*

---

*The career of Philby's maverick father, Harry St. John, also bordered on treason. British official in Arabia, later trusted adviser to King Abdul Aziz, Arabian explorer, convert to Islam and British intelligence agent at odds with Britain, his recommendation to the Saudi King that he switch alliance to Nazi Germany earned a royal rebuff and led to his brief internment in World War II.

ladies in the cult film *La Dolce Vita*, he makes a good living from selling Bofors guns to Arab governments and perhaps other services besides.

My boss in the Information Section is John Snodgrass, a gentle giant who has a tendency to disappear during dinner parties and take a nap in his host's bath, from where his wife rescues him when it is time to go home; an endearing trait, but not a point of etiquette recommended in Sir Marcus Cheke's handbook. Neither is my own first attempt at giving a lunch party. The house servant I have acquired is Mikhail, a Nestorian Christian who spent many years serving in the Assyrian Levies, raised by the Royal Air Force to guard their base at Habbaniya near Baghdad. To my chagrin his first course turns out to be a soup bowl of hot water with bits of cabbage and carrot floating in it. He claims this was the vegetable soup recipe he had learnt from the wife of an RAF corporal.

The British ambassador, Ponsonby Moore Crosthwaite (you could get away with such names in those days), is a bachelor of taste and a stickler for correct English usage. He abhors the use of adverbs. "They are lazy. An appropriate adjective or verb will always suffice to convey your meaning." (There is something in this). On one occasion an immature report which I had prepared for his approval – it may have been on the predicament of the large contingent of refugees from Palestine or else the aftermath amid Lebanon's ever-neurotic intercommunal politics of an abortive *coup d'état* attempt by a right-wing Christian group – comes back to me covered in corrections in the ambassador's red ink together with his copy of Fowler's magisterial *Modern English Usage*. The margin contains a pedantic rebuke, "Mr Munro, there are two anacoluthons and one litotes in this. Get rid of them! " It is a hard discipline, but makes for a change from the drafting, mostly in stilted French, of *protocolaire* letters of welcome and farewell that ambassadors spend much time iterating to each other in ritual token of the "excellent relations that prevail between our two countries".

The ambassador's antique mother acts as his hostess, which the Lebanese find quaint. He also requires all his staff to have white suits made for their roles as hosts at the annual Queen's Birthday reception; Beirut's tailoring standards not being up to Savile Row, we look more like a clutch of second-rate entertainers. He has however demonstrated a cultural affinity with Lebanon's history by taking over a handsome but derelict Druze manor house in the mountains as a weekend retreat, and restoring it with stylish taste. I find myself invited to join him there with whomever he has as guests. One of these is Freya Stark, traveller and doyenne of British writers on the Middle East and now retired to Asolo in northern Italy. We make a happy threesome as we walk over the stony hillsides, with Freya in flowing cotton dresses that snag on every bush and wearing her trademark wide-brimmed hat. She has the history of each village and community at her fingertips – a fascinating companion. The evenings are taken up with interminable games of Scrabble which somehow Freya always wins. On another occasion I find Sir Anthony Blunt, Keeper of the Royal Collection and revealed years later to have been the "fourth man" of Moscow's notorious spy cell. Perhaps he found the time during his sojourn in Beirut to connect once again with Kim Philby…

* * * * *

It adds up to a rosy existence, with time to keep a sailing dinghy in the port, and an Arab horse on which to participate in show jumping events around the country and even a race on the course beside the former French High Commissioner's residence. It brings regret to suspect some of the loyal Lebanese staff of the embassy have staked their shirts on me. An elegantly named "estivation allowance" enables staff to rent a summer cottage up in the mountains as a refuge from the city's torrid heat; the younger among us prefer to spend it on a beach hut. There is just time in the winter months to climb up to Faraya for a ski run or two after the day's work. I am introduced to the charms of this seductive city and its hectic society by the hospitable Asseily family and other Lebanese friends. Mates appear regularly from England to share the delights of the warm Levant. Among them Tessa Kaye turns up at the airport with her baggage tied up with string in a battered Harrods cardboard box – stylish if hardly practical – to be joined by my old-fashioned cousin Theodore from Zambia, with umbrella firmly clutched against sun or rain. My half-brother, Colin, passes through en route to London from his home in Tasmania. Together we search out the Kit-Kat Bar, a disreputable nightspot which he last patronised on a short leave respite in Beirut from his tank battles in the Libyan desert twenty years ago, and round off his trip down memory lane with an inspirational evening of belly dancing. A visit by a peripatetic uncle and aunt brings Clementine back into contact with the *Telegraph*'s Ian Colvin whom she last knew in Hitler's Berlin in the 1930s when she spent time there with her ill-starred cousin Unity Mitford; they have much to reminisce about. There is an evening of laughter with Osbert

Lancaster, whose bearded son, William, is acquiring Arabic in Shemlan. Osbert has been sketching scenes in the Holy Land. Outside Bethlehem's Holy Grail Café he longs to paint a cheeky pub sign with "Good Pull-in for Magi".

Best of all Grania Bacon arrives to join the embassy. Together we make the most of Lebanon's variety: Margot Fonteyn and the Royal Ballet in the ornate Temple of Bacchus at Baalbek, glee singing in the enchanting Greek theatre at Byblos, expeditions to mountain sites steeped in antiquity or to the ruins of Chateau Beaufort high above the UN-patrolled border with Israel with a pattern of kibbutzim settlements down below, sailing out of Beirut's busy harbour dodging tramp steamers and liners, the temptations of Jounieh's glittering casino with its hushed green baize tables and troop of Cossack horsemen, and the incomparable Cave du Roi with Aldo, master of the whisky sour, behind the bar. We visit the ruined stead above Sidon where the dramatic and reclusive Lady Hester Stanhope, who had once acted as official hostess to her uncle, Prime Minister William Pitt (the Younger), had settled and ended her days a century and a half before, a foremost figure among that cadre of romantic English women who have taken to a life in the Orient. Settled in the branches of an ancient yew tree we read from Alexander Kinglake's *Eothen* and Alphonse de Lamartine's *Voyages en Orient* of their visits here to Djoun to pay court. There are more far-flung trips north to Aleppo with its warren of souks and steamy Turkish baths (in one of which Grania's sudden materialisation causes the naked male clients to scramble for a prudish concealment behind their newspapers), Antioch with its marvellous Roman mosaics and a feast of Turkish delight, the dramatic Crusader castles of Krak and Sahyoun in northern Syria and the colonnaded ruins of Queen Zenobia's great city of Palmyra deep in the eastern desert. We pay a memorable Christmas visit to a friend in Jerusalem where we put up in the Dom Polski hostel, run by gentle Polish nuns in the Arab Old City still under Jordanian control. Halcyon days indeed.

There are narrow scrapes too. Crossing an icy pass over the Lebanon range in deep winter the Sunbeam Talbot starts to slide towards the outer rim of the narrow road with a deep chasm below. At the last moment the tyres regain their grip on the ribbon of soft snow at the verge and we are out of danger. On an evening trip to a mountain stream our party is held up at gunpoint and we are relieved of our cash; a prudent lesson – always park the car facing the direction of your exit. Then comes a dreadful day when, diving into a rocky pool on the Damour River, Grania surfaces with a fractured neck vertebra. A hideously painful drive by rocky tracks gets her back to a Beirut clinic whence she is evacuated to England a few days later by the RAF. It is months before she is able to come back, for much of which time I find myself on attachment in Kuwait. We become engaged soon after her return.

I am required to obtain the permission of my ambassador to get married. This turns out to be less than plain sailing. Revealing a misogynistic streak Sir Moore's immediate response to my request is a testy "Must you?" He relents however, though only to the point of allowing me a paltry five days for a honeymoon, on the grounds of pressure of work. For her part the rules oblige Grania to resign from the Diplomatic Service, thus exchanging gainful employment under the Crown for a life of loyal yet unrewarded service in diplomacy. We marry in Beirut in the pretty Anglican church of St George on the waterfront. This solid building will later be one of the few to survive the intense shelling of the city's centre during fifteen years of civil war. Our families come out from England; the cacophony and chaos of Beirut come as a shock to my father, an uncompromising proponent of British order who sees everyone east of Dover as faintly suspect and whose distinguished overseas career has been passed in North America and the British-governed parts of southern Africa. The church is packed with colleagues and friends, Lebanese and foreign. The Dean of St George's Cathedral in Jerusalem, Harold Atkins, takes the service in full canonicals and Cranmer cap. A good friend, Malcolm Davidson, flies out to be best man, before going on to Jerusalem to stand in for a spell at the British School of Archaeology there. Grania looks superb while I nearly expire in the heat of my inherited morning coat of heavy flannel. Our attendants, got up in satin, are the two children of friends in the Spanish Embassy, Luis and Maria-Luz Jordana. With taxi horn blaring we move on to a stylish reception given by the ambassador, and at last to the peace and quiet of the Achrafiyeh coach house. Our abbreviated honeymoon is spent on Rhodes, where, a copy of Lawrence Durrell's *Reflections on a Marine Venus* to hand, we explore every corner of this delightful island, the last outpost of the Crusaders in the Eastern Mediterranean.

* * * * *

For all the veneer of peaceful stability Lebanon's reputation for bouts of civil rivalry and disorder does not let us down. I wake one morning to the roar of the air force's Hawker Hunter jets over the city. Apparently the night has seen an attempted *coup d'état* by a fringe group of political fanatics calling themselves the Parti Populaire Syrien. The party has its historic heartland among certain Christian villages in the north of Mount Lebanon and has for objective the formation of an Arab crescent in the fertile lands stretching from Palestine northwards over Lebanon and Syria to the river valleys of Iraq. It is a madcap and futile affair; the minor acts of resistance are quickly stifled, while calm is restored and Beirut resumes its seductive ways. A flurry of theatrical trials of the group's leadership follow, which I find myself diligently reporting to London.

More bothersome for us is a renewal of controversy over the Arabic Centre up in Shemlan. The sensational arrest in 1961 of one of its Diplomatic Service students, George Blake, and his sending down for an unprecedented forty-two years as a Soviet spy (only to escape five years later over the wall of Wormwood Scrubs prison with the help of Irish republicans), have rekindled all the local suspicions of a nest of British espionage. Quite a bit of this does go on, for Beirut has become a key hub of Arab world intrigue. Shortly after I move over from the press section to the junior political slot in the embassy one of my more shadowy colleagues asks if I will do him a service by spending a night with a female member of the Egyptian Embassy, an invitation which I consider to be carrying foreign relations a touch too far, at least for me, and politely decline. The sudden crisis over the despatch of Soviet missiles to Cuba in late 1962 with its risks of a nuclear confrontation with the United States brings a flurry of nervous activity in the embassy with the dusting off of plans for evacuation in the event of wider hostilities. Morale is soon restored however by a comforting circular from the Foreign Office administration notifying staff that henceforward toilet paper supplied to overseas posts will be of upmarket tissue quality in place of the standard crisp parchment variety with its caution – GOVERNMENT PROPERTY – printed on each sheet.

A different challenge occurs when I collect a young scion of Oman's ruling family off the boat fresh from his English studies at a vicarage in Suffolk and transfer him to catch an onward flight to the Gulf. Despite my protestations of diplomatic immunity a zealous airport customs official insists on examining his suitcase. It turns out to be stocked with smart watches. Without turning a hair the young sheikh starts to place timepieces one by one on the counter. When there are half a dozen or so lined up the officer calmly closes the case and wishes us on our way. I pray no one has been looking.

Another test presents itself one weekend when it is my turn as the embassy's duty officer. The Lebanese watchman telephones in the afternoon to ask me to come round; he has a problem with an incoherent Briton who has turned up at the door. On arrival I find none other than the actor, Peter O'Toole, stretched out on the marble floor in an inebriated haze. I make out that after an intemperant weekend in Beirut he has missed his flight back to Amman from where he has to carry on by taxi to rejoin the crew filming *Lawrence of Arabia* over a hundred miles south among the desert valleys and rocky bluffs of the remote and spectacular Wadi Rum. He must be on set tomorrow morning or there will be serious consequences. I am expected to wave a wand to get him back in time. Money seems to be no problem but my attempts to charter a plane which will circumnavigate Israel's intervening and closely guarded airspace get nowhere. The only course, and an uncertain one given the lack of a visa and the restrictions on travel through Syria to Jordan, is to find a resourceful taxi driver; happily the watchman turns out to have a friend with a car who can oblige. While we await his arrival a slightly more sober O'Toole boasts of his prowess in swimming at night through the mines between Aqaba and the adjacent Israeli port of Eilat to visit a girlfriend. A tall story perhaps, but dramatic none the less with its shades of the legend of Leander swimming the Hellespont to Hero, and of Lord Byron's youthful emulation of the feat. With considerable relief we bundle him into his conveyance. He must have blagged his way somehow through the frontiers as the film turns out to be a winner.

A visit by George Brown, who would subsequently become Foreign Secretary under a new Labour government, makes little impact, although his evident Zionist sympathies need to be massaged. Winston Churchill calls by on board the *Christina*, the private yacht of his friend, Aristotle Onassis. President Chehab does him honour with the presentation of a priceless Phoenician glass jar from Lebanon's national collection. I collect it from the museum and stow it nervously in our flat for the night. Churchill's long-serving Private Secretary, Anthony Montague-Browne, is an old friend of Grania's family, so we go on board the luxurious vessel to hand over the trophy. The old statesman is however too frail to appear. The reaction of the local press to his visit is somewhat muted by recollection of Churchill's staunch support as Colonial Secretary in the early 1920s for the implementation of the Balfour Declaration's provision for a "Jewish Homeland" in Arab Palestine. Memories are ever fresh on this vexed issue.

Indeed a good part of our work in the embassy's chancery involves liaison with the headquarters of the United Nations organisation responsible for the thousands of Palestinian refugees who fled the turmoil that accompanied the violent birth of Israel in 1948; their crowded and impoverished camps are scattered through the Jordan valley and across Lebanon too. An enduring resentment over what they see as Britain's scuttling of her unsustainable political mandate in Palestine continues to fester.

The time for our return to the Foreign Office in London comes all too soon. Our farewell party, for which we choose the historic Ottoman Grand Hotel Bassoul with its arched windows overlooking the sea, goes with a swing apart from the expensive discovery that the equally venerable waiter has added tonic water to over a hundred Scotch whiskies. With many a backward glance we take passage for a delayed Nile honeymoon on the *Esperia*, one of the two handsome Italian liners that ply the Mediterranean ports. We plan to join up with the car on her sister ship, the *Ausonia*, in Alexandria a fortnight later for what turns out to be a tempestuous Christmas crossing to Marseille and a slow drive onwards to a snowbound England. It is to be 35 years before we find ourselves back in a war-ravaged, yet ever hedonistic, Beirut.

Beirut Tram – from a watercolour by Osbert Lancaster

Kuwait
1961

*There are now three superpowers, the United States, the Soviet Union
— and Kuwait*

Attributed to the late King Faisal bin Abdul Aziz of Saudi Arabia

In June of 1961 the sheikhdom of Kuwait gained her independence with the ending of 63 years under British protection. Iraq's revolutionary and pro-Soviet regime under the military leadership of Abdul Karim Qasim, and fresh from its bloody overthrow of the Hashemite monarchy three years earlier, lost no time in resurrecting a questionable claim to sovereignty over the newly established state, which dated back to Turkish times. The claim was backed up by the despatch of troops to the frontier with Kuwait. Faced with a threat of invasion the Ruler of Kuwait, Sheikh Abdullah Al Salem Al Sabah, was persuaded to implement his recently agreed defence pact with Britain in order to safeguard independence as well as to protect the country's by now substantial oil production in which British and American interests had the major stake.

A combined land, sea and air force consisting of an infantry and armoured brigade based in Aden and Kenya, Hunter aircraft from the RAF base in Bahrain and a naval task force including a contingent of marines embarked on the aircraft carrier, HMS *Bulwark*, was promptly despatched to Kuwait where they took up positions along the Mutla Ridge north of the town. Their arrival sufficed to block any Iraqi idea of an attack. A spell of intense diplomatic activity involving Britain and leading Arab states, inherently concerned at the return of British troops to Arab soil, led to a welcome decision by the Arab League that autumn to replace them with an Arab peacekeeping force composed of green beret units from Jordan, Egypt, Sudan and Saudi Arabia to police the frontier. Following the violent revolt against Abdul Karim Qasim's government two years later in 1963 the new Ba'athist regime recognised Kuwait's independence in return for a substantial cash payment. The British Centurion tanks were made over to the Kuwait army together with a military training mission.

* * * * *

The furnace of heat that hits me on landing at Kuwait airport in the middle of June comes as a suffocating shock, even out of a Beirut summer. All around are Hunter jet fighters and bulky Beverley transports of the RAF, enveloped in a dusty haze. For the next four months I am here to undertake liaison with the local press and with the groups of foreign correspondents over the purpose and progress of this sudden British military action to buttress the sheikhdom's fledgling sovereignty, while the embassy's press attaché takes a well-earned break of leave. I am not the only substitute; Sir John Richmond, transformed from British Political Agent into Ambassador with the coming of an independence he has done much to foster, has also been released. His temporary replacement is Alan Rothnie, a gritty Scot and firm disciple of the Keir Hardie school of socialism, who has been plucked from mid-career Arabic studies in Shemlan to take over the helm during this crucial period. He proves a sound choice, both in treating with a nervous Kuwaiti establishment and meeting the demands of the British military presence.

Alan Rothnie and I have our shared abode in the elegant old embassy building on the foreshore of Kuwait City, with its wide verandas dating from the days when representatives in the various Gulf sheikhdoms under British protection were appointed from New Delhi by the Government of India. There is a comfortable Lutyens-style feel to the building, which also serves as the chancery and consulate offices. One wing contains the small courtroom in which, prior to independence, British diplomats have for years past sat in judgement on non-Kuwaitis accused of minor legal offences – an archaic but effective judicial system now superseded by Kuwait's full sovereignty. Our needs are met by Gholam Reza, the antique butler who has been in British service since goodness knows when. If there is company we dress for dinner in "Gulf rig", a practical yet smart combination of dinner jacket minus the jacket and plus a silk cummerbund (an Indian tailor down in the souk quickly rustles one up for me). The only problem is the persistent heat of summer, which can be stiflingly humid when the *sharqiya* east wind blows, and for which our primitive and noisy air conditioning sets are quite inadequate. The electric ceiling fans are a poor substitute for punkahs. Kuwait's dwellings lack the stylish louvred wind towers that surmount the traditional houses of older Gulf towns such as Bahrain and Dubai.

The walled and dusty compound is spacious. Thirty years on would see a good part of its baked soil tilled to provide emergency rations for the staff besieged within its confines by an invading Iraqi army. Inside the gate near the shore stands a flagpole flying the Union flag. Tradition has it that individuals in domestic bondage in the households of the Al Sabah or other leading Kuwaiti merchant families can obtain their liberty if they are found clasping the flagpole when the Jack is flying. They are then issued with a handsome "certificate of manumission" on behalf of Her Majesty's government and can go free. I find a number of these grandiloquent certificates in the drawer of my desk. In practice requests for liberation are by now rare; it is said that one needs to be cautious in meeting these as the "slave" in question could be a valued servant such as the ruler's cook whose disappearance would not go down well. There have been instances too where the freedman subsequently regrets his hasty decision and seeks re-establishment in his master's comfortable household. It is all a social minefield.

* * * * *

The Kuwaitis keep very much to themselves. Their tightly knit society amounts to a guild of powerful and long-established trading and pearl fishing families, some Sunni and others Shi'a, and headed by the Al Sabah. They constitute a coastal enclave in a barren desert through which the pastoral bedouin migrate each year in the search for grazing for their herds. After occasional rains the *sabkha* salt flats can yield succulent truffles, which fetch a high price in the souk.

The sudden bonanza of crude oil revenues in recent years has produced wealth on an unprecedented scale through oil royalties, booming import business and the sale of lands for development. Much of this new wealth goes into the construction of ostentatious homes around the city, as well as the purchase of expensive overseas properties in Lebanon and elsewhere. Among their Gulf neighbours the Kuwaitis are regarded as a comparatively sophisticated and free-speaking society, offset however by a certain arrogance combined with parsimony in business. In Kuwait herself professional tasks are largely carried out by immigrant Palestinians (the young engineer Yasser Arafat among them), while labourers for the oil and construction industries arrive from the Indian subcontinent on the antiquated steamers of the British-owned Strick Line that plies the Gulf ports out of Bombay. It is not a popular posting for the Arabists of the Diplomatic Service. As one despairing ditty puts it:

> The summer temperature's sky high;
> The liquor permit may run dry;
> Mother, what a place to die!
> Kuwait.

The city itself retains a few of the old mud-walled houses and the imposing official *diwan* fortress of the Al Sabah, from which government is exercised. As yet there is only one modern hotel, now crowded with foreign journalists here to observe the military stand-off. One place of pilgrimage in the old town is the home of Violet Dickson, the indomitable widow of a pre-war Political Agent, Harold Dickson, who became a foremost expert on the tribes of north-east Arabia. Yet I find compensation for the city's brash appearance in the fascinating boatyards along the shore where sailing dhows are being constructed by local shipwrights using tools and materials that have not changed in hundreds of years. To cap it all there is the unforgettable spectacle each evening of trading dhows, their lateen sails spread, returning to harbour on an onshore breeze and silhouetted against the brilliant orange light of the setting sun.

* * * * *

The British employees of the Kuwait Oil Company live in yet another world in the neat isolation of their township at Al Ahmadi, some thirty miles south. It is their production and livelihoods that the military have in effect come to safeguard. Many of the families never set foot in Kuwait City except to pass through the airport. The oil company has a cunning strategy to entice them to re-engage on completion of a tour, with successive promises of larger house and garden, higher salary and more seniority. It seems to work.

There are new players on the oil scene in the shape of the Japanese-owned Arabian Oil company. It has begun to develop a marine field discovered off the coast at Al Khafji in the neutral zone which Kuwait shares with Saudi Arabia, the first of many offshore fields which would shortly be found to line the Gulf littoral as far south as Oman. Production has however been interrupted following an explosion and fire at the wellhead. The renowned American firefighter, Red Adair, has been called in to try to douse the conflagration, so far without success. The affable head of the Japanese operation, Itoh-san, invites me to drive down to see the spectacle. We head south on a rough cross-desert run by Land Rover and then take a launch out to the well. It is an awesome sight with flames leaping from the clear blue Gulf waters. Nearby are two old tankers, used to store the crude and trans-ship it to carriers from Japan. One of the vessels is blackened and blistered, the result says Itoh-san of another fire mishap in which several Japanese workers were killed. My expression of concern is brushed aside; "Prenty more Japanese in Japan," he remarks as we tuck into a picnic lunch.

* * * * *

The British military lose no time in getting their act together. A tri-service headquarters is to be established in the town. The army contingent, under Brigadier Derek Horsford, and his air force counterpart have no problem with this. But the Royal Navy puts up a defiant resistance when the flotilla commander aboard *Bulwark*, Admiral Fitzroy Talbot, insists on operating independently from offshore and routing all his communications to his fellow commanders through the Admiralty in London. Even the choleric General John Walker, who pays the occasional visit from his base in Aden, cannot challenge the resolve of the "senior service".

The soldiers have an uncomfortable time of it, dug into trenches along the Mutla Ridge. I find a company of the Manchester Regiment suffering stoically under flimsy camouflage netting with the air temperature well over 100 degrees Fahrenheit. Their brains must be roasting under their tin helmets. There is a risk of sabotage too. Derek Horsford looks a bit shaken after a flight to Bahrain. It turns out that shortly after take-off from Kuwait there is a loud explosion in the troop-carrying bay of the Beverley and the ramp door at his feet blows open. A bomb device has clearly been slipped aboard at Kuwait airport. The hatch connecting with the flight deck above opens and the RAF loadmaster puts his head through it. "Blimey, Brigadier, we've got mice", he remarks, and shuts the hatch. The Beverley drones on to Bahrain. Another sideshow occurs when two sappers out on patrol stray across the frontier and are picked up by the Iraqi military. Strangely they are presumed to be deserters. A rash decision is taken to interview the pair live on the radio, where one of them is asked how it feels to find themselves enjoying the liberty of Iraq. "One ******* Arab is very much like another to me," comes the gruff reply. The interview terminates abruptly, and the Iraqis sensibly tip the pair back over the border.

* * * * *

In the embassy itself we are under considerable pressure. The threat from Iraq has drawn a large and unaccustomed media contingent from Beirut and elsewhere to Kuwait City and its one raw hotel. There is not much news with which to feed them. I make friends with the correspondent of Egypt's leading daily, *Al Ahram*, who delights in telling anti-Nasser jokes that he would not get away with at home. One of the better ones involves a splendid *son et lumière* demonstration at the Giza pyramids in which the Sphinx plays a prominent part. At the end of the show President Nasser comes to congratulate the great effigy on a splendid performance, and offers to grant any favour. "I'd like an exit visa," the monument responds.

A major problem is the massive volume of telegraph traffic out of London, all of which has to be manually decrypted using the secure but time-consuming numerical subtraction system of one-time pads. Despite interminable daylight and nocturnal shifts we are often two or three days late in getting round to unbuttoning all but the highest priority of messages, on top of which our own traffic has to be encrypted for despatch. Action has frequently been overtaken by the time we decode an instruction; it sometimes seems one is waging the last war, not the current one. Eventually the Foreign Office relents and sends us a wizard from Hanslope Park who has spent his life on one-time pads and knows by heart many of the numerical keywords. He is also a dab hand at subtraction!

Opportunities for recreation are limited, nor is there much time for it; tennis in the relative cool of evening and the occasional volleyball game on the beach with the American Embassy, the only other diplomatic mission. The British Council, led by Onslow Tuckley, another cultured refugee from pre-Suez Alexandria, does its best to introduce the Kuwaitis to an appreciation of Shakespeare. There are one or two coffee-house cafés. Not a sign of a belly dancer however, and liquor is forbidden. It can only be sold to non-Muslim individuals armed with licences furnished by the British consulate and giving confirmation of their religious status. This profitable monopoly of liquor sales is exercised around the Gulf by the historic Scots-Indian trading house, Gray Mackenzie. Even this dispensation will eventually be cancelled with the prohibition of all alcohol. Years later I learn that local music shops have discovered they can do a roaring trade in a liquid with the archaic description of gramophone needle cleaning fluid. There is however one trick to enliven a café visit. Two aspirins in a glass of Coca-Cola give quite a lift to the spirits, apparently through a chemical reaction with the coca leaf ingredient in the beverage. The days of this short cut are however to be numbered when the company is obliged to remove the narcotic coca from its secret formula.

We have a visit by Sir William Luce, the British Political Resident and overlord in the Gulf, who is based in Bahrain. A former Governor of Sudan and of Aden he is a widely respected figure throughout the Gulf sheikhdoms. Much of his role is taken up with helping to settle the territorial and tribal disputes that constantly arise among the colourful assortment of petty sheikhdoms under British protection. The oil revenues that will transform their traditional existence are only just starting to flow. Bill Luce will himself be called out of retirement ten years hence to implement the hasty, though necessary, decision by a cash-strapped British government to withdraw military protection and dragoon the various sheikhdoms into fledgling unions and independence. Henceforward it will be for the United States to take the lead in the guardianship of the Gulf and its resources on behalf of the west. Even now some of us in Kuwait are beginning to question the value of maintaining an increasingly unpopular military presence to safeguard a stake in what is becoming a global oil industry.

Bill Luce's Gulf tours can involve bizarre experiences. On a recent trip to see Sultan Said bin Taimur, the reclusive and fiercely traditional ruler of Oman (shortly to be replaced under British auspices by his Sandhurst-trained son, Qaboos), he is taken to a bedroom in the Sultan's palace in remote Salalah to await the audience. Finding a smart new bathroom he settles down to enjoy a quick cigar, flushing the stump down the pan. Ten minutes later comes a knock on his door to reveal a black attendant with dagger tucked into his sash who proffers a dripping cigar stump with a grave warning, "This was found beneath the palace wall; smoking is punishable by death."

* * * * *

Kuwait can spring its own surprises. One torrid August afternoon when I am doing duty in the embassy, the watchman comes in with news that Sheikh Shakhbut, the Al Nahyan Ruler of Abu Dhabi, has turned up and wishes to see someone. This is a startling development as Shakhbut has the deserved reputation of having set his face against all steps towards the modernisation of his impoverished mini-state of salt water creeks and date palm oases to the west of Dubai's prosperous port. This has led to tensions as substantial reserves of oil have recently been discovered within his emirate. He is reputed to demand that the royalties be paid in gold and to keep this hoard locked away in his mud-brick fort, the only building of substance among a collection of palm-frond fishermen's huts. It is almost unthinkable that he should make a journey as far as Kuwait. I must see what is afoot.

In comes Sheikh Shakhbut, a wispy figure in white *dishdasha* robe under an *abaya* cloak. He is accompanied by an equally wispy young man carrying a battered brown leather suitcase which he deposits on my desk. As we sip our ritual coffee I enquire what brings him this far from home. In his guttural Arabic he comes quickly to the point. "You British are responsible for my overseas connections." I nod assent. "Well, I am travelling to America. I have come to Kuwait to catch the aeroplanes through Beirut and London." I nearly fall off my chair with surprise. How on earth...? He draws a grimy envelope from his pocket and produces from it two air tickets. "I have received these tickets in the post from someone called Morgan in New York, so I thought I would go. Do you know him?"

I am struck dumb. Here is what must be the boldest long odds mail shot of all time – and it has scored a bull's eye. The target, soon to be master of massive revenues, has taken the bait. But there is more to come. "So I need your help," goes on the sheikh. "What money do they use in America?"

"The dollar, may your life be long," I reply. "Will they take the Gulf rupee?" "No, I very much doubt so." "That is what I hear. Open it!" he says turning to the young man, who unfastens the battered suitcase. It turns out to be stuffed with rupee notes. "So you must turn these into dollars for me," commands Shakhbut. I find they amount to roughly eight thousand US dollars, a considerable sum in 1961. I ring the manager of the Kuwait branch of the British Bank of the Middle East, which also enjoys a monopoly of banking in Abu Dhabi at that stage. He is suitably astounded to hear of the act of banking piracy which has been conducted under the nose of his complacent enterprise. He explains however that he cannot raise this quantity of dollar bills in Kuwait and will have to send for funds from Bombay by air. It will take a couple of days. "Might the sheikh take traveller's cheques instead?" I put this to Shakhbut who is sceptical. "Is that currency?" he asks. "Well not exactly." No, it has to be dollars in cash to go in the suitcase.

Sheikh Shakhbut is none too pleased at the delay, though I assure him he will be well attended by his Kuwaiti hosts, the Al Sabah. Two days later he turns up again plus suitcase and companion. The bank manager is with me, armed with packets of bright greenbacks. We effect the switch, the suitcase is shut and off go the pair. Britain has done her duty. As for astute J.P.Morgan, they will be financing the prodigious development of Abu Dhabi and the other sheikhdoms of the lower Gulf for years to come.

* * * * *

By late September the British force is winding down. I go with Cairo's *Al Ahram* correspondent to the airport to see the arrival of Arab League contingents from Jordan and Saudi Arabia, while British infantry board their Beverley transports back to Kenya. The Saudi troops are of particular interest as the Kingdom severed its diplomatic relations with Britain back in 1956 following the ousting by British-commanded forces of a Saudi military contingent that was occupying the Buraimi oasis, to which both Oman and Abu Dhabi had fair claim. Our relations with the most powerful country in Arabia are still in the freezer. Moreover relations between the Al Saud and the Al Sabah of Kuwait have for well over a century alternated between bouts of alliance and open hostility. As the British units board their aircraft the Egyptian journalist cannot resist remarking, "Another British withdrawal." So it is, but in far more positive circumstances than the humiliating pull-out from Suez five years earlier that he has in mind. On this occasion the task of patrolling Kuwait's frontier is being freely handed over to a combined Arab force, a promising sign for the future.

My own departure draws near too. I am now lodged with a colleague from Shemlan days, Mig Goulding and his wife, Susan, as Alan Rothnie's wife has come with new-born babe from Beirut to join him in the embassy. I have also acquired a saluki puppy from some Al Mutair bedouin, camped with their camel herd near the town. Salukis are very much part of the Kuwait scene; to desert Arabs, for whom dogs are unclean, the fastidious saluki is in a different category, valued for its prowess in the hunting of gazelle in tandem with the hawk. With this handsome black and tan creature, named Sabah, begins for Grania and me an affair for years to come with these elegant dogs. By late October the puppy and I are on our way back to the seductive embrace of Beirut.

Egyptian Interlude
December 1962

People are startled at our choice of a trip up the Nile for a delayed honeymoon, lest we run into residual hostility over the Suez invasion six years earlier. As it happens the fears are groundless; there is a warm welcome from the moment we disembark from the *Esperia* at Alexandria. As we climb the broad stairs to the railway terminus to catch the express to Cairo, we are met by a smart figure in uniform and red tarboosh. "Are you Mr and Mrs Munro?" We are indeed. "Then please come with me." A porter seizes our bags, and we follow our guide along the wide station concourse to a café with tables under cheerful umbrellas. Several dignified officials rise to greet us and invite us to take coffee. We sit somewhat bemused and making small talk until one of the party, in splendid frogged costume, rises to say, "Mr and Mrs Munro, I am the stationmaster of Alexandria. We believe that you are the first British visitors to return to Egypt for several years. It gives me great pleasure to welcome you back on behalf of Egyptian Railways."

It is a moment of high emotion, and a dreamlike start to our journey. We all clasp each other warmly as I attempt a few inadequate remarks in return. Coffee and cakes are brought until we start to worry about missing the express. "Do not worry," exclaims the stationmaster. "The train will wait for you." And so it does. When protocol is eventually satisfied Grania and I are escorted past several carriages of irritated passengers to a private compartment and waved on our way by our hospitable hosts. It has been a memorable encounter; we have had a soft spot for Egypt ever since.

* * * * *

Two fascinating days in Cairo and Giza and we take the night train on to Luxor. One of the sleeping cars catches fire along the way, but we can forgive Egyptian Railways anything after that wonderful welcome. The famous old Winter Palace Hotel is virtually empty. I start running a bath to remove the dust of the journey; twenty minutes later the water still gushes cold through the massive taps. I complain to the servant who is posted outside our door. "How long have you run the water, *ya sidi?*" When I tell him, he assures me it will be hot in another twenty minutes – and it is. Quite something, this Edwardian plumbing. It is a privilege to have the Karnak temples and the decorated tombs of the Valley of the Kings virtually to ourselves. Tourism is at a standstill post-Suez. On to the grand Cataract Hotel in Aswan to visit the temple of Philae, not as yet submerged by the great dam which the Russians are building above the cataracts. We board a river steamer for the six-day return voyage upstream to the twin temples of Rameses II and his queen, Nefertari, at Abu Simbel in the Nubian Mountains. The handful of fellow passengers includes a group of evangelical Americans who enliven our evenings with hymn singing on the upright piano.

We reach Abu Simbel after nightfall and moor for the night. The temples are set in a low gorge of sandstone; three years later they will be cut into sections and relocated higher up the rocks in a remarkable feat of archaeological engineering to avoid submersion in the waters of the reservoir lake created by the Aswan dam. Our dawn timing has been carefully calculated to enable us to catch the beams of the rising sun as they briefly illuminate through its narrow doorway the altar within the dark chambers of the main temple. No such luck. We wake to find ourselves shrouded in thick fog, a rarity on the Upper Nile. A few yards from the landing stage we can just discern the grey outline of the colossal statues of the Pharoah on the façade. Forgetting piety for an instant, one of the Americans grumbles to his wife, "Have you brought me all this way just to see some more goddam sphinxes?" The guide puts a brave face on things as we grope our way to the temple entrance. High up on the door jamb I can just make out the carefully incised names of soldiers of the Royal Sussex Regiment who passed this way in 1884 with Sir Garnet Wolseley's force, sent too late by a reluctant British government to rescue General Gordon in Khartoum. At that time the temples were partly buried by desert sand. The sun is starting to burn through the thick mist, but sadly we cannot wait as the boat has to make its tight schedule back to Aswan. It will be another twenty years before I have the chance to see Abu Simbel in sunlight.

But it is not to be plain sailing. That evening a wind gets up, bringing waves that lap across our low decks. The worried captain decides to moor for the night. The delay brings consternation to those who have flights to catch. An Italian lady asks how she can explain her failure to return to her work in Rome. In a flash of inspiration I recommend she pleads *sforza maggiore*. She seizes on this and goes off chanting her new mantra. Fortunately Grania and I have a day or two in hand. We make it back to Cairo by temple stages, and on to Alexandria.

* * * * *

The *Ausonia* has brought the car from Beirut and we are bound for Marseille via Syracuse and Naples. It is Christmas week in midwinter so passengers are few. Inevitably a fierce tempest gets up on Christmas Eve which has us confined to our berths. For Grania it does not help that she is in the early stages of pregnancy. Christmas morning dawns and the sea is as brutal as ever. At midday there comes a knock on our cabin door. It is the steward. "Signori," he beseeches us, "I know you are suffering. But could you do us the favour of coming to the dining room just for a few minutes? You see, the chef he has prepared a wonderful display for the Christmas lunch and there is nobody there to see it. He is weeping with sadness. I promise that you need not eat anything. Just sit at your table and I will serve you a little spaghetti. The chef will show you his handiwork and then you can come straight back to your cabin."

Who could resist such a heartfelt appeal? We drag ourselves unsteadily along the passage and collapse into our seats. The big restaurant is indeed empty except for the captain and the ship's officers who, oblivious of the storm, are tucking with gusto into their Christmas fare. We sit wanly as out from the galley come the chef and his underlings, wheeling past us great trolleys on each of which lie superbly carved images in ice of swans and other exotic birds, all garnished with ornate confections. They must have taken all night to prepare. We can hardly bear to look, but manage what we hope is a friendly grimace at the artist. Honour appears to be satisfied however, and, with much show of gratitude, the steward helps us back to oblivion. We resolve that in future we shall make our posting moves by air.

Three days on and we offload the car in an icy Marseille for a hazardous drive the length of France to Paris and on to the Channel. At Le Touquet airfield the man from the Automobile Association points to the snowbound runway and says no Bristol freighter has landed for days. With chains on the car wheels we skid our way to catch the last boat out of Boulogne, and see out New Year's Eve in a freezing guest house in Folkestone. We ask for fruit at supper. "An apple or an orange?" enquires the waiter. No self-indulgence here; this is Fawlty Towers. A frugal sequel to a memorable Egyptian experience; in London the snow hangs on for another six weeks.

London
1963-1965

Diplomacy is like ploughing sand

Sir Ashley Clarke

There are stages in every working life, and not least in a bureaucracy, when we find ourselves at the coalface with a succession of intricate matters demanding close attention, and yet little sense of result; in effect the trees obscure the view of the wood. Such is my experience of three years on a Foreign Office desk engaged in responding to the tensions which afflict an alliance such as the North Atlantic Treaty Organisation (NATO) where a powerful common defensive purpose is offset by inevitable national rivalries and discords among its members.

For all its supreme achievement in ensuring that the Cold War stays cold and that Europe remains locked in a security stalemate, disharmony is never absent, mostly petty, occasionally more serious, whether in political form as with bitter Greek-Turkish antipathy over Cyprus, or in the military arena over the role of nuclear weapons in battle or fitful moves towards the closer integration of national forces and standardisation of their equipment. There are tricky negotiations in Whitehall to bring a newly independent Malta, who, with her strategic naval base, is seen as susceptible to Soviet influence, under the umbrella of the NATO alliance. Much time is taken up with a tedious exercise to coax legislation on the privileges and immunities to be accorded to other NATO forces in Britain through a querulous Westminster parliament. Overshadowing all these divisions is the visceral reluctance on the part of General de Gaulle to see a renascent France submerge her identity and independence of action in NATO's supranational structure. His peremptory decision in 1965 to withdraw French participation in the alliance's military command brings major upheaval and the removal of the NATO headquarters from Paris to Brussels.

For much of this period, until a worn-out Conservative government under Sir Alec Douglas-Home is replaced by a Labour administration in the general election of 1964, the Foreign Office is in the charge of R.A. (Rab) Butler. An eminent political figure, his lukewarm approach to foreign policy gives one the impression, intentionally perhaps, that he considers he should by right be sitting not in this grand room overlooking St James' Park but rather across the road in No. 10 Downing Street. Nevertheless Britain can still claim to be playing a global role in the field of international security. This is brought home to me when I am occasionally called to cross Whitehall to the Ministry of Defence in order to deputise for more senior Foreign Office mandarins at policy meetings of the heads of Britain's armed services. These are chaired by Admiral Lord Mountbatten, war hero and former Viceroy of India, whose imperious manner and incisive comments are treated with condign respect by the military chiefs in attendance. As staff officers bustle in and out of the map-hung room I seek a place near the bottom of the long table, feeling conspicuous in suit and tie amid the gold braid and medal ribbons. But there is no hiding for long; the military all having said their piece, "And what," demands Lord Louis, fastening me with a look tinged with disdain, "has the Foreign Office to say on all this?" I take a deep breath…

* * * * *

The pressures of the work are compounded by a hard taskmaster in the shape of John Barnes, an individual of rigorous intellect and short fuse. He would subsequently be posted as ambassador to Israel where we expected him to meet his match. A stickler for correct usage of English, style and syntax are for John every bit as important as substance. Interrogatives expressed in the "*num*" form when "*nonne*" is deemed to be more appropriate bring sharp reproof (please, which of them expects the answer "yes"?). Sir Ernest Gowers' magisterial work, *Plain Words*, serves as our Bible and sharpens the pen. As becomes the son of a Bishop of Birmingham, John is something of a biblical scholar. A proposal I submit on some aspect of our policy in NATO comes back adorned with the spare comment "too Laodicean". Recourse to Cruden's Concordance brings me to the Book of Revelation, chapter 3, vv. 15–16 in which St John castigates the church in Laodicea for being "lukewarm and neither hot nor cold" – point taken. One prime solecism in the Barnes liturgy is the misapplication of the verb "to anticipate"; he quotes a classic definition of its proper use given by his former ambassador in Washington, Lord Inverchapel, "James and Mary anticipated their wedding" – a sequence of events that is fast becoming obsolescent.

Policy discussion is conducted through tautly written "minutes" rather than via the ephemeral medium of the telephone. I chafe at seeing my diligent, if immature, contributions chopped by many hands as they move up the Office's over-elaborate production line. There are times when the volume of dictation overwhelms our "departmental ladies" as the typist staff are graciously known. Reserves can be called up from a pool of stenographers in some remote corner of the cavernous building. It can spring the odd surprise. One busy day my call for help comes in the shape of a charming middle-aged man wearing full facial make-up. His appearance brings all kinds of sensitivities to life, for the subject with which I am dealing carries a high security classification. After an exchange of startled looks with other members of the happy band in our "Third Room", I discreetly ring the lady in charge of the typing pool to check out his status, only to be given the blithe assurance that there is no problem as "he has a private income". So that's all right then...

* * * * *

Good friends from Lebanon keep in touch with us in London; their beautiful country will within a few years be torn apart by a quarter of a century of brutal civil war. A parliamentarian acquaintance from Tripoli – later to have a short-lived spell as Prime Minister – turns up and I take him to lunch at the Travellers Club in Pall Mall. As we taste our ritual mulligatawny soup amid the club's imposing surroundings he asks with a touch of impatience when the girls will appear. Oh dear; not quite the sort of club which, accustomed to Lebanon's boisterous nightlife, he has been expecting.

Home life proves rather more eventful than the daily pursuit of harmony within NATO, what with the birth of a daughter and a series of house moves as we search for a Thames-side home that is within our means. The first night in one rented house in Notting Hill is disturbed well after midnight by a loud knock on the door. The visitor turns out to be a young police constable who asks if we have a very thin dog. At this moment the saluki I had acquired out of a bedouin tent in Kuwait bounds down the stairs. "Ah, it's a saluki," says the policeman. "Surely, constable, you haven't got us up in the middle of the night to tell us the breed of our dog?" He then explains with apologies that he is from Notting Hill Gate station where a report has been received from their colleagues in Chiswick that some busybody member of the public had reported a woman in a car registered in our name exercising a "half-starved Gordon setter" there earlier in the day. Grania had indeed been giving the hound its run. By happy coincidence the constable turns out to have lived as a boy on an RAF base in Libya and is familiar with the bedouin's favourite hound. So no further action and he departs content. We wonder how many felons are burgling their way round Notting Hill while the police spend the night hours checking the condition of our Sabah. But then we British are always said to put animals first.

* * * * *

General de Gaulle's paranoia over a perceived threat of Anglo-Saxon dominance in Europe's destiny underlies his summary, indeed brutal, snub in 1963 to Britain's first application to join the European Economic Community. A terse French message in this sense goes to an aggrieved Harold Macmillan at 10 Downing Street, who charges the Foreign Office with drafting a response. This historic communication nearly goes astray in transit however. Finding that I am living on the road to Heathrow, I am asked, in the relaxed courier fashion of those days, to take the Prime Minister's reply out to the airport to hand it over to the British ambassador, Sir Pierson Dixon, who is catching an early flight to Paris for a meeting with the General. I sleep with this crucial missive safely under my pillow, only to fail to connect with the ambassador in the airport's terminal next morning. There is nothing for it but to burst through the security barriers, down the ramp and across the tarmac towards what I hope is the Paris-bound Viscount, chased by a posse of officials and police. I just make it up the steps into the aircraft as the doors are closing and thrust the letter into the hands of a distraught ambassador, who has begun to see himself going empty-handed into his crucial audience.

Keep the Flag Flying

A NATO ministerial conference with its litany of formal speeches, pre-cooked communiqués and ceremonious hospitality, and held in the grandly restored saloons of Lancaster House and in the Banqueting Hall along Whitehall where King Charles I once lost his head, forms the climax to two laborious years of repetitive bureaucracy and elusive consensus within a fractious defence alliance. A posting to the open spaces of North Africa comes as a welcome release from a despondent London which has as yet hardly started to exchange the long years of post-war impoverishment and social unrest for the "swinging sixties". It will be hard to leave our new-found home in a fine but dilapidated old house we are just starting to restore on the bank of the Thames and within the aromatic shadow of a brewery, yet a refreshing change to be back in the unpredictable welter of Arab politics.

Libya
1965-1968

The Arabs are Jews upon horseback

Benjamin Disraeli, *Tancred*

Arrival into Benghazi airport at two o'clock in the morning off the Nairobi-bound East African Airways Comet and with one very small daughter plus a newborn baby presents a test to parental stamina. It does not help to discover that, having been spared only a single hectic weekend between winding up my London job and setting off for North Africa, we are not expected for several days.

Benghazi itself, reputed location of the mythical Garden of the Hesperides and the underground River Lethe in Hades, is now joint capital along with distant Tripoli of an artificial desert kingdom created by the United Nations out of thirty years of harsh Italian colonisation, and then a rudimentary British military administration following the Second World War. It presents a run-down aspect. The dilapidation is compounded by brackish water and the pall of red dust that envelopes the town in a blast of stifling heat during the choking *ghibli* sandstorms that blow up from the Sahara. Many of the buildings still show scars of bombardment from the five marches and countermarches – the Benghazi Handicap in which my brother Colin took part in a succession of tanks – that flowed across Cyrenaica and the Western Desert during the early years of the war, as armoured forces from Britain and her empire wrangled with Italian and then more powerful German armies over this huge battlefield of sand and scrub, while successive generals made and lost their reputations in combat. Yet for all the town's drab appearance it feels good to be back amid the bustle, the colourful costumes and the spiced aromas that go with Arab markets.

We find Libya in an uncertain mood, still a tribal society of pastoral bedouin and townsfolk Arabs, with a few Berber groups and even a handful of families descended from the Moors, expelled from Spain four and a half centuries before. A constitutional monarchy of largely British creation since 1951, the country is governed under a parliamentary system in which the political groupings and senior appointments have become the preserve of tribal and regional interests, while rivalry persists between the two main provinces of Tripolitania and Cyrenaica. There is a prosperous community of Sephardic Jewish merchants, whose centuries of residence are about to be abruptly terminated in urban riots aroused by the Arab-Israeli war of June 1967. Libya has survived a first decade of impoverished independence, underpinned by British subsidies. Suddenly her economic adversity has been transformed by financial rewards from massive oil deposits, being brought on stream by American and British producers. Massive construction projects are under way, including a raw new national capital at Al Baida, up in the Jebel Akhdar range that fringes the eastern coast and near to the ruins of the Greek city of Cyrene, a marvel of the ancient world. There are new contracts, military as well as civil, to be had on every side, much to the advantage of predominating British enterprises.

Unsurprisingly the impact of this avalanche of activity on Libya's unsophisticated and passive society has induced an appetite for the darker side of business, not least among close advisers around the senescent King Idris. This dignified and reclusive ruler, hereditary leader of the puritan Senussi brotherhood and, after years of bitter resistance to a brutal Italian rule, strongly attached to the connection with Britain, is unable to hold the indulgence in check. As Anthony Thwaite mordantly puts it in a collection of poetry on his experience of Libya:

Simon of Cyrene carried the Cross.
No Libyan in collar and tie will carry anything.

These insidious ills are compounded by a growing political restlessness that receives its powerful stimulus from the current mood of nationalist identity and anti-western sentiment, now prevalent across the Arab world in the wake of Gamal Abdel Nasser's takeover in Egypt, the debacle of the

Franco-British attack on the Suez Canal and France's traumatic evacuation of neighbouring Algeria. Yet Libya, together with Cyprus and Malta, still forms a key element in a diminished British strategic shield within the eastern Mediterranean. Britain's stake in Libya's precarious stability and pro-western outlook, inherited from the Second World War and amounting to a degree of tutelage, is buttressed by the presence of substantial contingents from the British Army and the Royal Air Force, based in Benghazi and at Tobruk and El Adem airfield near the Egyptian frontier, along with a US Air Force base at Wheelus Field near Tripoli. Their presence however is by now contributing to these popular resentments, which are shortly to erupt in violent demonstrations and lead eventually to the regime's overthrow. As a struggling English-language student at the university puts it in an essay for his British tutor – "Libya is a country of agriculture and difficulture". Quite so…

* * * * *

The embassy occupies offices of the former Italian administration near the harbour. We find ourselves, plus a New Zealander nanny, a tight fit in an adjacent block of flats we call Peabody Buildings. It has its hazards; most alarming is the need to remember to turn off the taps before getting into the bath to avoid a sharp electric shock, as the water system is somehow live. A good night's sleep is rendered impossible by the packs of feral dogs that roam the city in the small hours. Indeed they can be vicious; the municipality's efforts to reduce their number by depositing poisoned meat goes badly awry when the meat ends up in domestic kitchens. Grania has a near escape while walking with our Kuwaiti saluki by the shore. Threatened by a roaming pack she is saved by the dog which, answering some deep atavistic instinct, charges the leading pi-dog and pointing his long head and neck between the dog's forelegs, flicks it into the air so that it lands on its back, the saluki's instinctive tactic when hunting gazelle with the bedouin. The pack takes flight.

Our basic domestic needs are catered for after a rudimentary fashion by Abdul Khair, a local of African stock and limited culinary skills. He does however provide one fascinating glimpse of the status of black Libyans within tribal society. Shortly after our arrival I find myself in charge of the post when the Consul-General, Robert Dundas, is transferred. One afternoon I join the other chiefs of our tiny diplomatic community on a long drive down the coast to Ajdabiyah to attend the funeral of a tribal sheikh who has held a leading position in the government. There is a huge turnout of dignitaries; we join the procession behind the coffin through dusty streets to the cemetery, after which we form up to pay our respects to the heads of the family. To my surprise the fourth in the line among the most senior figures, all smart in suits or tribal garb, is Abdul Khair, who had earlier prepared our breakfast and is still in his working clothes. We show no sign of recognition as I present him with HMG's official condolences. That evening however, with Abdul Khair back in the kitchen, no doubt in the process of concocting Libya's favourite dish, a savoury soup of mutton, tomato, chickpeas and hot pepper paste, I say how struck I was to find him high in the grand receiving line by the graveside. "Of course," he replies, "My mother was an *'abd* [in effect a bonded servant] of the family as they moved around the desert, and was wet nurse to the late sheikh. Because we shared her milk I remain a central part of the family. It is the bedouin way." So much for racial prejudice in Arab custom.

There is little opportunity however for social contact with Libyans, who keep very much to themselves. We find ourselves in a largely expatriate society of oil companies, engineers and academics, mostly British, American and Egyptian. The substantial British military presence also features in our lives with Sunday matins at the garrison church followed by drinks and curry in the officers' mess – "thirst after righteousness" as it is known. The wife of the manager of the local branch of Barclays Bank is notorious for insisting that ladies invited to tea should wear gloves – the intimidating memsahib image is very much alive. One of my predecessors had been Martin Buckmaster, a dyed-in-the-wool Arabist whose idea of entertaining his Libyan contacts was to buy a carcass of mutton in the market, chuck it in his Land Rover, and push off into the hills where he would hold a feast in some bedouin encampment, generally accompanied by a flickering outdoor film show on a bed sheet about life in Britain; all very romantic, and no doubt popular too, but by now Cyrenaica is outgrowing such antics. The town boasts one unhygienic restaurant, the original "Greasy Spoon", where we are not surprised to find the table laid with a tin of prickly heat powder alongside the cruets. Nightlife is restricted to a dingy section of the dilapidated Berenice Hotel, said to have been formerly the Italian army's bordello and now hosting second-rate Egyptian belly dancers and furtive drinkers. Competition for their custom is about to arrive in the shape of the gleaming new Benghazi Palace, complete with artless sign in its lobby to "Make our Bar your Randez-vous". A colourful place in the town is the old *funduq* or custom house, where merchants, farmers and nomads bring their produce and handicrafts to market; fruit and vegetables of excellent quality are cultivated around the wells and lagoons of the dusty coast.

* * * * *

We seek relief from a claustrophobic Benghazi in the Jebel Akhdar, or Green Mountain, the impressive escarpments of which rise from the dry coastal plain to the north-east. These well-watered and fertile uplands, cut through with steep *wadis*, extend for over a hundred miles as far as Derna, famed for its luscious apricots – *bukra fil mishmish* or "apricots tomorrow", as the Arab proverb runs. The *jebel* affords a welcome contrast to Benghazi's ubiquitous dust and brackish water. Best of all, the coastal hills are littered with the monuments of the classical Greek and Roman settlements that formed the ancient Pentapolis. The embassy is fortunate to have inherited a villa and cottage amidst the ruins of the region's greatest city, Cyrene, founded on the rim of a steep escarpment by Greek colonists around 630 BC, allegedly on the instructions of the Delphic Oracle, and inhabited by successive Greek, Hellenistic, Jewish, Roman and Byzantine communities for well over a millennium. They chose well; Cyrene, together with its port of Apollonia, the now submerged ruins of which provide a memorable experience for the snorkelling amateur archaeologist, is one of the classical gems of North Africa, in its cool and fragrant setting. Its great forum, on the rim of the Cyrenaican escarpment that drops down to the blue of the Mediterranean, is magnificent in scale and the Temple of Zeus, several columns of which are standing, is larger than the Parthenon.

During their brief and contested thirty-year conquest of Cyrenaica from Ottoman rule, the Italians made a start on excavation and restoration. But they could only scratch the surface of the vast site. The embassy's villa there was built for Marshal Graziani, the most brutal of Mussolini's military commanders during the Fascist era who, through a policy of forced concentration of the local tribespeople into camps, finally put an end to the determined resistance of the Senussi with the capture in the Jebel and subsequent public hanging of their commander, Omar Mukhtar. Vestiges of Italy's ambitious but forlorn attempt at agricultural colonisation are scattered across the Jebel Akhdar. The largest of these is on the fertile western plateau around Barce, where the plain is dotted with smallholdings, each with its identical farmhouse built for the Lombardy peasants who were uprooted in large numbers and sent off to farm the newly pacified African colony. Their tenure had hardly begun when in 1940 the region became a battlefield, and the farmers were summarily evacuated back to Italy. Their dilapidated homesteads are now in the hands of local bedouin for whom bricks and mortar are alien to a pastoral way of life; instead they find the buildings handy shelters for their flocks and pitch their own goat-hair tents alongside.

During the Italian period Barce became a substantial rural centre with a railway running down the escarpment to Benghazi. The service is now reduced to a once-a-week railcar. It is told that, in an early fit of enthusiasm for technical assistance, the British government arranged for the signalman at Benghazi to have a training spell at hectic Clapham Junction, where he suffered a nervous breakdown – probably an apocryphal tale but a cautionary one. Barce is now a tumbledown place, having been largely destroyed, with considerable loss of life, by an earthquake some years previously. A smart new town in concrete is under construction a few miles away. Meanwhile the inhabitants camp in what remains of their homes and shops. My courtesy call one morning on the local governor is interrupted by what appears to be an artillery barrage nearby. There are sounds of panic from the street outside, and bits of ceiling start to drop on us. The governor is quite unperturbed. "Just another *zilzal*", he says and takes a sip of mint tea. There is nothing for it but to stand, or rather sit, my ground. It would not do for Her Majesty's representative to blink first. Thankfully the earthquake rolls away.

The Barce plain is alive with partridge and quail, for the sport of which the officers of the British military training mission have cunningly contrived to have a gamekeeper on their strength in the shape of Colour Sergeant Crowdey of the Grenadier Guards. There is not a covey or a covert he does not know. On towards Derna near the rocky promontory of Ras al Hilal with its wrecked Italian Navy submarine pens lives Miss Olive Brittain, official beekeeper to the King and survivor of the line of indomitable British women who have taken up abode around the Arab world. It is said she arrived after the war in the company of a British officer, "Galloper" Evans, and that King Idris, much taken with her honey, set her up in an isolated Italian farmhouse where her bees feast off the rich flora of an enchanted valley. With time however has come paranoia; behind every bush lurks someone out to get her. Visitors are not always welcome; one popular tribute for gaining admission through her barricades is a Dundee cake from the NAAFI store in Benghazi. The house itself is grand but quaint. Caricatures of Winston Churchill and slogans hostile to Britain in Gothic script, relics of earlier occupation by the Afrika Korps, still adorn the sitting-room walls, and when she takes us into the kitchen a chicken flies out of the oven door of the old-fashioned range. Miss Brittain is however not a whit discomposed by her decrepit habitation.

We speculate whether her abode might be the Italian farmhouse deep in the *jebel* which was the scene in late 1941 of a celebrated commando raid led by Colonel Geoffrey Keyes on what was believed to be the headquarters of the Afrika Korps commander, General Erwin Rommel. Landing from submarines the group were taken inland to the farm by Libyan guides. In the event the raid was a failure. Rommel was away in Rome, and Keyes and a number of his party were killed in the ensuing firefight while others made it back through the desert to British lines. Keyes, who was awarded a posthumous Victoria Cross, lies buried in Benghazi's large war cemetery. It is in this well-kept refuge that I find myself attending the annual Remembrance Day parade by our garrison regiment of hussars – the only occasion on which I ever wear my newly acquired tropical white diplomatic uniform, in which under a peaked cap I feel more like a hotel commissionaire than a commissioned officer of the Diplomatic Service. (Many years later in Qaddafi's Libya I find myself laying a wreath at this still tranquil cemetery on behalf of a visiting tour group. When I point out Keyes' headstone to a Libyan accompanying us he reveals with pride that his father had been one of the local guides that met the commandos on the shore and led them to the farm.)

Further east lies Tobruk, a small and undistinguished port that was the scene of an epic five-month siege of Australian and British troops and their eventual relief in 1941, and has now begun to come alive again as the loading terminal for crude oil from British Petroleum's Sarir field way off in the Saharan sand seas. The crude is so thick that, were the flow in the pipeline to halt, it would become "the longest candle in the world". King Idris prefers to base himself here in Tobruk in a modest home, well away from the rough and tumble of Libya's political life. The area contains some of the most imposing war cemeteries of the North Africa campaign. Their styles reveal something of the contrasting national attitudes to warfare of the combatants. The huge German cemetery takes the form of a towered fortress with the walls of its inner courtyard emblazoned with the names of the fallen – a heroic yet resentful memorial in Wagnerian mould. The two extensive British cemeteries at Tobruk and at "Knightsbridge" nearby afford a complete antithesis. In the gentle Cotswold village style adopted by the Commonwealth War Graves Commission emotions of grief are eased by the neat rows of granite headstones marking the dead of the many nationalities that made up the Eighth Army, with members of a Senussi Libyan force too, and set in a neatly landscaped and well-tended garden setting. The mood is one of peace.

* * * *

May sees us transferred 700 miles west to Tripoli, where I take over the political section of our embassy's main branch. We welcome the change to the more sophisticated environment of Libya's main city, particularly as it comes shortly after Grania has suffered an unpleasant assault close to our villa and the children's nanny has been briefly carted off to a mental ward in the British Military Hospital in Cyprus for observation. There are regrets however to be losing the good company of Peter and Felicity Wakefield who have taken charge in Benghazi and become firm friends. The ambassador in Tripoli is the jovial Rod Sarell, affectionately known as "Hot Rod", with long experience of the Levant and North Africa and descended from one of the old-established British merchant families from Smyrna. We are lucky to inherit an elegant and cool Ottoman-period house on the harbour front, with raftered ceilings, veranda and a walled garden with a marble fountain. The flat roof sports a high wooden frame which handily provides the girls with a swing; only later do we discover that our Italian landlord has sequestered it there as a trophy from the Fascist period when it apparently served as a gibbet! (Sadly the house has since been razed and the gibbet is said to have been transferred by Colonel Qaddafi to be an exhibit in the national museum). The only serious drawback for us is the presence of rats which occasionally emerge from the dark cellar and scamper over our bed at night.

The city itself is in tidier shape than Benghazi. The British army garrison and the RAF presence at the airport have recently been withdrawn. There is however a strong British influence still in evidence; the main hospital and secondary school are British-run and the only supermarket belongs to the Gordon Woodruffe trading house. There are British advisers in key ministries, and the British Council, where an old Cambridge friend, Clive Smith, is on the staff and his wife is a nurse at the hospital, runs a major English-language programme. The modern business centre from the Italian period has arcaded streets in the style of Milan or Turin. Behind its walls lies the old castle, or *casbah*, of the Karamanlis and other rulers from the heyday of the Barbary corsairs and the Ottoman regency. The rest is a fascinating warren of old mosques, handsome but dilapidated courtyard houses in Moorish style, and booths where traditional apparel and attractive filigree jewelry are crafted, much of it by Jewish artisans. A modern contrast is provided by a glitzy casino in the Waddan hotel, frequented by American oilmen on a break from the desert – and where I once learn to shoot craps. By the seashore to the west of the harbour there is an intriguing memorial to the *Philadelphia*, flagship of a fledgling US Navy squadron despatched in 1804 by President Jefferson on his country's first ever naval engagement to punish Dey Osman Karamanli for attacks by Tripoli's pirates on American shipping. The *Philadelphia* ran aground and was captured. The prize was subsequently retaken and set on fire in a daring raid by Lieutenant Decatur; hence the reference to the "shores of Tripoli" in the battle hymn of the US Marines.

The surrounding hills that shield Tripoli from the desert are populated by Berber as well as Arab tribal groups. Some Berber families live a troglodytic existence in ample chambers excavated beneath the sandy slopes. We start to make Libyan and other Arab friends, including a descendant of the Emir Abdel Kader al-Jazairy, the tribal leader who led a prolonged resistance against the military might of France in Algeria in the mid-19th century. There is still an Italian feel to Tripoli. The non-Arabic daily newspaper is in Italian; I try to master the grammar with the aid of an old "Hugo". Some knowledge is essential as maintenance services are still undertaken by Italians, and otherwise we shall never get the clutch repaired on the Austin. My rudimentary vocabulary confounds our Italian grocer when, on the hunt for cheese crackers, I ask for "*biscottes per la chiesa*". He politely suggests I get my wafers at the cathedral.

It is a long and hot couple of days' drive to Tripoli around the Bay of Sirte, much of it across empty desert with the monotony broken only by the occasional pipeline terminal. On the historical border between Cyrenaica and Tripolitania Italy's dictator, Mussolini, had a triumphal arch erected to the grandeur of new Rome, and known to irreverent British troops as Marble Arch. It marks the spot where, according to legend, the frontier was fixed by a race around 400 BC across the Syrtic desert with a Carthaginian team, composed of the Philaeni brothers, starting from the west and a Greek team from the east. The Philaeni ran faster and met the Greeks two thirds of the way across. The Greeks protested their rivals had started early and only accepted the result provided the Philaeni brothers agreed to be killed and buried at that spot. This duly happened, and the frontier remains to this day. Such is the lot of the long-distance runner. When Grania and I drive through the arch in 1966 it still carries a warning, scrawled on its flank no doubt by an exasperated British military policeman on convoy duty, which runs thus:

> You will not laff should Jerry straff
> Safety first Stay dispersed.

The journey gives us our first glimpse of the magnificent Roman ruins at Leptis Magna, the port city that was embellished by Rome's warrior Berber emperor, Septimius Severus, who died at York in AD 211 while on campaign to resist Scots incursions over Hadrian's Wall. Nor does Leptis' connection with England end there; nestling in a glade today beside the lake at Virginia Water in Surrey is a clutch of antique marble columns. These were purloined from the ruins of Leptis by an enterprising Captain Smyth, RN during Lord Exmouth's naval expedition of 1816 which put a final end to the predations of the corsair centres of the Barbary Coast and culminated in the great bombardment of Algiers. The monumental stones were carried back for presentation to the Prince Regent, later George IV, who had them erected on this picturesque site in Windsor Great Park.

Leptis Magna lies in a region of fertile hills where Italian farmers continue to cultivate wide acres of olive plantations. Many still live out an irredentist fantasy of Italy's Fascist rule with a portrait of Il Duce prominent in the home. The aristocratic Contessa Volpi, widow of a former Italian governor, still keeps a home in an old Moorish palace. Their lingering idyll is soon however to meet with a violent ending and flight.

* * * * *

One of the enjoyable diversions of my work in Tripoli is to accompany Rod Sarell on his periodic visits to see King Idris and act as interpreter in their discussions. Mercifully Libyans speak a pure version of Arabic, derived from their Arabian bedouin roots, unlike the clipped and berberised dialect encountered among their neighbours further west. Sometimes Pam Sarell and Grania are invited along on these outings to join Queen Fatima. An early start and a four-hour flight in the RAF Varsity bring us to Tobruk in time for a relaxed family lunch with the King and Queen. After we have eaten, and partaken of the ritual three glasses of green tea poured out with ceremony by the King – the first with sugar, the next flavoured with mint and the third fortified with peanuts with the embarrassing result that most of the contents dribble down one's chin, much to the royal mirth – the ladies find themselves invited to join the Queen in a session on an exercise bicycle.

King Idris is a patriarchal figure, ever open about his problems of governance. He sets store by his long and close relationship with Britain though the sequence of events sometimes becomes confused; on one occasion he begins by asking after the wellbeing of the Prince of Wales. When we explain that Prince Charles is attending a school in the Scottish Highlands the King shows considerable surprise. It turns out that he has in mind King Edward VIII. He can also be frank about Britain's part after the war in persuading him to become sovereign of a new and divided Libyan state. "I am from Algeria," he once grumbles to us, "and you made me King of Libya. It is difficult." Indeed the Senussi movement, of which he is titular leader by succession, originated in the 19th century in Mostaghanem in western Algeria and quickly spread its puritanical and martial creed across North Africa. More firmly established in Cyrenaica than in Tripolitania its principal shrine is now located at Jaghbub, deep in the desert south of Tobruk. There is a moment of embarrassment on one of these visits when bluff General John Frost, who from Malta has command of British forces in the eastern Mediterranean, and whom we are bringing on a farewell call, sits displaying the sole of one shoe before the royal eyes – an insulting gesture in Arab protocol. The courteous King takes it all in his stride. It is however

69

some relief for us when his successor, General Rea Leakey, a hero of the German siege of Tobruk, turns out to be a more sensitive "model of a modern major-general".

There is however much more to Libya than the settled coastal strip, as we find on a drive through uplands and desert to the Touareg oasis of Ghadames, a picturesque outpost on the frontier with Tunisia along the old African slaving route. The town is a warren of mud-walled houses where the women have their existence on the upper level and the men keep to the ground. We arrive in a heavy downpour which heralds the end of a year-long drought, and are greeted as saviours. Three days later of incessant rain, with the streets now a muddy torrent, the locals are probably glad to see the back of us.

* * * * *

Early on the morning of 5 June 1967 I find myself seeing a visitor off to London at Tripoli's Idris airport as reports start to come over the radio of Israeli air attacks on her Arab neighbours. An Egyptian friend comes up to warn me that this will mean problems for us locally. I am puzzled to see why, given our good relations and Libya's record of political inertia. This complacent illusion is promptly dispelled as I drive back into the city to find our chancery building already under siege from a mob of stone-throwing youths, many with transistor radios clamped to their ears from which the siren voice of Egypt's firebrand propaganda urges attack on British and American establishments. Libya's radical and suppressed undercurrent has at last burst to the surface, and so it will continue for some days. The startled staff have already closed up the embassy's shutters and the metal security screen over the entrance. We are effectively incarcerated and embark on our prepared procedures for the destruction of all sensitive material in case the mob should force entry. The police are called to protect the building but can do little to hold at bay the fast-growing and angry crowd. We get reports of an attack on the Benghazi embassy which has been set on fire, and of disturbances right across North Africa in Tunis, Algiers and Rabat, where the old order of stability is also being challenged by popular uprising. It is a tense scene, and brings a stream of telephone enquiries from the media back in Britain looking for a story. There comes a desperate rapping on the shuttered entrance. We open it a crack to find a British fugitive from the mob seeking refuge. He turns out to be an Arsenal footballer called Spurling, who is in Libya to train the national team. We send him up to the roof to join those who are endeavouring, under a shower of stones thrown by the youthful mob in the street below, to burn our most sensitive papers by the laborious method of waving them in a smouldering bag around their heads on a rope. It is a primitive and ineffective device; several precious sheets float away over the parapet. All the while the exhausted radio operators in a nearby shack laboriously take down an incessant stream of communications in encrypted Morse code; small wonder some of them go off the rails – at a later date one of them takes a bread knife to his wife.

A major concern is for the safety of Grania and the two small girls in our house a short distance along the waterfront. Earlier on an embassy colleague, Rosemary Butt, had providentially managed to warn Grania by telephone to stay indoors just as she was about to go out in the car with the children. From the embassy roof I can see an ominous cloud of dark smoke rising from the vicinity. The telephone is now dead. Geoff Bishop nobly volunteers to scale the rear wall of the embassy and make his way over to our home. He returns to report that the family are safe; it had been a very frightening time however as Grania found herself trapped inside by a menacing crowd throwing stones and attempting to set fire to the house. Mercifully our Libyan cook, Hadi, had persuaded them that no British family lived there. Whereupon the mob had turned its attention to an adjacent house, providing the distressing sight of a female member of Libya's Jewish community being roughly manhandled while her home was set alight. Most of the billowing smoke we had seen turns out to come from a truck from the US Air Force base at Wheelus Field that has been overturned in the street.

Contact is made with the police to ask for urgent help in evacuating the family to the ambassador's residence in its safer location further along the shore. To their credit they respond with the despatch of a Volkswagen Beetle with a police driver to the narrow alley between the side door of our garden and the villa of Libya's absent Crown Prince Ridha, which is also one of the mob's chosen targets. As ill luck will have it we had arranged to give a diplomatic dinner party that very night; an ample gazpacho soup has just been prepared when the message comes to abandon the house. Grania packs the girls and some basic necessities into the back seat of the Volkswagen. With foresight she has hastily dug a hole in one of the flower beds in which to hide our few pieces of silver (their recovery several days later involves much cautious probing for the cache with the tines of a garden fork). Resourceful as ever, she decides not to waste the soup but to bring it along. She squeezes into the car and carefully deposits it on the front seat beside the police driver. At this point our saluki dog, determined not to be left behind, slips out the gate and leaps through the car's open window straight into the large tureen, spraying driver and vehicle with fresh gazpacho. The drenched policeman, in any case none too happy in his role of rescuing a British family, explodes with "Filthy British soup!" "No," Grania corrects him, "Spanish" as the car plunges forward into the mob and the midday heat.

The residence has already become a refuge for a number of nervous British expatriates. Our advice to our community is to stay put and keep a low profile until the hostile mood passes; the Americans in contrast have decided on the more controversial course of flying out their expatriates from the cities and the oil installations. The embassy in Benghazi has had its defences breached, and a relieving British armoured vehicle burnt out by a mob. Peter Wakefield arranges for several hundred members of the community in Cyrenaica to be given refuge in the garrison barracks, where they find themselves camped for some days. The military manage to entice Olive Brittain down from her distant bee farm. "Your name?", asks the corporal at the registration desk. "Miss Brittain," comes the reply. In disbelief he looks up to find a generous bosom adorned with the pink bow of the Order of the British Empire. "Pull the other one, dear. What's your real name?" He receives a sharp reprimand.

The rioting lasts for much of the week, incited continuously by defiant Egyptian broadcasts as victorious Israeli forces drive on through Sinai to the Suez Canal and into Syria's Golan Heights and Jordan's Palestinian West Bank territory. To little effect we attempt to nail the insidious Egyptian allegation of British complicity in Israel's campaign. Tripoli suffers some serious destruction, particularly of buildings in the Jewish quarter of the Old City. The remaining Jewish population, together with a good portion of the Italian community, see the writing on the wall and flee to shelter offered them in Italy. The country is the poorer for their abrupt departure, though against a background of increasing nationalism this is probably inevitable. On the third day of unrest we had been due to hold the annual Queen's Birthday reception, to which leading Libyans and many of the

British community are invited. This is of course a non-starter; moreover the residence is now a refugee camp. Late that afternoon, on looking out of the office across the seafront highway, from which the youthful mob has largely dispersed, I see a lone Libyan in tribal costume of red felt cap, white robe and toga and with a row of North African campaign medals displayed upon his chest, standing stiffly to attention and saluting the Union Jack flying on our roof. He must be a loyal veteran of the Senussi force that had fought under the Eighth Army. After a few minutes he drops his arm and walks away. It is a brave act at this difficult time, and one that catches in our throats.

* * * * *

Following the Arab defeat by Israel it takes some time to recover a close relationship with Libyan acquaintances. Abdel Nasser's nationalist rhetoric has taken hold. Indeed on the night when the Egyptian leader in an emotional speech announces his resignation such is the hysteria this arouses among young Libyans that many are collected into hospital in a rigid cataleptic state. Egypt's propagandist "big lie" about British involvement in Israel's military conquest fades soon enough, though Arab resentment over defeat is to impede progress towards a solution of the poisoned Palestine issue for years to come. The crisis has moreover stimulated latent undercurrents of sedition within Libya of which we are only partly aware. We try to assess these with our military counterparts in periodic meetings of the local intelligence committee, involving me in trips to Malta and to Cyprus.

A young Libyan friend, Omar al-Badri, does his best to account for the ferocious outburst of hostility over Britain's perceived machinations which has so caught us off guard. The Soviet military attaché tells me a revealing fable about Egypt's military performance put about by her Red Army advisers. A Russian colonel is attached to the headquarters of an Egyptian brigade in Sinai. All is calm, until he suddenly finds himself deserted as the staff hastily evacuate westward. He then sees a large cloud of dust coming from the east and an armoured regiment swings by in retreat. It is followed by a second force. The adviser is wondering what on earth is up when a straggler comes into view. The Russian manages to catch him and demands what has led to this flight. "There is an Israeli soldier back there," says the man, as he struggles to get free. "But one Israeli is no reason for everyone to flee?" demands the Russian. "We don't know which one of us he is chasing," comes the reply. Caustic humour from a disenchanted Soviet ally.

Grania and I with our two girls take a respite from the tensions which have followed the rioting with a break in Malta. The handsome mediaeval fortifications and fine old palaces of Valetta with its lively Christian festivals and handicrafts of finely worked silver and lace help to refresh our spirits. A welcome discovery is a branch of Marks and Spencer, though the rigorous application of the Arab boycott of firms trading with Israel puts Grania to removing all labels from the garments we buy before we can bring them back to Tripoli.

∗ ∗ ∗ ∗

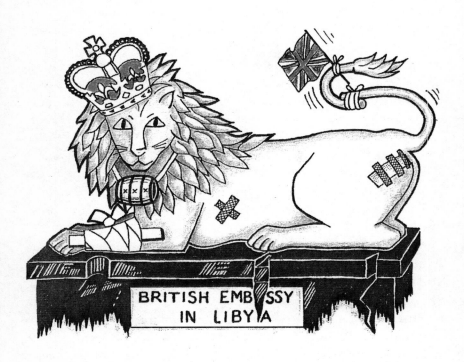

Bloody but unbowed; the card produced by the members of the British Embassy in Libya at Christmas 1967

The King's instinctive conservatism leads him to be wary of the spirit of nationalist republicanism that is evidently penetrating his country out of Nasser's Egypt next door. In this however he risks falling out of step with popular opinion. Defence against a possible military threat from Egypt now preoccupies him and he looks to Britain and the Americans to help with support for Libya's young military forces as well as with direct protection. A corvette has recently been acquired from Britain to inaugurate Libya's young navy. The King startles us by following up with a request for a submarine. Such a complex warship makes no sense; with the just launched Beatles anthem in mind I have to restrain myself from asking if he means a yellow one... We do however open discussions on the provision of a sophisticated air defence system.

For our part the violent riots in Tripoli and Benghazi, provoked by the outbreak of the Arab-Israel war in June 1967 and unfounded suspicions of British support for Israel's blitzkrieg attack, cause us to question the value to Libya and to Britain of retaining an army garrison in Benghazi. Given however the King's growing uncertainty over the popular mood in the country and his faith in an ultimate British shield, it will be a sensitive matter to obtain his blessing to our withdrawal. When we put the proposal to him over a solid lunch in Tobruk, we happen to choose a moment when he has a mouthful of chicken and rice. The King's monosyllabic reply in Arabic is indistinct enough for me to interpret it as assent. The withdrawal of the Inniskilling Dragoon Guards goes ahead, though we agree to retain the RAF's staging post at El Adem and the army training areas it serves, partly I suspect to satisfy Queen Fatima who has always found the El Adem NAAFI store indispensable for her wardrobe.

These adjustments to our long-standing defence relationship bring a visit by the Defence Secretary, Denis Healey. Strangely this is the first visit to Libya by a British minister for some years – an indication of the extent to which our political masters are content to leave the conduct of diplomatic negotiation in the capable hands of the diplomats on the ground. Our support is given for the award to Britannia Airways of the first contract for the transport by air of Libya's large national contingent undertaking the annual haj pilgrimage to Mecca, which includes our loyal cook, Hadi. Two years earlier we had encountered a dramatic sight in Benghazi when a dusty camel caravan, which had taken the historic and arduous route across the Sahara from distant west Africa, rode into town on its pious journey to Islam's holiest shrine. The British press also start to show an interest in Libya's increasing prosperity. Among our journalist visitors is the redoubtable Clare Hollingworth of *The Guardian*, famous for having scooped the German invasion of Poland back in September 1939. A veteran too of Algeria's bitter war of independence next door she startles us by swimming across Tripoli harbour before coming in for a morning briefing. The BBC's Gordon Martin comes up against Libya's primitive censorship process when his live report for the evening news bulletin down a precarious telephone connection is interrupted by a voice asking him to pause while the tape is changed.

In this aftermath of wariness we are thrown back on our own resources for diversion. I go riding out at the huge US Air Force base at Wheelus Field. The stables are run by conscripted roughriders whose "yee-hi" charges on western saddles are a total contrast to the polished routine of the cavalry riding school of the Inniskillings back in Benghazi. The weekly poker school I run with our embassy "spook" resumes, and amateur dramatics too. A production of Christopher Fry's *Ring Around the Moon*, in which I have a leading part, has its opening performance disrupted when I am summoned to fly east to Tobruk with Rod Sarell to see King Idris; a stand-in nobly reads the part, involving even greater "suspension of disbelief" than usual on the part of the audience. We take breaks to visit the theatrical Roman ruins at Sabratha, and to swim and fish from serene beaches all along the shore. To reinforce us in what has become a period of intense political workload an extra wireless operator is attached to the embassy. He turns out to be of all things a seer and magician, who moonlights as secretary of The Magic Circle, a wonderful bonus for our entertainment. Given his gift of second sight one wonders why we bother to encrypt the sensitive telegrams we exchange with London via his Morse code key and headphones in the radio shack on the embassy roof. In the new and restless climate that prevails we turn attention to contacts with the Libyan army, seen as a potential source of instability (as events will prove later). At one lively evening in our house we introduce some of the senior officers to the boisterous game of "Are you there, Moriarty". Perhaps they still play it...

* * * * *

That autumn Grania and I make an expedition through the deserts of Libya's southern Fezzan province down to the remote oasis of Ghat on the verge of the Tassili mountains. Our companions are Rosemary Butt and an old friend and amateur archaeologist out from London, Malcolm Davidson. As guide we have the pleasure of the egregious Dr Ayoub, a former sergeant in King Farouk's bodyguard in the Sudan who has somehow been transmogrified into the Libyan government's Director of Antiquities. He has made a particular study of the mysterious Garamantes civilisation that flourished in the fertile southern oases in the era of Roman occupation, and whose wasted monuments in the Germa oasis he is restoring with concrete and a somewhat heavy hand. According to the fanciful account of the classical Greek historian Herodotus, the Garamantes fought Ethiopian interlopers with four-horse chariots; they also bred an exotic strain of oxen that were obliged to graze backwards lest their low horns became impaled in the soil. For prudency's sake and running repairs we borrow a REME staff sergeant and an Ordnance Corps sergeant from the British Military Mission. The team is completed with local police and a peripatetic assortment of veiled Touareg nomads.

It all turns into a fascinating adventure; a mix of ancient societies, delicate rock engravings and cave paintings of wild beasts that date back to an era when prehistoric hunters roamed a fertile Sahara, pristine stone age hand axes lying on the desert floor, towering dunes and sandstone gorges, treacherous *fishfash* quicksands, diminutive Tiboo cameleers (with impeccable French) out of the distant Tibesti Mountains in Chad, and indigo-stained Touareg nomads with their obsolete Berber alphabet – *tamahaq*. Above all there is that indefinable sense of release that the desert can bring. One day sees an exhilarating charge for miles across the Murzuq sand flats, cans of Tennents lager on the dashboard wrapped in wet loo paper to chill them in the hot sun; great refrigeration but heavy on our precious water supply. Within one dark cave, its walls decorated in red ochre with primitive human and animal figures, Grania just stops me in time from stepping on a small snake the bite of which I am told is lethal. We camp by sparse wells, among bedouin who deplete Grania's supply of aspirin. The morning reveals more snake trails in the sand around our sleeping bags; the crafty Dr Ayoub has prudently taken his bedroll into a Land Rover. In the silent evenings under a brilliant panoply of stars we share visions of the future: "We white men must stick together," affirms Dr Ayoub, himself a full-blooded Nubian. At one oasis the rudimentary hospital is run by despondent Taiwanese who have run out of food as well as medicines;

recklessly we hand over supplies only to find we have left ourselves nothing but tinned Brussels sprouts and marmalade for the two-day run back to civilisation; so it's back to dodgy camel meat.

We make it to Ghat, Libya's most remote settlement in the mid-Sahara on the edge of the Tassili Mountains plateau. The local governor puts us up in the old fort, now rather a tumbledown affair where Grania and I are shown into a spacious if dilapidated bedroom. This, we are proudly told, is the stateroom prepared back in the 1930s for a visit by Italy's Governor General, Marshal Balbo, a famous aviator of the period who tried his best for Libya with Fascist Rome. The adjoining bathroom is furnished with gold-plated taps, though no water runs and the bath is full of wind-blown sand. It seems that the Marshal never made it to Ghat. The welcome to our party is however most hospitable.

It is said that on one occasion the Marshal flew himself from Tripoli for a visit to Tobruk. On arrival he was greeted by a local dignitary, to whom Balbo remarked that through the wonders of aviation he had undertaken in a day a journey that would have taken the sheikh at least a week by camel. "But what will you do with the other six days?" enquired the sheikh. Game, set and match to the timeless bedouin. Some years later in Brazil I re-encounter Ghat in an anecdote told by my ambassador, David Hunt, who served as intelligence officer in Field Marshal Alexander's HQ in North Africa. The German military intercepts they were receiving from the Enigma code breakers at Bletchley Park included an intriguing signal from Berlin to Field Marshal Rommel's staff which ran: "Olga Schmidt, the prostitute, will arrive at Tripoli. (Two code groups indecipherable?) her well, and send her on to Ghat." Evidently a beleaguered Afrika Korps garrison was in need of creature comfort – but what might the missing words have revealed about her treatment en route?

Our final stop is Sebha, the capital of the Fezzan province. There Dr Ayoub produces the doyen of the local tribes, Sheikh Mohammed Saif al-Nasr (or Sword of Victory), a grizzled and venerable warrior who regales us into the evening with tales of feuding. With relish he illustrates his uncompromising vindictiveness towards his enemies with a vivid account of how he once had the corpses of his slain foes dug up from their shallow sepulchres and replaced with the cadavers of dogs – a supreme insult in Muslim culture.

* * * * *

Life back in Tripoli seems tame. A routine of calls and canapés resumes, punctuated by occasional invitations to lively wedding ceremonies the distaff side of which involves Grania in somewhat off-putting encounters with the bride's hymen. The 'Id holiday following the fasting month of Ramadhan involves the traditional round of courtesy calls at the homes of former political leaders like Mustapha ben Halim who welcome us in. We enjoy the company of a variety of local characters, young members of Libya's aristocratic Al Muntasser family, Tariq al-Askari, a sophisticated scion of one of Iraq's powerful clans who knows by heart the scores of Mozart's operas, Augusto Ricciardi, a stylish Italian and friend to various British generals captured in the Western Desert, for whom he had acted as a notably lenient and congenial prison camp commandant back in Italy, and an eccentric Briton, Philip Bradburne, executive in an American oil company who moonlights as reader of the daily news in English on Libyan radio, to which he rides through Tripoli on a Vespa scooter with monocle, bowler hat and furled umbrella. An Italian doctor friend comes round one evening in a state of excitement. Having turned on his gramophone to play a record he is startled to find a conversation in Russian coming out of the speaker. Examination reveals a wire running up the wall and through the ceiling. He then recognises one of the voices as that of Ivan, a Russian embassy official who lives in the flat above. Pierluigi storms upstairs to remonstrate, to be met with a smooth welcome and a bottle of vodka. Not a whit abashed, Ivan seeks to excuse his clumsy exercise in eavesdropping with a solemn warning that Pierluigi's English wife, Angela, "is a member of Her Majesty's Secret Service". We let it rest.

The return to diplomacy is not to be prolonged however as we are soon posted back to London. We leave a newly enriched Libya, yet on the verge of social unrest and revolutionary upheaval. While her conservative establishment seeks improved defences against a perceived threat of Egyptian expansion, other elements in the population, including the military, have become seduced by Abdel Nasser's powerful nationalist message with its call to disengage from British and American tutelage. The government, under a young Prime Minister, Abdul Hamid Baqqoush, chooses to discount these new undercurrents with complacency. There are indications too that the relationship with Britain is starting to count for less among Libyans; the devaluation of the pound in 1968 sees a sharp drop in the value of Libya's growing assets from oil, much of which is held in sterling.

A year later the storm will break, when a youthful Captain Mu'ammar Qaddafi swiftly forestalls the plans laid by a group of senior army officers to take over government, a failed plot which may have had the King's acquiescence and of which we had been made aware. In the middle of the warm summer night of the coup, Peter Wakefield is called from bed in Benghazi in the early hours to decipher an urgent telegram from London. Crossing the street from his house to the chancery building, he finds himself grabbed by soldiers who march him up the road to the radio station. There he is confronted by a scruffy young officer who demands to know who he is. "The British Consul-General," says Peter, trying to look dignified in his Japanese *yukata* robe and bedroom slippers. "Who are you?" "I have taken over," comes the reply. "Go back to bed". A bizarre first encounter between a foreign diplomat and a Head of State. It will be 42 years before Qaddafi's revolution in Libya's backwater, with its radical anti-western ingredients and massive reverberations around the Arab world and far beyond, is brought to a bloody end in a rebellion by a people finally driven to despair under his manic and oppressive rule. For a weary King Idris though there is a safe and welcome exile in Egypt; as Queen Fatima writes to an English friend, "The slave is at last free."

London
1968-1972

It is an advantage in the F.O. to have a mad wife

David Hare, *Plenty*

B ack to London for four years in a fresh and absorbing field of managing the careers and appointments of diplomatic officers and their families, followed by a spell with responsibility for recruitment and the process of personnel selection. The appointment comes at a time when well-tried but paternalistic systems of management are having to be adapted to a changing employment environment in which individuals are claiming greater personal involvement over the direction of their careers. The long summer of a job for life and quiescent obedience to the decisions of the Service's managers is passing; a new generation, faced with wider options outside the frame of government service, is calling for more consultation and choice, as well as access to what is being reported on their performance and abilities. In step with the mood of the time the trades unions, known euphemistically as the "staff side", are finding new muscles to stretch. There is opposition too to the practice of reporting in confidence on the behaviour of officers' wives, for so long taken for granted as an unpaid adjunct to a diplomat's career. Female officers still face the discrimination of having to resign on marriage; the idea of a husband in the distaff role has yet to be accepted.

The Diplomatic Service under Labour's Foreign Secretary Michael Stewart is also being subjected to a thorough review of its role and resources, conducted by Sir Val Duncan, a leading industrialist. Among the report's key recommendations are a painful reduction in senior manpower and a greater emphasis on specialisation, including wider experience of trade promotion work abroad, an area hitherto regarded as something of a Cinderella activity by high fliers. These fresh ideas make for a challenging role for those engaged in administration of the Service. A traditional respect for the "gifted generalist" is starting to be queried in favour of the applied skills of the specialist. The upheaval is compounded by a controversial decision to bring the smaller Commonwealth Relations Office and what remains of the Colonial Office under the mantle of the Foreign Office, seen by some as a further dismantling of empire. The older dogs are having to learn new tricks.

✳ ✳ ✳ ✳ ✳

London too has seen changes during our three years absence. The "swinging sixties" have led to the unharnessing of fashion as well as of public inhibitions. No longer is the District Line train to Westminster and the City full of a morning with bowler hats, overcoats and neatly rolled umbrellas. No great loss perhaps; as Nicholas Elliot, the stylish senior spy back in our Beirut embassy days would put it – "Never judge a man by his umbrella." Yet I quickly learn to conform.

Our re-entry is not however to be straightforward, for we have arranged to bring back our Sudanese servant, Daoud, to our Chiswick home to help with the house and the girls. He comes under a curious immigration scheme whereby he is in effect indentured to our employ alone. We meet him at Heathrow and start by giving him an idea of the locality. Despite not having a word of English Daoud sets out that first evening to explore. By midnight he has not returned; a nightmare – could he have absconded already? Nor had he appeared the next morning, the first day of the Spring Bank Holiday weekend. So I call at the Chiswick police station to report a missing person. An avuncular Metropolitan Police sergeant straight out of the *Dixon of Dock Green* TV serial starts by asking for the individual's sex and how long they have been missing. Told it involves a male absent since the previous evening, he regrets he is unable to help at this point; under some bizarre anomaly in the law females can be reported missing after twelve hours whereas males have a full twenty-four in which to steal a march. If I come back that evening he can set a search in hand…

I duly reappear to be greeted by the same sergeant and we get down to details. I explain that Daoud is a Sudanese house servant, just arrived from

Libya. "Could you give me a description of this person, sir?" "He is short and dark, and has three deep knife scars across one cheek." "And do you really employ someone of this description?" comes the incredulous rejoinder. I explain that the scars are tribal badges and not the result of some criminal fracas, but the good sergeant remains sceptical. Helped perhaps by his misgivings a search message is quickly put out to squad cars throughout London. But Sunday still brings no news, nor Monday morning either. The police have found no trace of the errant Daoud.

We try a long shot and telephone the Sudanese consulate opposite St James' Palace. A charming voice answers in an impeccable English accent. "Are you by any chance looking for your *soffragi*? He is standing in front of me now! He was sent round to me from the Sudanese students hostel, where he spent last night. I'll give him a lecture and send him back to you in a cab." I can only express a profuse relief and appreciation; it is the Sudanese authorities and not the police who have come up trumps.

An exhausted Daoud is duly delivered to our door. Slowly we piece together his story. He had boarded a bus along the Chiswick High Road to nearby Hammersmith where he alighted to look around. Seeking a bus for his return he found the figure nine on his ticket, and this is where things started to go wrong. He took nine to be his bus route number, whereas it was in fact his original fare in pennies. So he then spent a dogged forty-eight hours on number nine buses, travelling between distant Aldgate in east London and Mortlake across the Thames, watching in vain for a Chiswick landmark and quite unable to communicate with the conductor. He passed two nights in bus shelters waiting for the first service to run. Eventually he found his way to the Libyan Embassy in Kensington whence he was sent on to the Sudanese hostel. Asked if he had not seen any police from whom to seek help, he insists the last person he would approach is a policeman. Daoud is not to survive with us for long and is soon packed off back to Tripoli – a lesson learned though he did lift our standing in the neighbourhood.

Incidentally Londoners for their part are said to have a particular affection for the number nine. There is a story that during the bombing Blitz in the Second World War Ernie Bevin, the irrepressible Minister of Labour, received a complaint that number nine buses had long intervals and then turned up several at a time. "Very sensible," replied the minister, "number nine always goes in convoy. Never lost a number nine yet."

Libya stays with us however. September 1969 brings Mu'ammar Qaddafi's sudden *coup d'état*, apparently pre-empting by a day a takeover planned by more senior army officers. A year later comes a knock on our door in Chiswick late one night. I open to find a haggard yet familiar face on the doorstep. It is an old friend from Tripoli days, Brigadier Ali Garrush, former commander of the Tripolitania Police and just released from a harsh incarceration in prison. We welcome him in, give him a square meal and send him on next day to join his wife and family at their home in Ireland. He has grim accounts to give us of the condition of others we know, who remain in vindictive captivity. For my part I am warned by the Office that I may feature among British diplomats on the black list of the new regime; it will be over thirty years before I feel confident to set foot again in Qaddafi's maverick land.

* * * *

In the Personnel Department I have charge of the section which handles appointments to embassies and consulates in Europe and both Americas. It is a huge parish. British foreign policy still has a global outreach; missions are consequently maintained in almost every state from the USA to Outer Mongolia (described by the first ambassador to be sent to that remote outpost on the Silk Route as more of an expedition than an embassy). Additional staffing demands are being created by the month as newly independent states are spawned across Africa and Asia, their raw capitals affording only basic facilities and perhaps civil unrest too. The elegant image of diplomacy is changing fast. Indeed there are new danger signals; one ambassador within my parish, Geoffrey Jackson in Montevideo, is taken hostage by a political terrorist group calling themselves the Tupamaros. His eight months in solitary captivity comes as a shock to a world that will later become all too inured to this brutal, and sometimes tragic, ransom tactic. In this initial instance a substantial sum is eventually paid through back-door channels to secure his release, a course which successive British governments will refuse to repeat.

It is a constant challenge to identify the horses best matched to the courses rather than falling back on courses on which to park spare horses. This carousel operates on an intricate but well-tried system of geographical grid patterns. Selected individuals then have to be proposed to ambassadors for acceptance. Occasionally it is necessary to gild the lily a touch. One also has to take care over wording. Phrases such as "he will be bringing his Dutch wife" can produce a wry smile; shades of frustrated merchant sea captains. The formulae used in the annual performance reports we receive can also lack precision; one worthy officer finds himself described in lukewarm terms by his head of mission as having a "Gothic" personality; what can one possibly make of that? But by and large we manage to get it right and meet our customers' preferences, albeit with an occasional bit of fun. The simultaneous appointment of a Marshall and a Snelgrove to the mission at the Vatican at a time when the august department store of that title is still trading in Oxford Street has a nominal felicity about it, as does a team of inspectors composed of Comfort and Joy and the despatch of Ayres and Gracie to the Gulf. The Service is tolerant of its sprinkling of eccentrics, not least among whom is the Permanent Under-Secretary, Sir Paul Gore-Booth, who also finds time to head the Sherlock Holmes Society and has been known to receive official calls by mystified foreign ambassadors in full costume of tweed cape and deerstalker with curved pipe alight. The Consul-General in Istanbul has been found by visiting inspectors to be using the vast ballroom floor of his splendid residence in the historic former embassy to lay out his model train circuit. We do however have to watch out for signs of "going native"; this brings the merry-go-round quickly into play.

Consuls, responsible for the care of British citizens abroad, can sometimes find themselves with challenging cases to handle. The resourcefulness of a Vice-Consul in one of my nearer posts, Le Havre, is put to the test when he is presented one morning with the ticklish problem of a British couple returning from holiday in Spain to catch the ferry home with the body of the husband's mother-in-law, who has had the misfortune to die during the trip, concealed in the luggage box on the roof of their car. The trouble is that the car, which was carefully parked outside their hotel near the port, has been stolen during the night. What should they do? Or the thieves for that matter? Call for the AA?

* * * * *

Two years on I take over the recruitment and selection of new entrants to the Service. There is a seasonal nature to this – an autumn spent touring universities around Britain to canvass candidates with the "Queen's shilling", followed by six months of intensive participation in selection boards and interviews for Civil Service appointment. Those who make it over the high hurdles for entry to the Diplomatic Service have then to be inducted through a spell of initial training. This period in the early 70s coincides with the first graduations from a greatly expanded higher education system. "New" universities are finding their feet all around the country, some like Sussex, Essex, Kent, York and Warwick on custom-built campuses, others such as Swansea, Exeter, Newcastle and Strathclyde enlarged versions of existing colleges. This explosion has its growing pains, including a much broader student community, female as well as male, whose members manifest an individualism and a scepticism of authority that has emerged from the unconstrained mood of the "swinging sixties". A radical approach in social politics is frequently matched by an uncommunicative offhandedness towards career options, a sharp contrast to the positive spirit of my own university days only a dozen years ago. There is also a chip on the shoulders of some of the newer establishments, which have persuaded themselves that the upper echelons of government service are reserved, if no longer for a private income and a silver spoon in the mouth, at least for Oxbridge and the established universities. Herein lies another myth to be challenged.

The Service is having its own debate too over the kind of recruits it should be seeking in the contemporary world. A long-standing preference for all-round attributes – the traditional British "gifted amateur" – is being challenged by a new breed of candidate with specialist academic or professional skills, for example in the sciences, economics or the law. Nor are we amateurs already in harness immune from the new vogue for formal training. I am packed off to the recently established Civil Service Staff College at Sunningdale to undergo a leadership formation exercise which includes a week of decision-making in an unstructured group, a form of business school challenge invented in the United States. I find the competition for authority within a "pack" starts to have an unsettling effect on one's personality. Next comes a week's course of introduction to the blossoming world of computers. Curiously more time is given to explaining what makes these electronic miracles work, involving supernumerary, and to me incomprehensible, lessons in binary arithmetic, than is devoted to teaching us how to apply the technology. The result is more trees than wood.

Yet candidates of good quality do emerge from this educational porridge. Britain is still living a post-war time warp where public and social service, for all their unexciting financial rewards, are regarded among young people as more virtuous than a career in business and commerce. The main competition for talent comes from the fast expanding academic sector. The three-day selection boards, run by the Civil Service Commission and involving IQ puzzles, committee work, problem solving, drafting and bouts of solid argument, are a demanding experience for both candidates and selectors. Gone are the more relaxed days of country-house sessions and the resilient myth of tests to see if aspirants eat peas off a knife.

My role on the selection panels is to engage candidates in an intellectual wrestling match on topical issues involving awkward moral or political choices. A few weeks into this combative act Grania announces she will no longer go out in company with me unless I stop picking arguments with everyone. I seem to have turned diplomacy on its head. It is intriguing to find that traditional academic disciplines tend to produce a sharper intellectual quality among our candidates than the social studies that have become so fashionable. A first-class degree however is not necessarily a passport to success; it can betoken a measure of inflexibility which will not cohere with the pragmatism that forms an inescapable element in the devising and application of policy, and not least in foreign affairs. One mature candidate is the winner of the BBC's *Brain of Britain* quiz programme. We expect him to sail through the tests with flying colours. Not so; he certainly has a massive store of data but turns out quite unable to put it to useful effect. "What should I do if I find myself in disagreement with ministers on some issue?" is a question often put by candidates. "Do your best to get your point of view across" comes our answer, "but if you find the kitchen gets too hot for you, then best to get out." Our selection panels tend to divide on the sensitive point of whether men and women differ in their intellectual approach to problems, with males adopting a deductive line while females give instinctive priority to intuition. From board experience I increasingly find this to be so.

* * * * *

The "milk run" to drum up recruits takes me all over the country – it's Tuesday so it must be Aberdeen/Aberystwyth/ Liverpool/whatever. Read the name board on the railway station to get your bearings. I go in tandem with a jovial character from the Inland Revenue, "Buster" Morovitch, who somehow contrives to make that unsociable institution sound appealing. We sally further afield too, to the Republic of Ireland. For under the terms of the 1921 Anglo-Irish Treaty the British government is obliged to continue to offer employment in the Civil Service – known as "the Imperial" – to Irish citizens, but cannot recruit to the armed forces. The irony however is that service in the British forces remains popular, while very few choose a career with the government. My first recruitment foray to Dublin in 1970 quickly runs into turbulence. This is not surprising as the latent inter-communal troubles in Northern Ireland have broken out only the year before in what will become a prolonged and bitter conflict; anti-British feeling is alive south of the border, not least among students. A sedate welcome in the Protestant stronghold of Trinity College is succeeded by a hostile reception from students in Cardinal Newman Hall of University College. We cut the session short. On return I recommend firmly that, the Treaty notwithstanding, public recruitment to British government service in the Irish Republic is now an unproductive anachronism and should be suspended. There are no more trips to Dublin. The next season however involves some bomb dodging to reach Belfast's Queen's University, when the taxi driver tells me to get out and take my chance walking from here.

It is not only Belfast however that is seeing unrest. Public opposition to the interminable war in which the Americans are engaged in Vietnam reaches a climax in 1968 with a mass march led by the firebrand president of the Oxford University Union, Tariq Ali, on the American Embassy and down Whitehall where an assault on the Foreign Office is seen as a possibility. Volunteers are called for to protect the building should this be necessary; those stout souls among us who enrol are put to patrolling the cavernous basements under the command of the Chief Clerk, a man with a distinguished war record in Special Operations, and are armed with pick helves with which to repel any attempt to force entry, an arrangement which would surely contravene health and safety regulations today. In the event there is a lot of noise but no rough house.

* * * * *

The time comes to practise what I have been preaching and broaden my own experience outside the Arabists' "Camel Corps" with a spell of economic and trade promotion work in Latin America. Rio de Janeiro is the destination of our family, now enlarged with twin boys – a blessing, yet a shock too. Grania and I must first go back to school with intensive lessons in Portuguese, given by Vittoria, a delightful "Girl from Ipanema" in the words of Brazil's sublime anthem. With her lively encouragement we clamber through an intricate grammar and an awkward nasal pronunciation. There is a hitch when Grania's anti-cholera vaccination has a reverse effect, landing her in a local isolation hospital while the borough pins mediaeval plague warnings on our Chiswick house. We could have done without this.

I am also immersed in an introduction to the mysteries of international finance and trade, guided by a friend in industry, Alastair Morton (who will later be responsible for forcing through the construction of the Channel Tunnel). These are thankless years for the British economy with poor labour relations, loss of export markets and severe controls on overseas investment. The decline of our major industries is brought home to me on an extensive tour of depressed manufacturing centres for which Brazil has always offered an important market. Rio promises to be a challenge, but also welcome relief from a perplexed Britain.

Brazil
1974-1978

Para o Inglês ver – to pull the wool over the eyes
(For the Englishman to see)

Brazilian saying

A dawn arrival out of a cold London winter at Rio's Galeão airport into a hot and steamy midsummer morning after a fourteen-hour flight on a ropey British Caledonian Boeing and with four small and querulous children is not an experience to be repeated too frequently. Add to this an interminable queue to reach an immigration official, invisible behind frosted glass, and then a hair-raising drive into the city along the Avenida Brasil, the sole artery connecting the city with the rest of this vast country and crowded with motorists who see the highway as a cross between a go-karting track and a fairground bumper car arena, and you realise that Brazil is going to be an experience. We decant, exhausted, via a decrepit lift into the top-floor apartment of an ageing building that yet enjoys a fine view across Guanabara Bay where the conical Sugar Loaf peak stands sentinel over the Atlantic gateway. It will be a bit of a squash for us all, and it does not take long before we discover that in the interval since the departure of my predecessor the place has become an incubator for one of the city's larger colonies of cockroaches.

These challenging first impressions soon fade however as we are swept into the daily frenzy of this dramatic city and its vibrant society. It only takes days for us to realise that Rio's citizens – known as *cariocas* – are among the kindest and most indulgent folk on Earth. For, returning for lunch from my office in the Consulate-General, a short walk along the waterfront, I find a small crowd gathered on the mosaic pavement in front of our block of flats, gazing up towards the top balcony. It appears that our three-year-old twins had decided to amuse themselves by dislodging two large terracotta urns filled with plants that had adorned the parapet so that they crashed to the ground twelve storeys below. Mercifully no pedestrian has been injured but a smart car parked on the pavement has a large dent in its roof. Its owner is in the process of addressing an apologetic Grania in voluble and, to us beginners, hardly intelligible Portuguese, with spectators adding their plentiful advice. It is going to be tough if we have to begin our tour here by buying the injured party a new car. We cast round for an interpreter and a helpful bystander comes up with some English. All of a sudden the whole mood changes as the boys' excessive mischief is explained. For Brazilians will forgive children anything. We are not to worry – *nao faz mal* – *crianças* – that's children for you. Our pressing offer to pay is declined. What a generous people!

* * * * *

The Brazil in which we find ourselves is going through one of her periodic phases of disciplined recovery from self-indulgent socialist experiment and inflationary collapse through the intervention of a vigilant and hard-faced military regime. Recent cases of urban terrorism have been fiercely suppressed and Rio de Janeiro is having a respite from the bouts of petty crime that seep inexorably out of the poverty stricken *favela* shanty towns scarring the granite slopes of the city's mountainous backcloth. Brazil's army is no stranger to government; ever since the deposition of the Bragança monarchy following the belated formal abolition of slavery in 1889, the military have seen themselves as the ultimate guarantors of the nation's wellbeing. Wisely this does not extend to a monopoly of governance; one British ambassador a few years previously has dismissed the army as "more spit than polish". Apart from the Presidency the senior posts in government are in the competent hands of a new generation of technocrats. Parliamentary debate has however been relegated to a largely packed assembly up in Brazil's raw new capital, Brasilia, far into the interior. Meanwhile internal security, and political authority and order are enforced with a heavy hand.

It takes a while to find our feet in Rio's hectic atmosphere. First priority is a move out of our decrepit apartment. Not only has it turned out to be infested, but Grania's psychic sense suspects it to be haunted too. Quite possible when we learn that the wife of my predecessor had died there. We are to discover that spirits can flourish in Brazil's fervent brew of African cults laced with Christian revivalism. After days of tramping round a stifling city we find an old-fashioned but spacious top floor close to Copacabana's spectacular beach, where elegant tanned bodies disport all day but sensibly hesitate to dip into the wild Atlantic breakers.

This is a proud city, indeed nation, that works hard and plays hard too. Cars display stickers with the patriotic message "Brazil – love it or leave it". The arts are in vogue, modern authors like Jorge Amado are writing compelling novels with a strong social message, football is a national religion, and to cap it all there is *bossa nova*, the new era popular music with its off-beat rhythm canonised in the seductive strains of "The Girl from Ipanema". Rio turns out to have attractions way beyond its beaches: the giant Christ statue that overlooks us from the Corcovado mountain amid the tropical Tijuca forest, a yacht-filled bay, a surfeit of elegant baroque churches, a sister opera house to that in Paris, delicious encounters with *churrascaria* grill houses serving black bean feijoadas, the delightful ride up the Santa Teresa hill on battered old trams, known as "bondes" from the London capital market from which they were originally financed, even the bronze lion over the entrance to the former royal palace, now housing the zoo, a replica of the one over the gateway to the Duke of Northumberland's Syon Park on London's Bath Road. Grania takes to her painting again and enrols at Rio's Belas Artes school, set in another former royal palace beside the Botanical Gardens, famed for their spectacular avenues of king palms. Our Portuguese is rapidly improving. It has to, for Brazilians make few concessions to foreigners who can't speak their mellifluous version of the mother country's nasal tongue. Like any new language it proves to have its traps for the unwary, and I am soon caught out. Thanking a stylish Rio hostess for an enjoyable dinner party, I describe the evening as *esquisito*; she looks a bit surprised. It turns out that in Portuguese the word is no compliment but retains its original and pejorative sense of agonising. We are not invited again.

Carnival, the brilliant annual pre-Lenten display of processions and samba, is about to burst upon the city. For a week the place goes wild. Every night sees the gorgeous costume parades of the competing samba schools to the thunder of drums and whistles all along the great avenue that proceeds from the monumental baroque Candelária church. Joyous balls are held in the city's clubs. Drink flows, notably the potent and seductive rum *cachaça*, the country's unique and devastating spirit, while pickpockets enjoy an open season amid the jostling crowds. There is nothing to compare with this great festival, now erupting all over Brazil. We join an all-night samba rave at the select Monte Libano club. Brazil hosts the largest emigrant Arab community in the world, mostly Lebanese and Syrians who started arriving in the Ottoman period a century ago. Today they move in the liveliest circles of society and politics. On Brazil's far-from-colour-blind social scale they begin as "*Turcos*", graduate through prosperity to become "*Syrios*" and with luck end up as "*Libanês*".

* * * * *

Exhausted, our daily lives resume. Work involves the promotion of business and trade, and there is plenty to be done. It takes me north to the plantations of Pernambuco, to historic Salvador with its seductive African-infused culture and cuisine, and to the old mining centres of Minas Gerais state. The halcyon days of British predominance in the economic life of South America is now a thing of the past. The scornful epigram at the head of this chapter is said to date back to the early 19th century when Rothschilds in London were approached to finance a Pernambuco sugar plantation. In an early case of due diligence they sent someone out by sea to take a look. The wily owners showed him acres of lush green stalks, whereupon the loan was promptly granted. In fact it was just wild grasses.

But trading and investment links do survive; in minerals, tobacco, beef, communications and shipbuilding, as well as banking and insurance. Indeed Rothschilds are financing a new iron ore railway. There is a British stake in heavy engineering too with firms involved in constructing the five-mile bridge to span Rio's bay as well the tunnels for São Paulo's new metro. Britain is however in the throes of a prolonged period of inflation and industrial unrest which is eroding her reputation and for which there seems no solution. It makes for discouraging work in this land of opportunity. A snap election brings Labour back into power under Harold Wilson, and the new Trade Secretary, Peter Shore, comes on a visit. He has little comfort to offer, though he confesses that his party has at last accepted that inflation can be a worse evil than unemployment.

Within weeks I find myself doubling up as Consul-General when Robert John, my boss, goes off on home leave. This brings consular responsibility for the whole of northern Brazil, from Manaus in the far Amazon jungle across miles of upland savannah to the Atlantic shore. It also involves interesting contact on behalf of our embassy in Brasilia with the powerful economic ministries; these have so far managed to escape exile to the new capital. The British ambassador, David Hunt, a laid-back classicist of prodigious intelligence, who would in retirement win the BBC's Mastermind competition, has himself only recently been dragged out of Rio's seductive society to the austerities of a villa in distant Brasilia under a threat from the Foreign Office of having his allowances cut off.

David Hunt has left behind him one of the most splendid residences in Britain's diplomatic estate, a neo-Palladian pile, built as recently as the 1950s as a post-war demonstration of British attention to Brazil, on the authority of Ernest Bevin, yet so soon to sit empty amid its spacious grounds – an instance of diplomatic vanity. In due course I am instructed to try to sell it, and manage to dispose of the mansion to Rio's mayor, Marcos Tamoyo, to serve as the new City Hall, a satisfactory outcome all round. His appetite is whetted when we suggest a ghost might come with the property.

The inventory produces surprises; we discover two rare 17th-century oil paintings by the celebrated Dutch artist, Frans Post, recording the early colonisation of Pernambuco by Maurice of Nassau and hanging neglected in an upper corridor along with a portrait by Sir Thomas Lawrence. The magnificent set of dining silver by the great silversmith, Paul Storr, turns out to be one of a series made for Britain's leading embassies at the end of the Napoleonic Wars and quietly transferred to Brazil from its original home in Hapsburg Vienna by a magpie ambassador in his baggage. Senior diplomats used to get away with a lot. I ignore instructions from a team of philistine Foreign Office inspectors to sell it all off.

* * * * *

An early visit to Brasilia, set in the flat scrublands of Mato Grosso state, turns out to be a disappointing experience. The vision of President Juscelino Kubitschek, back in the mid-1950s, as a way to compel Brazilians to leave the comforts of the coast and engage in opening up their country's vast interior, the new capital's design and architecture were put in the hands of two brilliant men with pronounced left-wing ideas on a modern urban society, Lucio Costa and Oscar Niemeyer. The former had undertaken his studies in planning at Newcastle University, while Niemeyer, a former member of the Communist Party subsequently driven into exile by the military regime, had collaborated with the French modernist architect, Le Corbusier, and was a pioneer of the use of pre-stressed concrete in construction. Brasilia gave this powerful pair an opportunity to put their revolutionary ideas into practice on a metropolitan scale. Their city, built beside a huge artificial lake, was to be an exercise in human engineering where families would live in clusters of apartment blocks, each self-contained with its shops and services and separated by broad highways on a geometrical pattern. The size of the government-owned apartments to be allotted to the occupiers was to be regulated by their seniority in state service. It was assumed that the car would provide the main form of transport; hence there were almost no facilities for pedestrians and no traffic signals (Niemeyer's wife had, it is said, been killed crossing a road). Addresses were reduced to coded combinations of numbers and compass points. The monotony of the blocks was to be relieved by a few monumental buildings, such as the Presidential Palace, the National Assembly, a Foreign Ministry fronted by a graceful pool and, most notable of all, a brilliantly conceived cathedral, the circular shape of which would represent a crown of thorns.

This magnificent concept for modern living soon turned out to have serious drawbacks. It became clear that the individualist spirit of Brazilians did not readily harmonise with such an anonymous and mechanistic environment; here was a city designed by Marxists but for capitalists to inhabit. Moreover no provision had been made for long-term accommodation of the army of workers from the impoverished north-east who were engaged in the construction of the capital. Their labour camps soon became satellite townships set out of sight on the broad plateau. It was not long moreover before many officials began to desert their futuristic and impersonal accommodation and build themselves villas in impromptu suburbs.

These cracks in the great edifice are apparent on the first of my visits to our embassy in the capital. Niemeyer's cathedral is indeed an inspiring building with its web of concrete and glass. But only ten years or so after the city's inauguration the living compounds look run-down and the concrete blocks are stained and peeling, not helped by a persistent drizzle. Many of the reluctant residents take the long flights back to the animation of their home cities for the weekend. I am so glad our lot has fallen in Rio and not in this raw outpost.

$$* \quad * \quad * \quad *$$

The Consul-General's role brings with it not only a car complete with flag but also three armed guards, furnished by the state police, who accompany me in a large black Chevrolet wagon on all official journeys. They are an oddly assorted and scruffy crew, with their holstered revolvers and brandished sawn-off shotguns that one suspects might go off at any moment. This heavy protection is a legacy of a rash of kidnapping of foreign diplomats by youthful revolutionaries in Brazil and other parts of South America. We deem the threat to have evaporated by now with the return of a measure of economic prosperity, but our guard has yet to be lowered. The ambassador in Brasilia and my colleague in São Paulo enjoy similar measures of protection. The team has some uses, such as helping to force passage through crowded traffic with their gun muzzles poked out of the windows.

There are times however when their zeal can be a liability. One evening, as I am leaving the office for our flat in Copacabana, Grania rings to ask me to bring back some tonic water as we have guests coming that evening. Accompanied by my attendant "heavies" I duly stop by our local Casas Sendas supermarket, where the man on the drinks counter passes over some bottles. When I point out that these are labelled as soda water he insists they are tonic. As I start to remonstrate the leader of my protection team appears at my elbow murmuring the Brazilian equivalent of "Is there trouble, boss?" When I explain he reacts, to my horror, by jamming his revolver in the assistant's stomach and demanding tonic water. "There is no tonic," stammers the assistant, "nowhere." "Get tonic," comes the stony reply. I protest to my gun-toting guard, who assures me, "No, senhor, you will have your tonic!" I turn to flee the shop, only to find the other two guards have produced their shotguns and have lined all the other customers up against a wall. At this point in rushes a boy who had been sent out to forage for tonic along the street. He carries a few precious bottles. "Take them, senhor, take them," cries the terrified assistant. I start to pay, but he has no time for that. Dumping some *cruzeiros* I hasten out, with my protector triumphantly bearing the bottles. The other guards retreat backwards after us, guns at the ready. I leap into the car and we speed off, Union Jack flying. Talk of smash and grab; all in a Consul-General's day. There is a cinema next door; its brightly lit façade advertises the current film. It is inevitably *The Godfather*.

We are to have other adventures with these faithful but motley "protectors" before their redundant role is finally terminated some three years later. A team comes out from the Special Air Services Regiment at Hereford every so often to check on their competence. On the first occasion it is led by Jeremy Phipps (whom I shall see again years later in Saudi Arabia as Director of Special Forces during the Gulf War). My mother happens to be staying with us during the team's visit. One fine morning finds her waiting with the children in our car on the drive of the ambassador's residence while Grania has gone inside. Suddenly the guards' wagon roars round the corner of the house with guns blazing from its windows and disappears into the grounds. Five minutes later it comes round again, firing away. It turns out that the SAS trainers have found the empty house to be an ideal location for a training exercise in firing on the move. For my mother it is very much what she has expected to meet in Brazil. On their next visit a Hereford team, led this time by Arthur Denaro (whom I shall also encounter commanding an armoured cavalry regiment in the Kuwait invasion), takes my guards for some firing practice on the police shooting range, only to find that one of the three has to put shell cases in his ears before firing to reduce the noise and another is incorrigibly gun shy. As for the range they find it out of use that day as the man in charge is planting gladioli bulbs to brighten up the butts. So much for Brazil's reputation as a police state. Arthur reckons the person most at risk from the erratic protection team is me in the car in front.

* * * * *

We all take a brief holiday on the little island of Jaguanum in the picturesque bay of Angra dos Reis, south of Rio. The only habitation is a hotel, a model of the originality of Brazilian architecture with the bedrooms separately bolted into the rock face of a cliff with sloping walkways linking them. A curious instance of twin inter-communication occurs when I am woken in the night by one of the little boys, Luke, tugging at my bed and crying out

"Daddy, wake up, James needs you." A raging thunderstorm is in progress. I stumble out into the dark and see in a sudden flash of lightning his brother backing away from a large dog as he tries to reach our room along the narrow boardwalk. Waves are crashing on the rocky shore way below. He slips and I just manage to catch him and bring him inside. Luke is back in his bed fast asleep. In the bright morning he has no recollection of the drama. Moreover he had woken me using words which at just three years old he had not yet acquired.

Brazilian friends to whom we relate the experience have no hesitation in seeing the hand of the occult element in Brazil's culture. For there is a deep vein of "spiritism" in the life of this society, which owes much to West African magical cults originally introduced by slave communities and subsequently fused with the pious Roman Catholicism of the early Portuguese settlers. We have noticed shops around the city which display a sinister selection of angelic and satanic effigies together with strange totems and powders. One hastens past with an uncomfortable sensation. At street crossings we often find makeshift shrines on the tarmac with candles, bottles of *cachaça* rum and cigars. Apparently these mark the site of fatal accidents and are intended to placate African animalist deities and their counterpart Christian saints. Yoruba words are used to identify different schools of belief – *macumba* and *umbanda* for white magic, and *quimbanda* for the blacker arts. Each New Year's Day a spectacular ceremony takes place on Rio's beaches when *orixás*, or priestesses, clad in flowing white robes, mark out their territories on the sand to hold services of healing for their devotees. Thousands of candles are floated out at midnight in an act of worship to Iemanja, the goddess of the sea – a brilliant sight.

We start to hear well-documented, if hard to credit, accounts of a peasant from Minas Gerais, Arigo, still living but excommunicated by the Catholic establishment, who has conducted, during trances when he is invested with the personality of a long-dead Austrian surgeon, complex internal operations without the use of anaesthetics or sign of bleeding. Friends also tell of one Lorival who performs similar surgery; one of them tells of having had a tumour removed from his liver by Lorival, operating with a kitchen knife on a table at the Jaguanum island hotel, and in preparation for which they drank themselves into a stupor on *cachaça*.

Anything seems possible within this paranormal dimension that has such a hold. Indeed we meet in due course with our own encounters with the occult. Grania finds herself sharing with a Brazilian friend of Scottish background a regression in time in which she has the vivid impression of an existence in an earlier century. A subsequent experience is just as bizarre. An old friend, Mozart Janot, whom we had known in the Brazilian Embassy back in our Beirut days and who was subsequently detained in prison for some years by the military regime on an unsubstantiated charge of having colluded with a group of armed subversives to whom by ill chance he had let his apartment, invites us to come one evening to a private "ordination" ceremony for female *orixás*. It promises to be a remarkable spectacle. We arrange to meet at his flat in Ipanema. That morning I awake to find myself afflicted with a fierce attack of conjunctivitis in both eyes and can hardly see. During the day Grania is suddenly incapacitated by a stomach bug. When I ring Mozart to explain that we cannot make it, it turns out that his other guest has just sprained her ankle climbing his stairs and cannot walk. "You are not meant to come," he adds, with no suggestion of surprise. The following day we are both fine again. One should not trifle with the spirits.

* * * * *

Mid-1975 brings the drama of the attempted apprehension of Ronald Biggs by Chief Superintendent Jack Slipper of the Metropolitan Police. Biggs is the fugitive ringleader of the celebrated Great Train Robbery on the London to Glasgow mail-train twelve years earlier. The first we get to know of this foolhardy adventure by Scotland Yard is when our consul, Henry Neill, a doughty Ulsterman, is telephoned one morning by a man claiming to be a senior detective just arrived from London to arrest Biggs, who has fled recently to Rio from his previous refuge in Australia. He had gone there, with his share of the money haul, after escaping from prison in Britain. His move to Brazil was apparently made in a hurry when Biggs, by now hard up, received a tip-off that he had been traced to Melbourne and was about to be arrested. No extradition treaty exists between Brazil and the United Kingdom.

Slipper asks the consul to witness the act of arrest. Unaware of the implications Henry Neill joins him and his detective band outside a modest hotel in Copacabana where Biggs is said to be staying. The detective has for good order's sake persuaded an uncomprehending policeman whom he found on nearby point duty to come along too. This will turn out to be one of a string of miscalculations, as Brazil's traffic police have no involvement with criminal matters. Accompanied by the hotel manager the trio proceed up to a room identified by Slipper. A man lying half-naked on the bed starts up in shock; "Good Lord, Jack, what are you doing here?" "Ronald Biggs, I arrest you..." as Jack Slipper recites the familiar formula.

Whereupon it is wigs on the green when an outraged Brazilian government reacts with an emphatic protest at what they regard as irregular and underhand action by the British police, while Biggs promptly claims asylum in Brazil. In this he has the law on his side, for he has since his arrival craftily lost no time in making a Brazilian woman pregnant, thereby ensuring under a curious quirk of the country's laws that as the potential father of a Brazilian child he has the right to stay. Game, set and match to Ronald Biggs, when a son is born to him some months later. A resentful Slipper of the Yard is obliged to fly back to Gatwick empty-handed, complaining that the Brazilian police do not speak English. He is greeted with derision by the British press.

We are left picking up the bits. Incredibly it turns out that the Metropolitan Police had indeed taken things into their own hands over the fiasco. No warning of their rash intention to make an arrest in a foreign state had been given to the Foreign Office, and possibly not to the Home Office either. This was in effect a stage in a long-running personal mission on the part of Jack Slipper to bring the train robbers to book. It had gone badly wrong. Biggs will now spend many years scot-free in Rio, enjoying something of a hero status and getting by as an odd-job man for members of the British community. It is some time before the Brazilian authorities get over their fit of pique. It will not however be the last we are to hear of Biggs.

* * * * *

In an uncovenanted though welcome consequence of this untidy episode I find myself taking over the role of Consul-General and with it responsibility for political liaison with those elements of the Brazilian government still based in Rio. For the next three busy years my vast parish covers the whole of northern Brazil. The state which I find myself visiting most frequently is mountainous and mineral-rich Minas Gerais, with its cache of precious stones and an historic treasury of old mining towns crammed with handsome dwellings and magnificent churches in the high baroque style, together with a trove of orchestral music of which the scores have been preserved from colonial times. Among our favourite spots are Tiradentes (Toothpuller), so named after an 18th-century rebel against Portuguese rule who doubled up as a dentist; Sao João del Rey, where we nearly lose a small daughter swept up in a sinister Carnival procession of necromantic figures wearing skull masks; and Ouro Preto, a vintage town dating back to Brazil's gold rush. Unlike the impoverished north-east this is a region of plentiful rainfall where peasant farmers cultivate staple crops of coffee and black beans. The roads twist through rugged hills; one can trail for ages behind laden trucks, many with homely aphorisms painted on their tailboards – "*A viuva e como lenha verde; Chora muito, e depois pega fogo*" (a widow is like green wood; she weeps aplenty, then catches fire).

Mineiros have a deserved reputation for obstinacy. This is brought home to me when one morning down in Rio I get a plaintive telephone call from Glasgow. The head of the Department of Trade's Scotland division is on the line to say that his office has been blockaded by members of the Drummond clan, protesting at the failure of a Scottish heavy-plant manufacturer to deliver on schedule a large equipment order placed by a member of their Brazilian branch, who owns a construction firm in Minas Gerais. Apparently the cousin has in desperation called up clan solidarity in support. The clansmen are refusing to depart without an undertaking that the order will be fulfilled. The stratagem works and they duly get their way.

The state's modern capital, Belo Horizonte, lies at the foot of an iron mountain, the high crest of which is being eaten away as the rich ore is remorselessly extracted for export. Not far away lies the small township of Morro Velho, the site of a long-established gold mine, owned by a British company. The miners and their folk were brought here from South Wales in Victorian times; their descendants, mostly Jones's and Evans's, still work the mine. They even have a cricket team. It is a little Welsh enclave in the hills.

They invite me to visit the mine, said at one time to have been the deepest in the world. This turns out to involve safety helmets and a descent down a dark and interminable shaft in a series of antiquated lift cages. At the bottom we follow a sloping gallery towards the sound of drills and voices. It is hot. Men are breaking up the rock face along a bright but sketchy seam and loading the broken lumps into a trolley. It must be back-breaking toil. Suddenly there comes an urgent shout repeated along the tunnel, "*Corre, corre!*" Fortunately I have just enough Portuguese to recognise the imperative tense of the verb "to run". Everyone pelts back up the gallery amid a rumbling sound and a cloud of dust. An adjacent workface has collapsed. By stages we all make it to the surface, where the embassy colleague who is with me suffers a mild heart attack. Two miners have been injured by falling rock, but a lucky escape on the whole. Hopefully I produce a piece of rock sprinkled with golden flecks; it turns out to be pinchbeck, the prospector's "fool's gold". I decide to give gold mines a miss for a while and concentrate my attention on a major contract for Britain to finance and build a steel mill in another part of the state.

* * * * *

The succession of British ministers and other prominent visitors, some engaging, others less so, seems incessant. Having transacted their business in dull and distant Brasilia, most elect to relax for a day or two in seductive Rio, and expect to be looked after in style. We owe much to generous Brazilian friends who help us out, either afloat around Guanabara's spectacular bay or in the dramatic scenery of their mountain retreats. A call on Dom Pedro of Bragança and Orleans, the patrician Pretender to Brazil's throne, evokes an earlier age of elegance in the old country palace up in Petropolis. A keen gardener, he takes particular pride in demonstrating a rare "mimosa pudica" tree, the leaves of which shrink coyly at the human touch. His son-in-law, Prince Alexander of Yugoslavia, holds a commission in the British Army. We first meet when he comes to the consulate to renew his British passport; on checking this out it transpires that his family, the Karageorgevičs, have an historic claim to British citizenship under the Act of Settlement of 1701 through their royal European lineage going back to the Electress Sophia of Hanover, mother of King George I. History is ever with us.

Princess Alexandra comes with her husband, Angus, on the way to opening a British trade fair down in São Paulo. We all have a ball, with police outriders doing gymnastics on the move on their Harley Davidsons, a special display of dance by the Portella Samba School and a midnight flit up to the Christ statue on the Corcovado mountain. The Royal Ballet comes out twice, led by Margot Fonteyn and Frederick Ashton, both of whom have roots in South America. During one of their visits we lay on an evening of samba, including the fascinating *capoeira* where the performers dance on their hands in an athletic tour de force originally developed, so it is said, by African slaves who had to use their feet in their fights as their wrists were shackled. During an act involving staves one shatters and a shaft impales itself in the wall between two of the principal ballerinas, missing their eyes by inches – a near catastrophe. A concert in Rio's ornate opera house, given by a visiting British consort of male countertenors, also falls flat when the Governor and his wife, our guests of honour, make their exit, disconcerted by the singers' falsetto tones. It is said that similar offence was taken by the *cariocas* a century and a half earlier when King João of Portugal, living in British-engineered exile in Brazil to escape Napoleon, brought castrati singers over from Europe to entertain his court.

A *bon vivant* Christopher Soames, Vice-president of the European Commission, has to be fed and watered – "too much lettuce in this salad". A variety of ministers troops through, both Conservative and Labour, one distinctly inebriated after a proving flight to Latin America on the supersonic Concorde. The Heseltines deplete Grania's sleeping pills. Patrick Jenkin has an eye for a samba with a dusky *morena* in a hot nightspot. A ponderous Edmund Dell, Secretary of State for Trade, upsets his Brazilian hosts by ungraciously walking out of a supper with lively cabaret that has been laid on to entertain him and his wife. Gerald Kaufman, Industry Minister and renowned film buff, is a more congenial guest. I spend a bizarre day with an energetic Dr David Owen, Minister of Health, traipsing round Rio's state hospitals in theatre gowns and slippers. Parliamentary delegations can be more tricky to handle; some Honourable Members choose to make no secret of their conviction that we diplomats live a sybaritic existence that is far from a reality.

Two years into our tour comes a welcome leave break at home. After nigh on three months however in what turns out to be a scorching English summer the plunge back into Rio's hectic pace comes as a shock, straight into a busy conference to promote Britain's new offshore oil industry. Peter Davies has held the fort well during our long absence; all is running smoothly though one of the staff may have tried to poison his wife... Family members visit to sample Brazil's splendours. Grania's brother-in-law, Adam Locket, turns up on a scientific expedition up the Amazon. So does my brother Colin from Tasmania. We fly down south with him and his wife to see the Iguazú waterfalls in remote savannah country where Brazil's frontiers meet Argentina and Paraguay. This spectacular horseshoe of cascades is one of the world's natural wonders. A short drive takes us to the Argentinian frontier post but no further; British diplomats are not welcome to that country's military regime. In a few years time we shall find ourselves at war over the Falkland Islands.

There is a moment of diplomatic drama when, with the ready aid of the Brazilian Navy, we smuggle a covert British delegation, sent under Lord Shackleton to consider the future of the Falklands, from a cargo ship out at sea through Rio's Galeão airport on their way back to London. We even field the Daily Mirror Punters Club, on a jaunt to sample the local horse racing. One of their party has the misfortune to drown while risking a swim in the treacherous Atlantic surf. The group blithely move on to São Paulo, leaving instructions for the consul not to reveal anything back home as the defunct is the manager of a bank in Epsom and moreover his wife does not know of his trip; yet another tricky consular case. One high point is a visit by the England football team, who contrive a diplomatic draw in a match against Brazil in the vast Maracanhã stadium that is heaving with spectators. We follow up with a reception for the team and are disconcerted to find only a handful of smartly blazered Football Association officials turns up. "Where are all the players?" I ask. "Oh we don't let them out," comes the reply. "They can be animals." Our hospitality service is sometimes complicated by the ambassador coming down to Rio on a social break from Brasilia's monotony. Derek Dodson is a stylish, if irascible, performer with a dramatic war record in the Balkans with the Special Operations Executive. He takes seriously Napoleon's advice to the French ambassador in Warsaw – "*Tenez bonne table et soignez les femmes*". Fortunately there are many sociable ladies to be found among Rio's much separated couples.

* * * * *

The visits of Royal Navy warships are always enjoyable events. These range from a Christmas entertaining the crew of HMS *Endurance*, the Falklands guardship, to the presence of two full-scale fleets in Rio's spectacular bay.

The Brazilian Navy models itself on the Royal Navy, and has several frigates of British design under construction in Southampton and in Rio's naval yard.

This close connection between the two navies goes back 150 years to the early 1820s when Admiral Sir Thomas Cochrane, Earl of Dundonald, was offered command of Brazil's infant naval force during the country's war of independence from Portugal. Cochrane, who retains an heroic status in the annals of Brazilian history, had a colourful career to say the least. Enrolled nominally in the Navy at the age of only five, he had by his twenties gained a reputation for daring exploits, as well as for insubordination, during Britain's incessant wars with France and Spain during the aftermath of the French Revolution and the subsequent Napoleonic era. He combined his service with a spell in Parliament, where he campaigned for electoral reform and an end to navy corruption. A dramatic elopement was followed by his conviction in a Stock Exchange fraud in 1814 which led to his being cashiered and sentenced to one year's imprisonment. Undaunted by this disgrace he hied himself off to South America to take command of the Chilean Navy and played a significant part in that country's successful rebellion against Spanish rule. He sailed his ships on to assist in Peru's independence struggle before accepting the invitation of the Brazilian Emperor, Pedro I. Cochrane succeeded in obtaining the surrender of Portuguese forces throughout Brazil's north-eastern provinces in return for which he was created Marquis of Maranhão. He went on to engage his enthusiasm for national liberation movements in the struggle of Greece against Ottoman suzerainty. In 1832 he was finally rewarded with a royal pardon and was reinstated in the Royal Navy with the rank of Rear Admiral of the Blue, rising eventually to the senior position of Admiral of the Red and to the honorary rank of Rear Admiral of the United Kingdom shortly before his death. He is buried in Westminster Abbey. It is no wonder that, with such a record of derring-do, Cochrane has served as a model for the fictional sailor heroes of Captain Marryat, CS Forester and Patrick O'Brian.

The first of these major naval visits lands us with a bit of ticklish, and tiresome, protocol. Two separate squadrons are to join up in Rio for a shore break and to exercise with the Brazilians. Shortly before the fleet arrives, a signal comes from the Admiralty asking us to be sure to arrange separate programmes of calls and hospitality for the admirals in command of the two flotillas – Admiral Leach flying his flag in the cruiser HMS *Blake* and Admiral Cassidi with the aircraft carrier, HMS *Ark Royal*. Apparently the two admirals do not get on and are better kept apart! We really could do without this finesse. With our long-suffering naval attaché, appropriately named Captain Hardy (by happy coincidence his army counterpart is called Nelson), we unscramble our carefully laid plans. The following days involve the admirals in an intricate exercise in Box and Cox, while some 1,500 officers and ratings off a dozen ships, including a nuclear submarine, make the most of the attractions of Rio. The city's ample harbour seems filled with the Royal Navy; it is said to be the largest assembly of British warships since the Coronation Review off Spithead over twenty years earlier.

Two years later in 1977 we get a second fleet visit led by the cruiser, HMS *Tiger*. They make a brave sight steaming into Guanabara Bay in the early morning light. This time there is only one admiral in charge, the debonair Martin Wemyss. There have been growing strains with Argentina over the Falkland Islands; perhaps this show of gunboat strength is in part intended to get up Argentinian noses, something with which the Brazilians, with a history of rivalry with their bumptious southern neighbour, are happy to go along. A ritual joint ceremony of remembrance is duly performed with a Royal Marine band and in soaking rain at the city's memorial to Admiral Cochrane. In the midst of the hospitality that follows Ronald Biggs suddenly re-emerges to complicate things. He has been keeping a low profile since arriving three years ago, doing odd jobs around the town and frequenting its bars, while keeping a careful eye on the wellbeing of his small Brazilian son, his security against deportation back to Britain.

A few days into the visit I am woken by the telephone at two in the morning. It is an excited admiral, who announces that Ronald Biggs has been enticed on board one of the frigates and that he has ordered the frigate squadron to put to sea immediately in order that a citizen's arrest can be effected by the Royal Navy once they are clear of Brazilian waters. Drowsiness rapidly shed, I insist that such a kidnap must in no way happen. Biggs has to be put ashore forthwith; we cannot afford a repeat of the Scotland Yard episode. A crestfallen Martin Wemyss presses for the operation to go ahead; this is an opportunity not to be missed – a major publicity coup for the Navy – the four frigates are already "getting up steam". "Then they must get down steam," I insist. "I am sorry to spoil the Navy's fun, but there is just too much at stake here."

Biggs is returned to terra firma, albeit reluctantly. It transpires that he met up with a group of senior ratings in a bar, and they invited him back to their mess on *Ariadne* in the early hours. The officer of the watch spotted the fugitive and warned the admiral. Action stations followed, though war is fortunately averted. We do however manage to exact some measure of revenge. For it transpires that the whole affair is a mischievous put-up job on the part of a *Daily Mail* correspondent who is in Rio to report on the fleet's visit and has sought to engineer a scoop. By fortunate chance the following day this journalist feels unwell and comes to our press attaché, Robert Chase, for advice on a doctor. Here is our chance. After a quick call to the admiral we tell him his safest course would be to see the ship's surgeon on board HMS *Tiger*. The latter is briefed by Martin Wemyss to put the wind up his patient and then send him along to the admiral's "cuddy" for a roasting. This last bit does not go entirely according to plan however, for, as Martin subsequently puts it to me, "I found he was another Fifeman, so we had a dram together." Oh well…

* * * * *

We make a visit to Manaus, one thousand miles up the Amazon at the furthest western extremity of my consular district. This extraordinary city, set deep in the damp Amazonian jungle at the confluence of the great river's two main branches, the Rio Negro from the north and the Solimões, flowing out of the Andes far to the west, is still inaccessible by road; it can only be reached by boat or by air, a four-hour flight from Rio. It was founded in the late 19th century by European rubber merchants, many from Britain, who made fortunes from the sap of the rainforest's wild rubber trees, tapped by native Indian *seringeiros*. Such was the city's prosperity in its heyday that the rubber barons had a luxurious opera house built, for which all the fittings and even the bricks were imported from Europe. It is reputed that both Caruso and Pavlova gave performances there. The wealthy merchants sent their dress shirts and collars all the way back to Liverpool by ship to be laundered and starched. Despite its remoteness the city was the first in Brazil to have electricity and a tramway. Its floating docks were imported from England and the customs house was modelled on the town hall of Halifax. The rubber industry had its savage side however. One of my predecessors as Consul-General in Rio, the Irish republican hero Sir Roger Casement, subsequently tried for treason and executed in London in 1916, had, following his previous denunciation of King Leopold's exploitation of the tribes along the River Congo, played a significant part at the start of the century in exposing the vicious conditions of slavery under which local native Indians were forced to labour, gathering rubber in the upper Peruvian reaches of the Amazon.

With the ending of the rubber boom Manaus fell into a decline which lasted up to the mid-1960s when the government gave the area an important economic stimulus as a customs-free zone. The connection with Britain continues with a monthly shipping service from Liverpool operated by the Booth Line, which goes right up into the river ports of Colombia and Peru in the shadow of the Andes where oil has recently been discovered. We have an honorary consul in Manaus, an Englishman who is agent for the Booth Line. His main job is to run the company's well-stocked supermarket, the only place in all Brazil where foreign groceries can be obtained.

On arrival I find an intriguing consular case. A young student from Exeter University is passing his summer vacation making an adventurous solo voyage by dugout canoe from the distant upper reaches of the river in Peru down to its mouth at Belém. Found paddling along in darkness one night by the incredulous crew of a Brazilian border-patrol boat his passport has been confiscated and he is marooned at Manaus. He is curiously passive about his bold adventure and its evident dangers, saying he took it on as he could not think of anything else to do. He just looked in an atlas for a long river and set out. He hopes to connect at Belém with a Booth Line boat and work his passage home, raking over a cargo of combustible Brazil nuts in the infernal heat of the ship's hold. There have been several scrapes on his way down river, including encounters with alligators which resented his camping on their sandbanks. It would all make a great story, but he seems curiously uninterested in writing up the experience. Fortunately it looks as though his passport is about to be restored and he can be on his way in his precarious hollowed tree trunk.

With a colleague, Stewart Brookes, we take a few days trip into the jungle creeks by boat to see the spectacular rainforest and do some fishing. The historic opera house of Manaus has recently been restored and is a fabulous sight with its ornate decorations, frescoed walls and plush seats, many equipped with strategically-placed brass spittoons. A few months earlier the Royal Ballet had inaugurated the restoration with a full performance of *The*

Sleeping Beauty, an experience which was for the company an unforgettable one. We eat in the town's only restaurant where the meat menu might have been taken from the inventory of the London Zoo, with tapirs and armadillos among its rare fare. Manaus is still an outpost amid what remains of Brazil's native Indian tribes, a few of which have yet to have contact with Europeans. The encroachment of western timber, mining and agricultural interests into their forests is presenting an acute dilemma for the government. Since early times Christian missionaries, often Jesuit, have sought to bring the Indians out of their isolated and primitive state and into more decorous "Mother Hubbard" garments, an activity which continues to arouse controversy. Tribal artefacts in the form of decorated clay bowls and bright necklaces made from feathers and the scales of huge Amazon fish are produced for sale. But the frontier between integration and separation remains an uneasy one.

The journey into the wilderness is fascinating. It is autumn and the annual summer floods have receded, as we float among the pillar-like trunks of great trees, above us their tight canopies of green vegetation dotted with the vivid blooms of orchids. It is a plant collector's paradise; a Rio friend, the indomitable orchid painter Margaret Mee, now into her seventies, still sets out with *caboclo* guide by dugout up the remote tributaries to search for the elusive moon orchid in bloom. Yet it is a scarce life for those who inhabit this rainforest. One evening we embark in dugouts to look for alligators by torchlight. There is a kindly warning not to put our hands in the water as the creeks are infested with piranha. The reptiles' eyes shine back in the darkness of the swamps; we catch a young alligator in a net and lay it in the canoe. Suddenly there is a violent shock as the dugout strikes a submerged trunk in the dark. We tumble about and I end up with the beast on my chest. Grania nobly hauls it off. The boatman has somehow managed to keep our tree trunk the right way up.

* * * * *

A short break in the high Andes of Bolivia and Peru involves a spectacular railway journey to visit the dramatic Inca ruins of Machu Picchu high above mountain ravines the sides of which are bright with wild lupins, and an interesting experiment with narcotic coca tea to alleviate our altitude sickness. In the hotel in Cuzco tourists are busy throwing up, while the staff go round patiently with mops and buckets. Flying into La Paz, perched up at 14,000 feet, the Brazilian pilot invites us to the flight deck while he sees if he can dislodge an avalanche on a nearby mountain. The engineer seated at his controls beside us collapses unconscious onto the floor. When I point this out to the captain he is unconcerned and grabs an oxygen mask, telling me to hold it over his colleague's face until he comes round. Indeed flying is often an adventure in South America. An overdue revolution in Portugal and her African colonies has brought many professional Portuguese to seek refuge here. Brazilians tend to treat the citizens of their former mother country with derision, and are not too happy with this influx. On an early morning flight to Salvador the pilot comes on the intercom to give us the usual details. His heavy Portuguese accent provokes shock and alarm among his passengers and a barrage of calls to turn around immediately as he can't possibly be relied upon to find our destination.

We are however coming up to five lively and productive years in a Brazil that has recovered her confidence and prosperity, and are in danger of becoming seduced – in the words of a previous ambassador – by her "tropical, insidious charm". The military regime is starting to ease its heavy suppression of the nation's lively politics, and a vibrant economy is starting to take off again. We have recently helped to steer important business Britain's way, including a major steel-mill project in the interior, though it has to be said that negotiations in this competitive business environment do not always follow Lord Queensberry's cherished rules, but call for the occasional diplomatic blind eye to be turned.

For our own part we have made many good friends, and have had the company of excellent colleagues. It is however time to return to London. This is brought home to us when Luke, the younger of our twins and with a proper sense of primogeniture, asks his mother, "When daddy dies, will James be Consul-General?" I am running out of things to say in my speeches at the annual dinners of the Societies of St George and St Andrew; what is more a Foreign Office strapped for cash has withdrawn funding for the traditional reception in honour of the Queen's Birthday, a high point in the large British community's year. We have also been descended upon by a team charged by the Labour government with taking a razor to the costs of Britain's worldwide diplomacy. A left-wing academic deems the standard of the fare with which we try to reciprocate the generous hospitality of our valuable Brazilian contacts to be extravagant. When she suggests that a typically British bowl of humble spaghetti would be more appropriate, my murmured protest of "when in Rome..." produces the tart rejoinder "and look what happened to the Romans". Mercifully their final recommendations for reducing Britain's overseas outreach prove too draconian even for our ministers, and the report is quietly pigeonholed. We have had a scare too when the telephone rings at home one day and a male voice warns us in Portuguese that he intends to kidnap the boys. A police guard is put on the apartment for a time. Worst of all, the handsome green Amazon parrot, tethered temporarily to a stake in our twelfth-floor window box so that he does not interrupt a lunch party, has been blown away in a gust of wind. Stephen Egerton, another Arabist about to dip a toe into South American waters, is coming out to take our place. Good luck to them both. With fond farewells we, all six of us, fly off home via Orlando, Florida – from one Disney World to another. We shall miss those rum-soaked *caïpirinha* cocktails.

Foreign Office – London
1977-1981

Diplomacy is the art of letting the other person have your way

Anon

Having resisted invitations to make a career move to the more lucrative pastures of international business (mid-life crisis?), the next four years are spent looking after a succession of three front-line departments in the Foreign Office. It is back to the daily run to Westminster on the District Line, with occasional forays into the parishes abroad. Life starts with a pitchforking into east and central Africa, a region in the throes of political upheaval and conflict that coincides with a lingering flourish of British post-imperial engagement in the affairs of the Dark Continent. As ever this involvement has its east-west dimension, underpinned by concern lest Soviet alliance with newly independent and half-fledged regimes should put at risk the security and the benefits of long-established western investments and trading relationships. There are Commonwealth bonds to be preserved here, and major development programmes too.

The huge constituency that I inherit, extending from the Indian Ocean across to the Atlantic, presents a scene of turmoil as newly independent regimes jockey to assert authority and adjust frontiers established a century earlier as the arbitrary product of colonial appetites. Ethiopia is entering upon a bloody civil war in the wake of the revolutionary overthrow of its imperial family by Marxist officers who, abetted by Cuban and East German surrogates of the Soviet Union, have embarked upon a reign of terror (their leader, Mengistu, will later flee to seek a refuge in Mugabe's Zimbabwe).

Next door in Somalia the tide has swung the other way with the expulsion of a Soviet naval base at Berbera and an appeal for western assistance, at the same time fostering an uprising by Somali tribes in Ethiopia's desert Ogaden province. Habitual Somali raiding goes on into the northern province of a Kenya where a precarious intertribal harmony has at last been established under an ageing Jomo Kenyatta. Next door Idi Amin's bloodthirsty regime in Uganda continues to defy western efforts, led by Britain, to unseat the tyrant through economic and political sanctions. Tanzania, a prickly cradle of "African socialism" under Julius Nyerere, is struggling to absorb a radical Zanzibar, where the African population has revolted against its former Arab rulers. Out in the Indian Ocean diminutive Seychelles has ousted an oligarchic regime and presents a potential Soviet naval springboard; Mauritius too has become a controversial refuge for islanders whom Britain has summarily expelled from the remote archipelago of Diego Garcia to provide a strategic airbase for the United States.

To the west the former Belgian colonies of Rwanda, Burundi and vast Zaire with her rich mineral deposits are riven with intertribal tensions that threaten to break out into civil war. The autocratic President Mobutu in Kinshasa continues to pillage his ramshackle country on a scale comparable to the example set by King Leopold a century earlier; it goes against one's grain as we help to shore up his kleptocracy against possible Soviet encroachment. Neighbouring Angola, having secured independence from Portugal, has adopted a Marxist government under Russian and Cuban tutelage, while breakaway forces in the south are waging an intermittent civil war with South African support and pose a threat to the security of Zaire's copper-rich Katanga province. And over all this minefield hangs the shadow of an outlawed white regime in Rhodesia, now deep into a guerrilla war, and where successive British attempts to negotiate a multiracial settlement have so far proved forlorn. Africa has indeed become the Tom Tiddler's ground of the Cold War.

No wonder therefore that our policies towards this theatre of instability tend to be guided by opportunism and expediency. At the same time the approach is blended with a political mindset determined by Cold War rivalry as well as by the still vital shades of a former historical role. Additional focus is afforded by the close personal interest being taken in Africa by the recently appointed and youthful Foreign Secretary, Dr David Owen. Following in the steps of the experienced and respected James Callaghan, now Prime Minister across Downing Street, he can show a hasty, and sometimes petulant, touch with his officials in seeking to make his mark. Perhaps there is a touch of insecurity here. One's recommendations for action frequently appear to be challenged by him on principle, to the point where, in the style of the popular Whitehall television serial *Yes, Minister*, one is tempted to submit proposals contrary to what one considers to be the appropriate course, in the confident knowledge that they will be reversed and we shall end up with the right answer. Among other things the doctor has prohibited the use of Latin tags in official correspondence, a step that comes strangely from the medical profession; out of the window go those ornamental, if pedantic, aids to concise drafting, to be replaced by pedestrian English. *O tempora, o mores!* Moreover Britain no longer has a strong diplomatic hand to play. Resources to sustain an active overseas role are tight as the country enters upon a depressing period of economic decline with inflation in double digits and wide industrial unrest. The government has had to go cap in hand to the International Monetary Fund for an emergency loan.

* * * * *

So where to start? My department finds itself squeezed into a remote eyrie under the eaves of the former India Office, possibly designed as bedrooms for Victorian servants. One has to negotiate a labyrinth of corridors and staircases, some grand and marbled, others mere holes in a wall, to consult with ministers or other departments. Visitors frequently lose their way, for lack of Ariadne's ball of string. It is discouraging to learn from my helpful personal assistant, Marie, that my predecessor was wont to drink a glassful of vinegar a day. Meanwhile *The Times* newspaper is thundering against the Foreign Office for our failure to take some – unspecified – action to halt the bloodletting in Addis Ababa, where the purges of the Marxist Derg have led to the slaughter of tens of thousands of Ethiopians in the name of the revolution. There is also concern, shared in Buckingham Palace, for the imprisoned surviving members of Africa's royal family of longest lineage, rulers of a country against which Britain mounted a military expedition a century earlier, yet saved from brutal Italian colonial suppression fifty years later. A colleague in the German Embassy takes the dismissive view that this media concern for the hapless Ethiopians, not reflected elsewhere in Europe, can only be attributed to the British love for dumb animals. Meanwhile Somalia's autocratic leader, Siad Barre, announces he is coming to London to seek aid. Domestic politics suddenly come into play here. It transpires that the Prime Minister's constituency in Cardiff contains a substantial proportion of Somali voters, descendants of generations of lascars who arduously stoked to keep the Merchant Navy steaming round the world. We are quietly instructed to be as helpful as we can to our less than welcome visitor. Funds are found from somewhere while we press him in vain to go easy on Ethiopia.

It is not all upheaval and warfare. A call comes one morning from a marine biologist at Newcastle University who asks if I am Administrator of the British Indian Ocean Territory, a series of remote atolls from which the islanders had recently been controversially offloaded to Mauritius to make room for an American strategic airbase. Looking across at a certificate on my wall appointing me to this office, I confirm this is so. Liaison with the military engineers building the airbase is conducted for us by a Royal Navy officer with the intriguing name of Portwine, whose existence, to judge by his occasional reports, seems little short of idyllic. It turns out that the air force are at the heart of the professor's problem, for which he is seeking help. He explains that he is leading a joint expedition with the military to measure the growth of the coral bed on one of the islands in the Chagas Archipelago. The studies will take one year with two scientific teams, each spending six months on the job. Their arrival and rotation will coincide with the RAF's half-yearly supply flights.

The problem he brings to us stretches credulity. One of the two divers recruited for the expedition is a woman. The RAF's regulations however forbid the carriage of female passengers on aircraft that are not fitted with flush lavatories. There is no problem on the outward flight as the aircraft will be a VC10, equipped with all mod con, and with a return flight in a year's time. But the intermediate six-month sortie to the territory is to be undertaken by a more rudimentary Hercules. Consequently the lady diver will have to stay marooned on the atoll (minus any public convenience) for the full twelve months. The air force are apparently proving inflexible over this regulation. Can the Foreign Office intervene with them? When I ask whether the medical nurses whom the Services are providing for the expedition must also last out the year, this turns out not to be the case. For they have, in RAF parlance, been "bucket trained". In the event we try to help, but to no avail; it appears that the bucket rule is immutable. As for the training course involved, it defies the imagination.

* * * * *

The shoring up of Zaire against the excesses of despotic rule by President Mobutu and his predatory family takes up too much of our time and energy. This vast and shambolic country with all its copper and other valuable minerals has seen little change since Joseph Conrad drew attention to its exploited plight as the personal Congo fief of Belgium's King Leopold eighty years ago in his classic novel, *Heart of Darkness*. Today its chronic scene of corruption and intertribal conflict continues to arouse a guilty sense of obligation with many Belgians. We find ourselves drawn with our western partners into expensive programmes of food and other essential aid, designed to stave off a humanitarian catastrophe while also keeping this key country onside in Africa's Cold War sideshow. Inevitably a good portion of these funds will end up in the pockets of the leadership. This chagrin is compounded for me following a meeting in Brussels of international donors when we British delegates find ourselves prevented by fog in London from flying home and are forced to catch an overnight truck ferry from Ostend to Folkestone on which we find all the bunks are reserved for holders of heavy-goods vehicle licences. After an excruciatingly uncomfortable night on upright chairs we are decanted at five in the morning onto a train that cautiously picks its way through the gloom to London's Victoria. Meanwhile our Zairian counterparts, replete with western largesse, are winging home in the first-class comfort of Air Zaire – known less charitably as "Air Peut-être". Life can be unjust.

A crisis is not long in coming. In the middle of May 1978 a group of some 4,000 former members of a militia force of the former separatist regime in Zaire's copper-rich Katanga province, who had been given refuge by Angola's hostile Marxist government, cross the frontier with Cuban military support in a sudden attack on the large mining town of Kolwezi. The population are taken hostage, including some 3,000 Europeans, mainly Belgian and French and a few Britons working in the area's copper and cobalt mines. A torrent of destruction ensues with the massacre of many Zairians and nearly 200 Europeans. With his army in disarray President Mobutu seeks urgent military help from France and Belgium. As the scale of the killings becomes clear a plan is rapidly put together for air drops by French and Belgian parachutists to retake the town. The logistics however prove difficult for this distant operation, requiring American assistance over air transport and parachutes. Britain for her part comes up with the gesture of an airborne medical unit.

I find myself coordinating our part in all this activity. Concern for the welfare of the British hostages has led to the opening up of the emergency centre, at that time a couple of rooms with rudimentary communications high up in the Venetian-style tower of the Foreign Office building. I shall be camping there for the next few days, and nights too; at least there is a great view over the park. The first I learn of the military plan is when the senior planning officer from the Ministry of Defence comes in with an outline of the joint operation that has just been cobbled together at a meeting in Germany. He turns out to be a naval submariner, Captain Hayhoe – surely only our own country could be so dotty as to have an underwater sailor plan an airborne assault into Central Africa? We have met once before when he brought his nuclear submarine into Rio on one of our naval visits. He lays out the scheme for the departure for Zaire the next morning of the French legionnaires and Belgian paratroops, with the British contingent making their way in RAF transports. To my natural assumption that the armada will presumably take their route down the western side of Africa, he confirms this is so for the others, but he has arranged for the aircraft carrying the British force to fly down the Nile and on to Lusaka in Zambia.

This comes as startling news. It will, I can see, present a considerable challenge to secure political clearance for overflights from the chain of countries concerned. For, as I point out to Hayhoe, there has been no passage of armed British military units along the sensitive Nile corridor for at least a quarter of a century, and in the case of Egypt since the Suez affair. Moreover our relations with certain of the states involved, notably the Sudan where the revolutionary President Numeiri hasn't spoken to us for months, and Zambia too given the Rhodesia problem, are none too amicable. In allowing a mere twelve hours for us to turn back the clock of recent history and secure permission for the necessary refuelling stops along this route, he has given me a major headache. "But we British have always gone down the Nile", is his impenitent rejoinder, "That's what I told them."

With major misgivings we fire off emergency telegrams to our diplomatic missions in Cairo, Khartoum, Nairobi and Lusaka stressing the humanitarian nature of our military foray and with instructions to make urgent approaches, despite it being the middle of the night. I take a gamble that the aircraft should be able to make it across Ethiopia and Tanzania without detection. By fortunate chance the route chosen by our naval planner is one I know of old, having bumped along it in BOAC Solent flying boats for school holiday journeys back in the 1950s when my parents lived in Southern Rhodesia. As a bright spring dawn begins to break into our tower refuge, the replies start to arrive. *Mirabile dictu* (as Dr Owen has forbidden us to write) they are all affirmative, even welcoming. Egypt's President Sadat goes so far as to offer refuelling help at Heliopolis and Jomo Kenyatta comments that surely the RAF need no introduction to their old base at Eastleigh, while the only reservation from Zambia's President Kaunda is to ask that troops do not wear uniform in the city. I have to pinch myself; perhaps our legacy of hesitation in recent years over further military engagement within Africa has after all been self-inflicted.

There is little time to ponder however. Captain Hayhoe materialises to find out what the night has produced. Greeted with the news that the Nile route is open, he departs for the Ministry of Defence with the dismissive observation, "Told you so, old boy. Britain always goes down the Nile." I do get a certain satisfaction in giving the RAF at Brize Norton the thumbs up to take off.

All is not harmony however. The French have endeavoured, not for the first time, to put Belgian noses out of joint by stealing a march and setting off early. At our end things are complicated by the fact that we have entered upon a Bank Holiday weekend, with a deserted Foreign Office that is not to be disturbed by some bush war in Africa. Dr Owen's Private Secretary tells me that the Foreign Secretary wants to be kept in touch with developments. He will however be out of contact for much of the next twenty-four hours as he is due to give a speech up in Southport, Lancashire, after which he will travel through the night by various trains right down the west side of England to his constituency in Devonport. He will ring me at intervals. It is a sign of the times that no limousine or security cover is thought necessary for a senior minister's overnight journey.

By that Saturday evening the leading RAF VC10 has cleared the British base at Akrotiri in Cyprus and is nearing Cairo, followed in slower time by the three Hercules transports. The telephone rings; it is the Foreign Secretary in a public callbox at Manchester's Victoria Station. There are railway noises in the background. I tell him the state of play and he rings off to catch his next train. A couple of hours later he is on the line again for a report on progress. On their way to Khartoum, I tell him; where is he? "Birmingham New Street," comes the reply, to a background of clanking railway carriages. I look across at the Bartholomew's school map of Africa I have pinned to the wall and wonder whether I should not also have one of the network of the old Great Western Railway. The next call comes from Bristol Temple Meads station; I hear the coins dropping into the box. This is becoming bizarre. Our military contingent is meanwhile somewhere over Kenya on what looks like a far more straightforward journey than that being navigated by the Foreign Secretary. Who will get to their destination first?

The final call comes from a platform at Exeter St Davids; not much further to go. "Where are they now?" "Heading across Tanzania for Lusaka," I reply, glancing quickly at my map. "Tell them to turn right and go for Kamina." Dr Owen evidently suspects that, with the French "paras" not having waited to make their airdrop on Kolwezi, we may miss the action. The Ministry of Defence are however doubtful about this late change in the flight plan, so we carry on to Lusaka. Over the following days the rebel forces are quickly chased out of Kolwezi while Belgian troops evacuate the large expatriate community. They leave a grisly scene behind them however, with many dead. There is only a limited call for our medical assistance.

* * * * *

Concern over how to shore up Mobutu's shaky control over his distant Copperbelt province brings me out to Kinshasa a few weeks later. The ragtag Zairian units are being reinforced by troops from Morocco and Senegal. The capital has become a decrepit place, overcast and damp much of the time and insecure too. The embassy residence where I am staying is a villa on the Congo River, where the banks are covered in lush lemon grass. Mobutu's gaudy presidential yacht is moored further along the shore. It comes as a shock when our ambassador, Alan Donald, sends me off to bed behind an iron grille, handing me the key through the bars in order to lock myself in, plus a loaded revolver to keep under my pillow. I worry much of the night lest it go off.

The visit has other surprises in store. Returning home one evening we stop at the driveway gate. Alan appears to be speaking out of the window into the empty darkness. It seems he is talking to a security guard. Peering out on my side of the car I am startled to find myself greeted in French by a diminutive figure, wearing little more than a loincloth and holding a rudimentary bow. His head hardly comes up to the window. "The guards are pygmies," Alan explains. "As armed guards are not permitted, we use these tribesmen. They are brilliant marksmen with bow and arrow and can even hit a bird in flight." After a round of unproductive meetings the next morning we try a round of golf on Kinshasa's run-down course. The grass grows long on the neglected fairways. "Don't worry about losing your ball," says Alan. "Little boys will pick it up where it lies and try to sell it back to you." An enterprising kind of green fee.

It becomes a priority to find more open routes to the sea for the country's mineral exports. The road and rail channels through to South Africa are impeded by the need to pass through boycotted Rhodesia. One attractive alternative is to try and reopen the Benguela Railway, built and still operated by a British company. Its long and lonely line runs west from Zaire across Angola to the port of Lobitos on the Atlantic. Unfortunately the tracks go through the heart of Angola's own civil war between the Soviet-supported Marxist government in Luanda and a South African-backed rebellion of southern tribes, led by Jonas Savimbi. The line is at a standstill as trains have been attacked and bridges damaged by the rebels.

The only way to get it running is to provide armed protection for repair gangs and for trains. We press Judith Hart, the Minister for Overseas Development, to put up some of her scarce funds for a survey of the line of rail and manufacture of armour-plated wagons for the squads of guards. After some hesitation (the corrupt Mobutu is far from being her favourite African leader) she gives her agreement. A firm of railway engineers by the old-fashioned name of Henderson and Busby are given the task and the armoured wagons eventually materialise. It is all curiously reminiscent of former colonial warfare. A small point that we tiptoe around in making the case for aid funds is that the soldiers who ride in them will not be African but Soviet-backed Cubans.

* * * * *

Meanwhile our efforts together with our European partners to bring an end to Idi Amin's bloodthirsty tyranny over Uganda are getting nowhere. By now his tally of massacre and execution is reckoned to have reached at least a quarter of a million. His removal is an objective close to the hearts of Dr Owen and Ted Rowlands, the minister responsible for Africa. A trade boycott by western countries has limited effect, and the French have to be cajoled a bit. Appeals to the Kenyans to block transit of goods, particularly oil, have gone unheeded. In late 1978 however the "President for Life and Conqueror of the British Empire", by now a cross between a monster and a clown, overreaches with a foolhardy invasion of his neighbour Tanzania in blind revenge for the asylum given to mutinous elements in his army. The Tanzanians seek our help over equipment in order to repel the attack and drive Amin's forces back across the Kagera River. Here at last is an opportunity. But as ever we have to scrape around for funds. Pressed by the Foreign Secretary we contrive to hijack a small sum from monies intended for sending British Army bands on goodwill tours abroad. This will pay for some inflatable boats in which the Tanzanian troops can cross the river. Given the need for haste I send a colleague round to Lillywhites, the sports equipment store in Piccadilly Circus, to see what can be obtained. The main requirement however is for trucks. This is well beyond the Foreign Office's paltry means. So back we go to Judith Hart, always a fan of President Julius Nyerere and his socialist ideals. She is clearly keen to help, but how to classify the provision of Bedford military trucks as part of a civil development programme? Her conscience is salved by a decision that the vehicles should not be painted khaki but white – QED. Amin's forces, despite some support from Libya's maverick Colonel Qaddafi, soon crumble before the Tanzanians. With the capture of his capital, Kampala, the Muslim Idi Amin flees to isolated refuge close by Mecca at Taif in Saudi Arabia. For the Ugandans and for Britain too it is a case of good riddance.

* * * * *

Amid all this upheaval I suddenly find myself switched back from Africa's endemic turmoil to the more familiar ground of Middle East affairs, in effect swapping a package of percussion caps for a powder keg. My new department covers Arabia and the Gulf together with Iraq and Iran. This turns out to be a baptism of fire. In Iran popular protest has been growing against Shah Mohammed Reza's programme of secular modernisation. Led by the Shi'a clergy and fuelled by economic dislocation and the repressive actions of the secret police, this resistance has been suppressed with increasing ruthlessness but now bursts out into an open, indeed seismic, revolution the shock of which is going to reverberate around the region and beyond for years to come. Britain's long and dominant engagement with the Gulf region and Iran, going back a couple of centuries to the days of the "Great Game", makes us a principal target of malevolence for whatever regime emerges out of the upheaval.

We start with another jolt for Dr Owen. No sooner do I reach my new office in the Middle East Department on a cold and snowy January morning than I am summoned to see the Foreign Secretary over Iran's growing chaos. Entering his grand ornate office with its views over St James' Park I am greeted by, "Hello, Alan. What are you doing here?" "I have just taken over the Middle East Department, Secretary of State." Seeing his disbelief, I add, perhaps without great conviction, "It's a region I know well." David Owen brushes this aside and calls for my Under-Secretary boss. To his surprise in comes John Moberly, a new face though an old Middle East hand. "Who are you?" barks the Foreign Secretary. "Where is Michael Weir?" "I took over from him this morning," replies John. The Owen fuse is understandably shortening. He goes on up the scale and sends for the Deputy Under-Secretary. In comes Sir Anthony Parsons, just returned from a turbulent spell as ambassador in Tehran. "Hello, Tony. Nice to see you back. Let's have a word later." "But you sent for me, Secretary of State. I have taken over today from Johnny Graham." David Owen cannot believe his ears. Somehow the administration of the Foreign Office has contrived, on the eve of a major crisis in the Middle East, to replace all three of his relevant senior officials on the same Monday… But there it is; we shall all be seeing a lot of each other over the weeks ahead.

* * * *

Shah Mohammed Reza and his family have suddenly taken flight for Egypt and within days Iran's powder train is alight with mass demonstrations in Tehran during one of which the British Embassy is torched. The country's spiritual leader, the aged Ayatollah Khomeini, who has for long preached against the increasingly despotic style of Pahlavi rule from his exile in Iraq and more recently in Paris, flies back to wild popular acclaim. Units of Iran's powerful military forces now switch their allegiance to the uprising and the country's Islamic revolution is complete. This swift and radical change of regime has somehow taken by surprise not only Britain but other major players too, not least the Americans and the Soviets, the former indecisive right up to the end and the latter disconcerted by the evident lack of appeal of the communist Tudeh Party. It is startling to find that, lulled by over-sanguine estimates from the embassy in Tehran of the survival of the Pahlevi regime, no serious planning appears to have taken place for the eventuality of the monarchy's overthrow and replacement by an Islamic, or even a Marxist, regime. Tony Parsons dons a hair shirt and devotes much time to trying to explain the misjudgements to political and business audiences. He has surreal tales of his weekly audiences with the Shah during the final months. By the time he reached the palace through demonstrating crowds his ambassadorial Rolls could be daubed with slogans calling for the Shah's death. The royal guards would parade and salute as if nothing were amiss. In discussion with Mohammed Reza Tony would attempt to bring the royal attention to the mood of unrest across the capital. By way of example he ventured that one vocal grievance in the bazaar was the constant breakdowns in electricity supply during the hot summer. The monarch's response was to go over to the door and switch on the lights in the audience chamber. "How can this be, ambassador? My people have the same as me." He had retreated into an ivory tower, surrounded by sycophantic courtiers and insulated from the public outrage.

The long and controversial history of Britain's imperial connection with Iran, coupled with our major stake in the country's defence apparatus and economy under the Shah's faltering leadership, make us a target for the new republican regime. The large British community finds itself in serious danger from mob attacks. So I find myself back straightaway to a hectic stint in the emergency suite up in the Foreign Office tower. Against a chaotic background the RAF and other western air forces undertake a rapid evacuation of western communities. At the same time much thought needs to be given in Whitehall as to whether anything of our extensive interests in Iran can be salvaged from the debacle and how to establish a relationship with the amorphous and resentful leadership that is starting to take shape. There are major strategic concerns too, given the possibility that a radical Iran, having detached herself from the Shah's western alliance, will be tempted into a pro-Soviet orbit. It soon becomes plain that the Central Treaty Organisation, an alliance between Turkey, Iran and Pakistan and western states designed to resist southward expansion by the Soviet Union, has received a *coup de grace*. Iran's revolution has blown a great hole in this Cold War shield. Overnight we put together a blueprint for the dismantling of a redundant alliance.

A post-mortem study is also called for of how the accumulating signals that a political hurricane was imminent came to be discounted. In large part we put the misjudgements, perhaps complacency, down to instinctive reluctance to interrupt the momentum of a close association with the powerful Pahlavi monarchy that has been bringing major benefits to Britain. In other words, and not for the first time in Britain's relationships in the Middle East, the wish to see a successful and valuable alliance endure became father to the thought. To search out and establish contact with the emerging centres of opposition would have put Britain's political and economic stake at risk. In effect we have turned a blind eye to trouble until it is too late, just as others have done.

The Shah, who soon moves on from initial refuge in Egypt to Morocco and thence to the Bahamas, asks whether he and the Empress Farah can be given shelter in Britain. This presents an acute dilemma. Ever since he succeeded his deposed father, Reza Shah, under British auspices in 1941, Britain has remained a constant source of support, with a leading part in Mohammed Reza's restoration to power following a coup in 1953, and in his subsequent programme of national modernisation and pursuit of a temporal grandeur which would set the conservative Shi'a establishment against him. To refuse asylum now involves a measure of betrayal. Yet to accede to the appeal is bound to jeopardise our relations with Iran's new rulers. After much deliberation a regretful decision is taken to refuse. Sir Denis Wright, a retired ambassador to Iran who has remained close to the Shah, is asked to act as emissary to carry this sorry news to Mohammed Reza in the Bahamas. It is an unworthy outcome and does little to allay the hostility of the new regime in Tehran. Events will however soon prove it to have been justified, as a subsequent decision by the Americans to admit the Shah for medical treatment provokes a violent mob seizure of the US Embassy and the taking of its personnel into a prolonged captivity.

Iran's Islamic Revolution sets off a chaotic period of settling of scores before an authoritarian theocracy is established under the supervision of inflexible and rancorous Shi'a mullahs. Moreover the insurrection brings a toxic religious ingredient into the political tensions of the whole region, while resurrecting old animosities between Persian and Arab. Within months a bitter territorial war breaks out with neighbouring Iraq and her ruthless dictator, Saddam Hussein. Some years later I come across a diary of an uncle of mine who happened to be visiting Tehran in October 1925 in the week when the Shah's father, Reza Pahlavi, a private soldier in the Cossack Brigade who had risen to become Prime Minister, deposed with British support the absent Shah of the three-hundred-year-old Qajar dynasty and, assuming the Peacock Throne, set Iran on the path of reform. This *coup d'état* appears to have been a bloodless one, greeted with nothing more noisy than displays of fireworks. The diplomatic corps, minus perhaps Russia's Bolshevik regime that had been aiming to extend its sphere of influence, applauded the event. The social round continued undisturbed, the head of the British Legation, Sir Percy Loraine, marked the day with a snipe shoot while the French minister held a ball. What a contrast to the mayhem and violence with which we are now contending!

* * * * *

The Islamic Revolution fosters a new sense of threat among Iran's Arab neighbours, particularly the former sheikhdoms along the Gulf's shore that have in the last few years emerged from decades under British protection into independent statehood, bolstered by fast increasing revenues from crude oil. The apprehension is shared by the Saudis; already threatened on their southern flank by an Egyptian-backed civil war in mountainous Yemen and despite having military forces trained and equipped by ourselves, the Americans and the French, they see good reason for worry over whether Shi'a Iran's new mood of religious fervour will spawn wider regional ambitions, and a possible challenge to the Sunni Kingdom's custodianship of Islam's two holiest shrines and the annual Haj pilgrimage.

Having successfully guided the welter of Gulf sheikhdoms into fledgling nationhood following the decision ten years earlier to withdraw from a costly defence role east of Suez, Britain has however turned her face away from her close association with the Gulf Arabs, leaving Iran and the Americans to guard the area from external threat. Indeed certain of our Labour ministers show a measure of antipathy towards the Gulf minnows, seeing their traditional autocratic ways of governance as anachronisms that are unlikely to survive, and perhaps do not deserve to do so. Despite the success of a recent visit by the Queen and Duke of Edinburgh to Saudi Arabia and other Gulf states – resulting in the Royal Yacht *Britannia* returning home with a hoard of treasure from her generous hosts the like of which has hardly been seen since the depredations of Sir Francis Drake on the Spanish Main – the proposals we now put forward for a re-engagement with these states to bolster their sense of security now that Iran is no longer onside meet with little enthusiasm at the top. We shall have to bide our time. Meanwhile there is regrettably little substance to our Arabian relationships.

* * * * *

A brief distraction arises out of Aden, in the far south of the Arabian peninsula. A strategic port surrounded by tribal fiefdoms, Britain's contested withdrawal from her former colony has been followed by the establishment of a Marxist state with the grandiose title of the People's Democratic Republic of Yemen (PDRY), and dependent on economic and military support from Cuba and East Germany under Soviet auspices. Relations with Britain remain strained, particularly following the recent perpetration of an assassination attempt in the open street in London.

One Saturday morning I receive an urgent call to a meeting in Whitehall with the Metropolitan Police Special Branch. It appears there are surveillance reasons to suspect that a group is about to arrive from Aden to collect some weapons. Clearly this calls for vigilance. I ask the police to maintain a discreet and unobtrusive watch on Aden's embassy building on the Cromwell Road in west London over the weekend and to report any unusual movement. They assure me this can be done.

I reach the Foreign Office on Monday morning to find the tabloid press alight with protests over the high-profile closure by the police of a section of one of west London's busiest streets. Oh dear – "discreet" is evidently not a term that exists in the police vocabulary. David Owen is on the line demanding to know what is going on. No sooner have I tried to put the record straight there than I am rung by the agitated PDRY ambassador asking to pay an urgent call. Mohammed Adan is a sensible diplomat with previous experience in Moscow. Not unreasonably he demands to know why his house has without warning been picketed by the police, his visitors interrogated on entry and his kitchen refuse bins searched. Even the Russians had never treated him in such a way. I conjure up an unconvincing response that there is reason to think his level of protection ought to be raised. A curious way of going about it, is his rejoinder. With a knowing look he goes on to ask if it has anything to do with the party coming to London for their arms. "Arms, ambassador?" I hope my show of surprise carries conviction. His explanation comes as a thunderbolt. A group of disabled ex-servicemen are on their way to have artificial limbs fitted at the Queen Anne Hospital in Roehampton, England's leading centre for prosthetic rehabilitation. Certain of them have lost their arms. Collapse of stout party, as Punch magazine used to say; the police are stood down and peace returns to the Cromwell Road. Still, one can never be too careful.

* * * * *

Ten years since our departure from Tripoli echoes of Libya's rough revolutionary road unexpectedly resurface. Walking to a meeting in the City a sudden voice calls, "Mr Alan. Mr Alan". It appears to come from behind a pillar. I stop and out steps none other than our old contact Colonel Aun Rahuma, one of the would-be architects of the military takeover that was pre-empted by the more radical Captain Qaddafi back in September 1969. A long-term refugee from his country's uncharitable regime he starts to talk of dark conspiracy. I steer well clear, for through my association with Libya's old regime I may well be among those foreigners on what passes for a black list. Recent publicity about the supply by Qaddafi of quantities of explosive to the Irish Republican Army has brought Libya's impulsive young leader back into the public eye. At a dinner with Arab friends we find Mohamed Heikal, a grand figure of Egyptian journalism and for years a close political adviser to the late President Nasser. He has a revealing tale to tell about an early encounter with Mu'ammar Qaddafi, of whose credentials to lead a revolution Nasser was sceptical. One of the youthful leader's earliest acts on taking over power in Libya had been to ask to pay his ardent respects to his hero in Cairo. A date was set and Heikal was sent to greet Qaddafi at the airport and bring him to his host. During their drive into the city Qaddafi's attention was taken by a gaudy hoarding on a cinema which was advertising the film *Mutiny on the Bounty*. Heikal had got no further than to say it was the story of a mutiny on a Royal Navy ship before Qaddafi jumped in with ideas for giving support to what he had taken to be a fresh blow to the British arch-enemy. The love affair is to be short-lived; Libya's maverick leader manages to provoke a border war with his Egyptian neighbour a few years later.

* * * * *

May 1979 brings a change of government with a landslide Conservative victory in a General Election that sees an exhausted Labour administration cede its authority over a country that is faced with major social and economic strains. The abrupt nature of the change is brought home to me on the first evening when I find Ted Rowlands, the Minister of State to whom I have been working, standing forlorn on the platform of Westminster Underground station trying to find his way home, having had to surrender his official car and driver. The return to power of a Conservative government under Margaret Thatcher comes as a breath of fresh air, bringing with it a new lease of life to Britain's diplomatic engagement with the Middle East region. The virtual collapse of the economy following the social unrest of the preceding "winter of discontent" has done harm to our standing abroad. In the Foreign Office a strike by the communications staff means that we have to go on bended knee to get key telegraph traffic transmitted, or even ask favours of our allies; the French have helped me with some urgent messages to our embassy in Saudi Arabia, where interminable civil conflict in the Yemen is threatening to spill over the southern border into the mountainous Asir province.

The appointment of Lord Carrington as Foreign Secretary provides an opportunity to resurrect the argument for a closer involvement with the Arab world. The region is once again at sixes and sevens following the shock of what some see as Egypt's defection to sign a treaty of peace with Israel in the wake of the US-brokered Camp David agreements of the previous autumn. The leaders of the oil-producing Gulf countries, with whom Britain has had such a long-established security and trading relationship, are also unsettled by the potential for subversion presented by Iran's new mood of sectarian zealotry and the pledge by Ayatollah Khomeini to "export the revolution". We have a shared interest in strengthening their defence capabilities; this is no time to be cold-shouldering old friends. Moreover we have reason to seek their help in opening the valves of their desert wells to ease the economic pressures caused by a sudden and painful surge in oil prices.

The upshot is a green light and an extensive tour by Tony Parsons and myself, taking in Saudi Arabia and four of the five smaller Gulf states, to discuss how Iran's revolution has shifted their scenery. With many years of pre-independence service to his account along the Gulf coast, plus his recent experience in Iran, Tony Parsons is ideally placed to revitalise the strands of our close links. I go ahead to have a few days first in Tehran to see at first hand how we may stay on terms with the new regime for all its cascade of anti-British rhetoric. The flight out finds me almost the sole passenger on a jumbo aircraft with a full cabin crew in attendance; until recently this has been one of British Airways' busiest routes. On arrival comes the strange experience of passing from the grimy streets of a concrete city centre into the gracious parkland of the British Embassy's vast compound, a grand legacy from the era of Lord Curzon and the Pax Britannica. A grim reminder of recent tumult is however provided by the scorched walls of the Chancery building, scars of its attack by a mob shortly before the revolution reached its climax. The porticoed residence sits unscathed among the trees, a house with its place in history for having been the setting for a ceremonious tripartite dinner during the meeting in Tehran in late 1943 between Churchill, Roosevelt and Stalin, at which decisions were taken on the opening up of a western front with the invasion of France.

Our ambassador, Johnny Graham, takes me to see the revolutionary regime's first Prime Minister, Mehdi Bazargan, a liberal figure whose period in office is to prove brief as his views come into conflict with the more rigid Islamist ideals of the mullahs; to draw a parallel with Russia's Bolshevik Revolution, he will prove to be Iran's Kerensky. His greeting is courteous, if on the wary side. Atavistic suspicions of British imperial designs are not long in emerging however when he alleges we are provoking a bid among the population of Iran's oil-rich Khuzestan province, many of whom are of Arab origin, to attach their lands to Saddam Hussein's Iraq across the Shatt al-Arab waterway. His paranoid conviction of British duplicity over a fanciful act of territorial rape appears deep-seated, and our attempts to allay it do not get far. We are in for a period of estrangement, though the door still seems open to contact. We go on to the embassy's summer compound in Gulhak, a suburb of the sprawling city further up the mountainside. Here is a lesser residence and solid houses in which the staff used to pass the hot summer months in greater comfort. A capacious tent covers much of the lawn, ready to accommodate diplomatic receptions that will no longer be held. A grand pro-consular era has met its abrupt end.

* * * *

I meet up with Tony Parsons in Saudi Arabia for a marathon tour taking in Riyadh and the oil-rich Eastern Province, Bahrain, Qatar, Abu Dhabi, Dubai, Sharjah and finally Muscat. For me it is a first introduction to the lower Gulf sheikhdoms, still uncertain of their recent independence and worried by Iran's sudden switch from a stabilising role to a potentially hostile one. I am particularly struck to find that the ten years since I was last involved with the region have seen Britain replaced by the United States as the prime target of Arab resentment over the continued existence of Israel. No more do our contacts, with a knowing look and a forefinger placed beside the nose, ascribe the latest crisis or setback in Arab affairs to "Breetish Intelligence", an unjustified though enduring myth from the days of empire. Yet for the eight of these mini-principalities forged by Britain into a single federation, the United Arab Emirates, unity remains elusive. The embers of old tribal feuds are ever ready to re-ignite, bringing British diplomacy back into play to help douse the flames.

As an old friend Tony Parsons gets a warm welcome from the assorted rulers for his assurance of Britain's re-engagement in the security undertakings given at the time of their independence. Riyadh is still a shuttered desert town of puritanical traditions, though with a sprinkling of modern offices and villas, harbingers of great changes to come. Much of government continues to be handled in Jedda where foreign embassies are quarantined. Hisham Nazer, the Saudi oil minister responds robustly to our request for help in easing the surge in the price of crude oil, arguing, not without justification, that he sees no reason to hasten the depletion of his country's precious asset in order to feed the west's insatiable and unrestrained consumption of the black gold.

Among our other ports of call Bahrain and Dubai have gained a modern façade, though at some cost to their elegant traditional architecture. The bonanza impact of unprecedented oil revenues is to be seen everywhere. The diminutive Sheikh 'Isa of Bahrain, sometimes to be found holding court in London's Dorchester Hotel, appears to govern his tidy island with a benevolent hand, Qatar's backwater has a palatial hotel and a new handicrafts museum, Abu Dhabi's Sheikh Zayed is using fast-increasing oil revenues to adorn his desert fief with palm-girt highways and a smart corniche, Sharjah's Sheikh Sultan, armed with a degree in agronomics, has invested in a virtual Scalextric layout of over- and underpasses for non-existent traffic, while Oman's young Sultan Qaboos, who holds a commission in the British Army, sports an elegant new palace, decorated out of Bond Street, to go with Muscat's fascinating old town. A new generation of leadership is taking over from their feuding predecessors, known to earlier British administrators by affectionate nicknames like Electric Whiskers and the Prophet Jeremiah.

Among this gallimaufry one of the most engaging figures we call upon is Sheikh Rashid al-Maktoum. Under his guidance Dubai, with its picturesque wind towers atop the old merchant houses and its sheltered creek, has become a busy port where sailing dhows cluster to ferry goods along the Gulf and across to Iran, as well as running illicit gold into India under the noses of a Royal Navy patrol. As we sit around, taking Arabia's cardamom-flavoured coffee in his diwan chamber overlooking the bustling quayside, Sheikh Rashid, his miniature pipe alight, has his customary grumble about claims to various wells and palm gardens which had been arbitrarily distributed between different sheikhdoms by Britain a decade earlier in preparation for independence. He has it in for two former officials in particular, Julian Walker and Martin Buckmaster. "Where," he enquires, "is Mr Walker now?" We reply that he is now our ambassador to Yemen. "And where is Mr Buckmaster?" "He is our deputy ambassador in Yemen." Sheikh Rashid shoots us a mischievous look. "What," he asks, "have the Yemenis done wrong to deserve this?"

Muscat in July is like a furnace. We have the compensation however of staying in the historic British agency on the shore, looking out to the twin Portuguese forts that still guard the entrance to the horseshoe bay. Sadly this handsome relic from the days of the Indian Raj will before long be razed to make room for modern pleasure domes. The young Qaboos is, to his credit, working to bring his oil-endowed and singular country out of the feudal seclusion in which his anachronistic father had sought to freeze it up until 1970, when with British support Sultan Qaboos staged a coup, sending the old skinflint into involuntary retirement in London's Dorchester Hotel. In those archaic days anyone going about within the town after the gates were shut at dusk had been required to carry a lantern; even the wearing of dark glasses was forbidden by this antediluvian ruler. Sultan Said bin Taimur's deep prejudices against modern society had provided the inspiration for a witty, if tongue-in-cheek, despatch to the Foreign Secretary by a former

British Consul-General asking for a search to be made for the B flat clarinet score in a makeshift Omani national anthem. This jingle was said to have been concocted in honour of the ruler, who incidentally saw all music as profane, by the Royal Marine Bandmaster on a visiting naval ship and was known to the bandsmen as "Gawd Strike the Sultan Blind". The jolly tune had been recorded at the time, but, so the story ran, was unfortunately obliterated when the Sultan had inadvertently sat upon the disc.

At his handsome new palace Sultan Qaboos, curved dagger tucked into his belt as Omani tradition requires, welcomes us in stylish surroundings. He has recently succeeded, with British and also Iranian military help and through a bold programme of civil development, in overcoming a bitter and prolonged civil war, fomented by attempts by his Marxist neighbour in Aden to rouse revolt in Oman's eastern Dhofar province. The religious upheaval in Iran has however brought a new threat to security, particularly given Oman's sovereignty over the inaccessible Musandam peninsula that faces Iran across the strategic Hormuz Straits at the entrance to the Gulf and astride the world's busiest oil shipping lane (and where in the 19th century a posting to the isolated British telegraph station along the wireless line to India gave rise to the expression "to go round the bend"). The meeting provides an opportunity to urge more rapid liberalisation of the autocratic system of government which Sultan Qaboos has inherited, as well as words of reproof over Omani involvement in the breaching by air of international economic sanctions on the outlawed regime of Ian Smith in Rhodesia.

So we have much to talk about in earnest with our Gulf contacts as, under the dark shadow cast by Iran's revolution, we take steps to re-engage with their security, no longer with garrisons as in earlier days of empire, but through diplomatic support, bolstered by military training and equipment.

* * * * *

Trouble is also brewing at the head of the Gulf where Iraq's bellicose despot, Saddam Hussein, is about to respond to Iranian border provocations by unleashing an ill-considered invasion of his neighbour, where the Shi'a tradition of martyrdom is now aflame. The Foreign Office's inexorable carousel characteristically chooses this critical moment however to order another change of scene, as I find myself taking charge of the movements and careers of the Service's five-thousand personnel around the globe. The sudden switch has been brought about by the appointment of my predecessor as a private secretary to Prime Minister Margaret Thatcher in Downing Street. This return to the administration may have something to do with having, in a fit of professional zeal, qualified during my earlier stint for membership of the Institute of Personnel Management. It is a case of poacher turning gamekeeper as I resign my position on the committee of our union and go back to matching horses for courses and vice versa. The work will bring its own challenges as the service enters a stage in the art of staff management where old assumptions of a job for life and "one size fits all" no longer apply. Individuals are rightly seeking greater choice and consultation over the course of their careers, staff associations have become more militant, and assessments of performance are required to be more open (painful as this may prove for some). Account is having to be taken of the need to find appropriate berths (to coin a phrase) for female officers being accompanied overseas by their male spouses, and gay members of the Service too, in posts where local social customs or legal considerations do not present obstacles. On a more bleak note I am also charged with making a cull among more senior colleagues whose numbers are blocking the promotion of younger talent; a necessary operation perhaps but a disagreeable one.

With some regret I hand over the Middle East Department and its chronic crises to David Hannay, whose first-hand experience of Iran is highly relevant to the current upheavals in the region. An early flurry on the personnel front comes with a long-awaited settlement of Rhodesia's civil war and agreement on her independence as Zimbabwe under a black-led government. Old colonial hands are uprooted from rural retirement to help see the new country through the process of transition and constitutional change. Even the policeman on our local beat in Chiswick, Constable Holloway, finds himself snatched away, helmet and all, to maintain law and order. Iran too continues to present challenges. As our relations continue to deteriorate, we become embroiled in a tedious game of diplomatic bluff with a succession of tit-for-tat expulsions of personnel from our respective embassies until one of us sees fit to blink.

The work is not without its lighter moments however. The Queen's annual reception for the diplomatic corps in London takes place in November at Buckingham Palace. As we are still at a stage where for historic reasons full diplomatic status has not been accorded by the court of St James to the Vatican, the Pope's representative in Britain is not permitted to join the foreign ambassadors who thread a long line through the reception rooms awaiting presentation to Her Majesty. I find myself in charge of a cunning arrangement, no doubt devised over many years, whereby the Papal Nuncio is concealed behind a pillar and is produced as if out of a hat, or perhaps a biretta, to be greeted as the Queen passes that spot. There is no limit to diplomatic guile. April Fool's Day provides another opportunity for a bit of fun, when I discover that I still have a business card of Kim Philby's, which he had given me in Beirut some while before his escape to Moscow. On 1 April I get the cardboard slip passed to Teddy Youde, the head of administration, with a message that it comes from a man down at the door who asks to see him. Having thus lit the touch paper we stand back to watch. Fireworks are not slow in bursting as the mercurial Chief Clerk calls for the building to be locked tight and Scotland Yard mobilised in double quick time. I hasten to come clean before the April Fool gets out of hand; to his credit Teddy administers no more than a good-humoured reproof and returns the precious card.

* * * * *

Some of the most difficult living conditions overseas are experienced by staff in the Soviet Union and other countries of Eastern Europe behind the Iron Curtain, particularly during the winter months. In Moscow they find themselves crammed into solid and soulless apartment blocks in flats allocated by the Soviet Foreign Ministry and where maintenance receives a low priority. I take an opportunity of making a pastoral visit to have a first-hand look at how things are. Moscow in the snow is a cold and silent city. The embassy itself, formerly the spacious residence of a wealthy merchant in pre-revolution days, has all the chancery offices squeezed into its ground floor while the ambassador occupies the grander storeys above the shop. It is an uncomfortable arrangement, but everyone makes the best of it.

Life for the embassy staff is pretty monotonous, particularly in the depths of winter. At least they have access to basic western foodstuffs from an in-house commissariat, replenished with stores brought down from Helsinki. Morale is not helped however by the fact that our relations are going through one of their more frosty patches with the Soviet Union's geriatric leadership. There is precious little on offer by way of diversion, and some of that needs to be off limits on security grounds. I am reminded of a well-recorded tale of a letter, sent in 1943 from a cheerless wartime Moscow to the head of the Foreign Office by the ambassador, Sir Archibald Clark Kerr, which ran:

> My dear Reggie,
>
> In these dark days man tends to look for little shafts of light that spill from Heaven. My days are probably darker than yours, and I need, my God I do, all the light I can get... So I propose to share with you a tiny flash that has illuminated my sombre life and tell you that God has given me a new Turkish colleague whose card tells me that he is called Mustapha Kunt. We all feel like that, Reggie, now and then, especially when Spring is upon us, but few of us would care to put it on our cards. It takes a Turk to do that.

I take a break from my rounds to stop at the government foreign currency shop to look for a Siberian fur hat for Grania. Kiril, the ambassador's driver, comes with me to interpret. He is quite a character; when he is not on duty driving the official Rolls-Royce he moonlights as a stunt driver for the Soviet film industry with car chases across frozen lakes and so forth. Having found an elegant bonnet of silver fox we make our way to the pay desk. Surprisingly the only western credit card accepted by the Russians is Access. As I fumble in my wallet to get out my card the impatient cashier grabs one of the plastics from it and inserts it in her till. I see that she has got hold of my account card with Ladbrokes betting agency. Finding it does not work she grumpily demands to know what it is for. My explanation leads to a remarkable reaction when she thumps a bell on her counter. Bidding everyone within earshot to gather round she flourishes the Ladbrokes card and announces, "This Englishman has this card for betting on horses!" There are murmurs of astonishment; an elderly man turns to me and says, through Kiril, "Sir, you must live in a wonderful country." I agree this is so, but resist the temptation to add that it has taken sixty-five years of communism and my Ladbrokes card to convince him. Off we go followed by warm farewells. It strikes me later that it was fortunate that the cashier did not find the precious visiting card which Kim Philby had given me in Beirut, and which I had forgotten was tucked away in my wallet. That would have given the Russians something to think about... As Kiril drops me off at the embassy, I ask how he makes his way back to his home in one of the massive and indistinguishable apartment blocks on the outskirts of the city. "In the Rolls," he replies. Indeed it turns out that he often parks the stylish barouche outside his block for the night. "It certainly impresses the neighbours," he adds. Some twenty years later Kiril is to write a book about his time as chauffeur to Britain's ambassadors on behalf of the KGB.

An even more bizarre twist to the security picture occurs within the embassy. The ambassador, Curtis Keeble, asks me at breakfast if I have remarked the handsome chambermaid who looks after the residence bedrooms. Wondering what he can be driving at, I acknowledge she is certainly attentive and well found. "Well," he goes on, "do you remember the sensational publicity in 1965 when our ambassador, Geoffrey Harrison, had an affair with one of the housemaids in a honeytrap set by the KGB, and had to resign from the Service? This is the same woman." How then, I ask, is she still employed in the embassy fifteen years on? "The Foreign Ministry won't move her." Male guests beware...

* * * * *

I fly on to chilly Belgrade to find a down-at-heel city. Some of the first stirrings of popular opposition to communist rule post-Marshal Tito are to be seen on buildings daubed with graffiti. Recalling the old joke that Aeroflot does not publicise its accidents for fear of alarming the passengers, I choose a seat next to the emergency exit. A superfluous notice above the window says in English "Do not open in flight". I was not intending to do so. The next stop, in Budapest astride the Danube, comes as a tonic after Moscow and Belgrade. In their subtle Magyar way the Hungarians have worked out ways to create a measure of style and prosperity under the noses of their Russian custodians. Here too is a happier embassy. There is no shortage of pleasant recreation, with diplomatic tickets to the ballet, an exhilarating morning ride across the wide steppe, gypsy melodies to go with the delicious goulash and even games of chess played on floating boards in the city's open air thermal baths with deep snow all around. Yet the walls still have their ears.

Prague comes next on the itinerary, and a frosty reminder of Soviet domination following the crushing of the "Prague Spring" twelve years ago. A foretaste of this sombre mood comes when the runway lights are switched off as soon as we touch down. The chancery and the residence are located in grand buildings on the hill overlooking the Voltava River and the historic Charles Bridge. It was formerly the palace of Austro-Hungarian nobility and, remarkably, still contains the family's collection of art and objets de vertu. It is rather like living amid the Wallace Collection. The ambassador, John Rich, has an amusing anecdote that illustrates the pride the Czech establishment takes in the monuments of this fine city, which, unlike Budapest, was mercifully spared allied aerial attack during the Second World War. A local contractor was recently engaged to restore the stucco facing on the residence walls. On completion the Foreign Office carried out the customary security sweep to check for any electronic devices. This turned out to be a wise precaution as a quantity of suspicious wiring was discovered to have been embedded in the new stucco. A brainwave on the part of John Rich produced a neat remedy without disturbing diplomatic protocol. He rang the head of the Prague Fire Brigade to warn him of a serious fire hazard caused by strange wiring that had appeared beneath the facing of this historic building. In no time the firemen were up their ladders removing the offending wires and making good the surface, and for free. But Prague in the snow is a silent place today. We join an evening mass in the old cathedral; the service has a furtive air, quite unlike the defiant exuberance which came as a surprise to me at a crowded celebration of the orthodox sung liturgy in Moscow's spectacular Novodevichi Monastery a week earlier.

My final call is in Warsaw. Departure from Prague is accompanied by one of Czechoslovakia's few remaining treasures – a glass of genuine Pilsner lager at the airport. It is a particularly interesting moment to be visiting Poland, as the Solidarity Movement, which marks an unprecedented stage in popular resistance to the Stalinist regime, is beginning to present a real challenge to authority. Its strike actions and vociferous demonstrations, and the provocation these present to the Soviet Union, are not entirely welcome to some of Poland's neighbours however. Hungarians in particular have been grumbling that the volatile Poles can always be relied upon to go about things the wrong way and spoil other peoples' games. It is a pleasure to find my fellow guest in the recently built embassy residence, a severe modernist cube faced in black granite that sits uneasily among the neighbouring villas, is Margaret Drabble, here to give talks on the English novel having just completed the re-editing of *The Oxford Companion to*

English Literature. Some of the leading Solidarity figures are invited to dinner. They seem full of confidence that they can turn the tide of Soviet domination.

* * * * *

The dining table for this occasion is dressed with some very handsome pieces of silver. Later I ask our ambassador, Kenneth Pridham, (he who, when I was so wet behind the ears twenty years before, had sent me off to have lunch with a "German ex-U-boat commander"), about the origin of these striking trophies. He explains they form part of an historic collection dating from the early 19th century and known as the Beresford Hope silver. He goes on to relate a fascinating and dramatic story of how they came to adorn Britain's embassy in Warsaw. A description of this valuable cache, written by Mary Henderson, wife of a former ambassador in Warsaw, had appeared a few years previously in *Apollo*, the arts magazine. The following account is the version of its colourful history, as related that evening by Kenneth Pridham.

The collection of fine silver pieces was originally formed by General Viscount Beresford, an illegitimate son of the Marquess of Waterford who rose to become one of the Duke of Wellington's most successful commanders during the Peninsular War against Napoleon. One of his most notable military exploits was to mount an unauthorised military expedition in 1806 to capture Buenos Aires, at that time under the faltering rule of Spain. The attack proved a total failure; Beresford was held a prisoner for six months before making his escape in the guise of a washerwoman. Nevertheless it was seen at home as an heroic endeavour and led to his being presented by the Patriotic Fund of Lloyds members with an inscribed silver-gilt cup, while a table centrepiece in the form of a dolphin by the famous silversmith, Paul Storr, was given by British merchants in Madeira. Lord Beresford went on to amass a large silver collection, which passed on his death to his Hope stepchildren.

In due course it came into the possession of one Harold Beresford Hope, a young member of the Diplomatic Service who was posted to Berlin in 1913. While there he had an amorous affair with a Polish lady. As ill luck would have it, she found him at a ball one evening accompanied by another partner. In an act of supreme drama she pulled out a revolver there and then

Emergency food supply reaches an encampment of the Al Howeitat bedouin in southern Jordan desert, April 1959.

The Royal Ballet perform in the Temple of Bacchus during the 1961 Baalbek Festival in Lebanon.

Rod and Pam Sarell and the author with King Idris and Queen Fatima and their family at the royal villa in Tobruk, 1967.

Libyan demonstrators gathering in front of the British embassy in Tripoli on the first day of the June 1967 Arab-Israel War.

Defence Secretary Denis Healey MP with Rod Sarell, Libyan escorting officer and the author in Tripoli's Old City, 1968.

HRH Princess Alexandra and her husband Angus Ogilvy with Brazilian Marines escort in Rio de Janeiro, 1974.

Energy Secretary Patrick Jenkin MP and the author enjoying a samba in a Rio de Janeiro nightspot, 1974.

Chris Barber and his Jazzmen playing at the Queen's Birthday Reception in Algiers, 1985.

The author with Grania (kneeling), Dutch colleagues and Touareg guide near Tamanrasset, Algerian Sahara, 1975.

No road to the Dr Livingstone Mission Hospital; Bruce Fieldsend and the author in northern Malawi, 1989.

A friendly welcome for the author from King Fahd of Saudi Arabia, Jedda, 1989.

With Grania, decorously garbed in her "Lady Anne Blunt habit", in the old fortress of Ha'il, northern Saudi Arabia, 1990.

"Our Men on the Spot" ran the caption in The Times; *Air Vice-Marshal Sandy Wilson and the author at Dhahran airbase, Saudi Arabia, August 1990.*

Prime Minister John Major with Chieftain tank of the 14th/20th Hussars and crew members on the Saudi frontier shortly before the advance into Kuwait, January 1991.

The ambassador loses his bearings along the old Hejaz Railway, northern Saudi Arabia, 1992.

Relic of an earlier war; the wreckage of a Turkish locomotive sabotaged by Col. T.E. Lawrence and the forces of the Emir Faisal north of Medina during the First World War, Saudi Arabia, 1992.

and shot herself dead in front him. Harold himself met an early death from typhoid four years later in Athens. It is said that in delirium he threw himself out of a window. It turned out that in his will, in what was presumably a gesture of remorseful atonement to the country of his paramour, he had bequeathed the silver collection "for use in the British Embassy, legation or mission in Poland if such ... shall be established in Poland at my death or within five years from the date of my death," The legacy was to include "a complete dinner service and ornaments for the dinner table".

Poland regained her fragile independence as a republic in 1918 at the end of the First World War. The silver collection was sent out to the newly established British legation by cruiser and under naval guard in 1921, where it remained in use until Britain's diplomats were withdrawn in 1939 following the outbreak of the Second World War and Hitler's invasion of Poland. At this point it was locked away in the strongroom of the embassy building, which came under American protection until Pearl Harbor brought the United States into the war, and subsequently under that of neutral Sweden. When the embassy was reopened in 1945 the strongroom was found to be empty and with a large hole knocked through the bricks of its rear wall. There was no sign of the silver; the Swedes claimed to have no idea what had happened during their watch over the premises. Embassies were alerted to look out for pieces of the great collection in salerooms and a ceiling of £2,000 per item (a fair sum at the time) was allocated for their recovery.

Some months later Aliki Russell, the wife of a British diplomat and herself a former Greek beauty queen, had her attention attracted while she was rummaging around in a Warsaw junkyard by a large and much discoloured old silver bowl. On inspection it turned out to be a dish-cover inscribed with the royal monogram. After it was identified as coming from the Beresford Hope horde other dish-covers came to light and were bought back. The hunt was now on; other items from the collection, including the Buenos Aires cup, were found with dealers in various locations as far apart as London, New York, Sweden, Holland, Italy and Israel, including candelabra, soup tureens, ice buckets and a venison dish. It is said that one of the huge tureens came to light when once again the eagle-eyed Aliki Russell found herself being given a shampoo in it in a New York hairdressing salon. There were even arrests made with prices negotiated through dubious back channels. With the recovery of nearly a quarter of the full collection however the trails ran cold and the Foreign Office called a halt to the expense. A few items which surfaced subsequently were declined, and the much reduced collection went on display at the Victoria and Albert Museum and then at the National Museum in Warsaw prior to being returned to the British ambassador's new residence in 1964. According to Kenneth Pridham a finger of suspicion over the theft was pointed at a junior official in the wartime Swedish embassy, as the pattern of recoveries appeared to match certain of his subsequent diplomatic appointments around the world. When I ask whether this has been taken any further with the Swedes, he suggests this might prove awkward, as by an ironical twist the official in question is currently his Swedish opposite number in Warsaw! Seventeen years on the silver makes a glittering setting for our lively dinner with leaders of Poland's emerging opposition to the heavy hand of Soviet communism.

It is all quite a story. A curious sequel comes my way in London a few months later when we are suddenly asked by the Metropolitan Police if a request could be made to the Swedes for one of their diplomats to be questioned about the theft; evidently the case is not cold. When I put this proposal however to our newly appointed ambassador to Stockholm, Donald Murray, he understandably points out that it will make for an inauspicious start to his mission to seek the interrogation of a senior Swedish diplomat. We agree to let things lie.

* * * * *

The time has come for another move. Abroad is not possible as Grania, who is working with an illiteracy programme in our local council, has been in hospital for an operation. Periods of secondment to gain experience away from diplomacy are in fashion, so I opt to go to the Ministry of Defence where there is a call for an Arabic speaker to run the department covering the provision of military equipment and support to our friends in the Middle East, work which chimes well with my experience of the region and its chronic insecurity. The Arabic will need refreshing, so first it's back to school. This spell coincides with a period of convalescence for Grania at Osborne House on the Isle of Wight, a dignified medical establishment out of another age, expertly run by the Royal Navy in a part of the Venetian palace built by Queen Victoria and Prince Albert as a family base over a century earlier. I join Grania there, combining immersion in Arabic vocabulary and grammar with a visit round the old Queen's homely chambers, walks in the landscaped grounds down to the Solent, rounds of golf on the private course, nautical outings to nearby Cowes and black-tie dinners hosted by the Surgeon Captain who runs the show. A chauffeured Rolls-Royce brings patients to and from the Portsmouth ferry. We are put up in a magnificent bedroom originally occupied by Edward VII when a young Prince of Wales; the walls are hung with royal portraits and Highland scenes by Winterhalter and Landseer. It is all a vestige of more gracious times. The faded splendour helps to hasten recovery, while I scrape through the Civil Service Arabic interpreters examination; "Are you still having to take exams, Daddy?" asks a despondent Luke who is about to sit for the Common Entrance examination to his secondary school.

Ministry of Defence – London
1981-1983

*Better they do it imperfectly than you do it perfectly, for it is their country, their
war, and your time is limited*

TE Lawrence, *Seven Pillars of Wisdom*

It comes as a relief to find myself made welcome in the Ministry of
Defence, having in effect parachuted from outside into one of their senior
jobs. As might be expected there are cultural differences between the Foreign
Office and the Home departments of government. For example, while the
former tends to operate on paper, perhaps because its main lines of
communication run overseas, policy in the Defence Ministry is more often
developed and applied through meetings and verbal communication. There
is to be much tramping through London's traffic between the ministry's vast
headquarters in Whitehall and my new location in the centre of colourful
Soho. My department, situated in an anonymous and unimposing office
block, has for its neighbour a fine old town house that now appears to serve
as a rest home for Soho's "fallen women".

The work brings responsibility for the promotion and the monitoring
of Britain's supply of military equipment to countries right across the Middle
East from Egypt to Pakistan. Given the present tensions in the region there
is plenty to do in a field of activity that is highly competitive, frequently
controversial – and sometimes murky; there is no shortage of shadowy
individuals, some plausible, most less so, keen to offer their services as go-
betweens in arms deals. A fine line needs to be trodden between the
development of legitimate marketing opportunities on behalf of Britain's

still extensive defence industries, all major providers of employment in factories spread throughout the country from the Clyde down to Southampton, and the expediency of a sale in terms of broader foreign policy objectives. Political sensitivities at home also come into play. Certain key markets, notably Saudi Arabia, call for a direct engagement in the negotiation and management of major military contracts, a new experience for a diplomat accustomed to a more tactical role in the devising and pursuit of foreign policy.

The smaller Gulf states too are in the process of building up their military capabilities in the face of potential threats from Iran, now deeply embroiled in hostilities with Iraq. Iran herself is off limits for military sales; indeed much time has to be spent in an attempt to unravel the major undertakings previously entered into with the Shah's regime for the supply of tanks and other fighting equipment. A good portion of this materiel is switched to Jordan. Iraq is also in the market; under Saddam Hussein she sources much of her equipment from the Soviet Union and from France. But there is residual respect among her powerful armed forces for British weaponry and training, dating back to the days of the monarchy; many of Iraq's senior officers received their early training in Britain. For our part we have, in a forlorn attempt to restrain the two combatants, forsworn the supply of any "lethal" war items to Iraq, though the line is a fuzzy one and is already presenting problems.

* * * * *

Egypt is one of our major customers through joint manufacturing projects for infantry missiles and Westland helicopters. My first contact with Margaret Thatcher comes about in a meeting in a comfortable sitting room in No. 10 to brief her for a forthcoming visit by President Mubarak, the former chief of the Egyptian Air Force who has recently succeeded Anwar Sadat, assassinated during a military parade by Islamist zealots among the soldiery. The gathering provides an occasion for the Prime Minister's reputation for not suffering fools to be demonstrated to the full. A senior Foreign Office minister present, Humphrey Atkins, commits the sin of dropping off in his armchair during Mrs Thatcher's opening review of objectives for the visit. Spotting this solecism she barks out "Do you agree, Humphrey?" Jerked back into the present, the luckless Atkins mutters a ready concord. "Humphrey," comes a rapier reproof, "you are paid to advise me, not I you!" The rest of us take the chance to study the pattern on the ceiling.

Soon after this, I join John Nott, the Defence Secretary, on a visit to Egypt to discuss our defence cooperation. It is my first return to Cairo since our honeymoon trip nearly twenty years earlier. There are a few handsome new buildings along the Nile, but the city seems more ramshackle and crowded than ever as Egypt attempts to throw off the stifling years of state socialism and embark on a new era of enterprise, buttressed by the benefits of a growing oil and gas industry. After a day of talks and a couple of armament factory visits our host, General Abu Ghazala, invites us to make a tour of Upper Egypt's antiquities. We fly on in the comfort of the RAF VC10 to Luxor, where a raucous late night with belly dancing in the night club of the Winter Palace leaves our party considerably the worse for wear for a hot day of temple trotting both there and on to Aswan. The wily John Nott and his wife duck out of the celebrations and arise as bright as buttons. We make it up to Abu Simbel in Nubia, where the aircraft squeezes down onto a sandy strip. At last I get the chance to see the great monument of Rameses II in brilliant sunlight; it had been shrouded in dense fog when Grania and I made the long passage upstream back in 1962. I have arranged with our accompanying *Daily Telegraph* defence correspondent, an obliging ex-major general, that we compose together his nightly despatch to London for the following day's issue. The travel diary that emerges serves as my daily letter home to the family. Newspapers have their uses.

We fly on to Saudi Arabia and Jordan. Memories of Britain's recapture of the Falkland Islands following their seizure by Argentinian forces earlier in the year are still fresh in the minds of our hosts. The congratulations which the victory evokes come as an embarrassment to the Defence Secretary, who had in fact found himself sidelined by Mrs Thatcher in favour of the service chiefs in the overseeing of the conflict. Indeed it is the firm opinion of many of my Ministry of Defence colleagues that the confrontation might have been avoided had those involved in the Foreign Office taken warning signals more seriously, and that the subsequent official enquiry into the crisis had the elements of a whitewash – a view with which I find myself in some sympathy. Prince Sultan, a doyen among the world's ministers of defence, has positive things to say about Britain's close and valuable association with the Saudi Air Force, despite finding himself taken aback a touch when John Nott rounds things off with a somewhat insensitive gift in the shape of an ornamental porcelain dog, an animal of low esteem within Islam's bestiary.

* * * * *

With the war between Iran and Iraq now into its third inconclusive and bloody year much time is taken up in a tussle between the Ministry of Defence, the Foreign Office and the Department of Trade over restrictions on the sale of defence-related equipment to the two combatants. It is proving increasingly difficult to maintain our basic objective of impartiality and restraint through refusal to supply any military materiel that can be classed as "lethal"; the considerable benefits Britain continues to derive from our valuable trading relations with both belligerents, particularly Iraq, have to be set against the war's impact on wider stability in this key oil-producing region plus a climate of public and parliamentary opinion that is openly hostile to revolutionary Iran. Moreover in the case of the latter country there remain significant contractual obligations over the fulfilment of orders for armour and naval vessels paid for by the previous regime. There are divergences within our own government. While the less-than-scrupulous Alan Clark at the Department of Trade presses for maximum flexibility in the interpretation of our "non-lethal" guidelines and the Ministry of Defence is keen to help equipment makers with their export business, over at the Foreign Office ministers and officials endeavour to strike a pragmatic balance that may avoid prolonging the conflict. The resulting exercise in semantic consensus and compromise will in due course lead abortively into the courts and come to roost in frustration a decade later with a hanging out of soiled linen during a four-year-long public inquiry conducted by Lord Justice Scott.

The Iraqi military are now in the market in a major way for ground and naval weaponry as well as aircraft. My chief, the industrialist bus maker Sir Ron Ellis, holds at least one clandestine meeting with Saddam Hussein; some of the equipment we are supplying to third parties in the region may be finding its way to Iraq. But the "non-lethal" watchword is carefully observed, bringing gall to a British defence industry that sees our exercise in self-denial lead to substantial equipment sales by the Soviet Union, and the less scrupulous French too. At least one enquiry from the Iraqi army borders on the preposterous, when a visiting general asks me whether we could resume manufacture of the Churchill tank flame-thrower, a dinosaur of the Second World War. Apparently they consider this long-outlawed weapon to be the only way to block the suicidal attacks on foot across the minefields of no-man's-land by Iran's fanatical Revolutionary Guards.

* * * * *

There is much flitting up and down the Gulf to be done in pursuit of equipment sales, often at short notice. Some suppliers are diligent over support and training for the fledgling local forces, while others prefer to make a sale and walk away; much of our time is taken up with keeping demanding customers happy, for business is brisk the whole length of this shore as Iran flexes her revolutionary muscles with territorial claims and naval interceptions. In response the Royal Navy finds itself back on its old station. It is a pleasure to take a break in Bahrain with a visit to the private beach of the hospitable Ruler, Sheikh Isa al-Khalifa, who, so it is reported, enjoys entertaining there the wives of personnel on the island's RAF refuelling station, seeing them off with broad smiles and a Rolex. Happy days… Oman, now coming out of long seclusion under Sultan Qaboos and with a close association with Britain's armed forces, is a major customer. His jovial uncle, Sayid Fahr, Minister of Defence and married surprisingly to a connection of the Douglas-Home dynasty, is a popular visitor to Whitehall where his custom of generously tipping the lift operators is much appreciated. His ample frame also keeps in business the tailor I find we share in Savile Row.

A new boss, James Blyth, fresh from running Lucas Aerospace, has bold ideas on marketing. His most ambitious is to hire a roll-on roll-off cross-Channel ferry, fill its ample car decks with tanks and guns and all kinds of sophisticated electronic toys, and set it sailing for a month of calls along the length of the Gulf from Kuwait down to Oman. I join the cavalcade at Abu Dhabi, where our luckless ambassador has recently had to be moved at the insistence of Mrs Thatcher, who on a recent visit to this oil-rich sheikhdom chose to be affronted to find him wearing a safari suit. It is an awesome sight to see in place of the usual holiday fleet of France-bound Ford Cortinas the procession of heavy armour and equipment rumble ashore, heading to dusty firing ranges for demonstrations, and then lumbering back aboard in the gathering dusk; a cross between a lethal version of Barnum and Bailey's circus elephants and a military Noah's ark. It is no surprise that one of the most popular items on board turns out to be the excellent floating restaurant we have brought into a region that is still in the gastronomic era of the "Greasy Spoon".

* * * * *

The Saudi Kingdom is by far our major customer – and one of the most demanding. Britain's association with the forces of the Al Saud goes back well over half a century. Along with the Americans we have for some years played an important role in the support and training of the Royal Saudi Air Force, one of the largest in the Arab world. Its fleet of British Aerospace Lightning fighter aircraft and Strikemaster trainers is getting a bit long in the tooth; my department takes the lead in negotiations for their updating – business of real significance for Britain's aviation industry. These are nervous times as Iraq's land and air war with Iran, including ballistic missile attacks, goes full swing, bringing with it a potential threat to Iraq's Arab neighbours, while to the north, Israel, goaded by the sallies of Palestinian guerrillas, launches a ferocious invasion to tear the heart out of Lebanon. I have a desk in Riyadh's smart new air force headquarters building, an opportunity to taste the unhastening rhythm of Saudi bureaucracy with its regular break for the noon prayers and a respite during the heat of the summer's day. The Saudis are in the market for new defence technology, such as airborne early warning systems – the "eye in the sky", a field in which the Americans have a significant lead. My final months at the Defence Ministry will however bring the satisfaction of seeing a fresh chapter of cooperation open with the supply of the sophisticated Tornado along with other air and naval materiel under the Al Yamamah project, a massive windfall resulting from the inability of the American administration to obtain support in Congress for the supply of the latest F15 aircraft, following pressure from the influential, and myopic, pro-Israel lobby. This will be the largest overseas contract to have been awarded to British enterprise – and one which is to afford ample food for speculation on the part of an insatiably inquisitive British press. The aircraft are to be built at Wharton, a location that involves me in escorting Saudi air force delegations up to Lancashire and an obligatory introduction to the illuminated nightlife of nearby Blackpool.

There are also negotiations to be taken forward over major support contracts with the Saudi National Guard, a parallel force created to balance the army and with responsibility for national security. Both the Air Force and the Guard have teams of British military advisers attached to them. The National Guard, fief of Crown Prince Abdullah, has its own imposing ministry near the Prince's palace to the east of the city. Recruiting largely from among the bedouin, its establishment reflects a tribal hierarchy dominated by the influential Al Tuwaijri clan. The cool and grandiose interior is sheathed in dark mahogany. Each heavy door bears the title of the department within; one leads to the pest control section, charmingly described in English as the "Department for Beating Small Animals" – a somewhat over-literal use of an English dictionary.

All this activity involves a shuttle every few weeks between Soho Square and Riyadh to join our negotiators in the front line, sometimes at disruptively short notice. It comes as a shock, perhaps a salutary one, after the traditional role of adviser and advocate characteristic of diplomacy, to find oneself directly engaged with the success or failure of intricate business deals which also carry major political implications. Our negotiations are often laborious. For their part the Saudis, ever tough traders, are well versed in the finer arts of commercial negotiation, from the pricing of jet engines for the air force down to the cost-benefit of the medical disposables to be provided for the National Guard's spanking new British-run hospital in Jedda. The Guard's chief official, known to us as T2, and a wily negotiator withal, takes a mischievous pleasure in playing us off against our American competitors in sessions around his great boardroom table, and with muttered asides to his acolytes which put my Arabic to the test. Some British contractors too can be a trial; Cable and Wireless, who manage the Guard's communications network, we refer to as "Wobble and Careless". Fortunately our well-tried negotiating teams contain colleagues far more numerate, and patient too, than me. One of them, Dick Evans, later to be an outstanding chairman of British Aerospace, has shrewd advice on tactics; "Never look behind you, even when you realise your point is lost; it will only weaken your resolve. If you have to withdraw, start afresh from where you find yourself." Sound counsel, yet not easy to adhere to at the exhausting end of an all-night session on contractual minutiae during a fearsomely hot August, with only glasses of sugared tea and cans of Vimto, a nauseatingly fizzy pop drink, for sustenance. One longs for the blessed break that will arrive with the call to prayer that heralds the Ramadhan dawn.

Riyadh, although the main seat of government, is still a shuttered and dusty town with a sprawl of grandiose villas and patterned ministries beginning to spread out from the old mud-walled centre with its bustling souks and historic Mismak fortress on "Chop Square" where public executions take place. The foreign community is small and lives mainly within walled compounds, where it makes its own entertainment away from the puritanical scrutiny of the religious police. Existence amidst the Kingdom's conservative and God-fearing society calls for a positive frame of mind on the part of the outsider. Alcohol is taboo, though it is curious to see how the local supermarkets are inspired to group such goods as sugar, yeast and grape juice together on the shelves. For the more daring there is a raw spirit known as *siddiqi*, cooked up by oil-company chemists who hope to end up with an ethyl rather than a toxic methyl distillation. Otherwise the tipple is "Jedda gin", a crude fermentation involving sugar, yeast, lemons for flavouring and water, all to be left standing for a week in the heat in a covered bucket. At the end of this period, if the brew has not already blown off the lid, it is certain to blow off your head. The few diplomats marooned here spend time smashing liquor bottles to unidentifiable smithereens before dropping the shards into their dustbins. Yet there are pluses too; there is warm hospitality to be found in Saudi homes, while the dunes that surround the city and the spectacular limestone Tuwaiq escarpment off to the west offer splendid recreation for the adventurous.

I manage an occasional escape from the monotony of the British Embassy guest house with its unvarying menu of cardboard omelettes to spend the weekend down in Jedda with our ambassador, James Craig, fluent Arabist and wise in the ways of the Arab world. He has recently reappeared in the Kingdom after a period of forced rustication back in London in an act of retaliation by the Saudi leadership for the showing on British TV a year ago of a controversial drama documentary, *Death of a Princess*, involving an alleged instance of adultery by a young female member of the Al Saud. Jedda is a livelier and cosmopolitan town, and gives the chance to go snorkelling with colleagues along the vivid coral reefs of the Red Sea shore with their shoals of brilliant tropical fish, an unforgettable experience. One visit coincides with the annual reception for the Queen's Birthday in the embassy garden where gaudy-crested hoopoes strut across the lawn. There is a risk of an unwelcome gatecrasher however in the shape of the dethroned Ugandan tyrant, Idi Amin, who has taken up a Saudi offer of Islamic refuge in Taif, up in the mountains beyond Mecca, to get him out of everyone's way. He appears to harbour the delusion that he owes it to his former sovereign to attend and pay his respects. The Saudi police officers at the door are given strict instructions by the military attaché that if a very large African gentleman turns up, he is to be refused entry. Another trip to Jedda is for the inauguration by Crown Prince Abdullah of the National Guard hospital over which we have worked so hard. With its marble floors and the latest in technical equipment this is a palatial edifice. As is often the way in the Kingdom the event turns into an engaging mixture of gracious ceremonial, relaxed informality and near disaster. While princes and other dignitaries enjoy rides around the wards in a fleet of golf carts the smoke from the ritual sandalwood incense burners succeeds in setting off the hospital's network of fire alarms with a cacophony of earsplitting hooters that no one has any idea how to silence.

✳ ✳ ✳ ✳ ✳

Nor are the frequent seven-hour flights between London and Riyadh always straightforward. The only carrier with direct flights is Saudia, the temperance airline which everyone loves to hate. Arrival at Riyadh's cramped downtown airport calls for stamina when one is decanted well after midnight to face an hour or more of queuing to clear customs and immigration and with the prospect of an early morning start to often tense discussions with British contractors and the Saudi military. Saudia's Lockheed Tristar aircraft are getting on a bit. On one return leg some technical emergency arises forcing a steep dive into Paris while the captain recites a devout prayer over the Tannoy system. It seems to do the trick, though we then find ourselves marooned all day at Charles de Gaulle with no way of getting on to London until I find myself impelled to organise a near riot on the part of the stranded passengers.

There are however lighter moments. The British Airways run into Dhahran's vast airfield on the Gulf coast means an onward hop on the Saudia shuttle up to Riyadh. Security concerns resulting from sporadic Iranian attempts at sabotage, connected with Saudi support for Iraq in the neighbouring war, have led to the installation of newfangled screening for passengers boarding internal flights. Lining up one early morning for the Riyadh run, I find myself behind an old bedouin whose surprising item of hand baggage is not the usual falcon but a canary in a wooden cage. Sensibly enough he tries to resist the command to put the songbird through the X-ray process, but is finally obliged under noisy protest to do so. Anxiously we all crane our heads to see if a hairless and irradiated creature emerges from the tunnel; all is well – it emerges fully plumed and carolling away.

On another morning a tattered tribesman ahead of me, clad only in headcloth, white *thobe* and sandals, keeps setting off the warning each time he passes through the metal detector. Repeated body searches produce nothing. The police sergeant in charge proceeds to lose his composure, while all of us held up in the queue start to worry about missing our connection. Under a fierce and public interrogation light suddenly dawns when the bedouin pulls up his robe to reveal an iron leg. Not to be made a fool of, the sergeant calls out his troop of militia with rifles at the ready and orders to take the offending prosthesis apart and examine it for weapons while its owner hops about. It takes an age for loss of face to be recovered and the leg restored to its severed limb. We just manage to catch the flight. Most memorable of all however is the day when I find the Dhahran terminal festooned with great banners showing a Saudi man and his fully covered wife side by side, together with a bold slogan in Arabic and English. The English text contains the enigmatic injunction "Do it at home to save time at the airport". Do what?...

* * * * *

The time approaches to say farewell to the Ministry of Defence and return to diplomatic life with an embassy of my own. It has been a fascinating spell despite the erratic demands of its heavy schedule on family life, and a valuable opportunity to see my own service, warts and all, from the vantage point of a home ministry and the military. I shall find this standing me in useful stead later on. For all the occasional anti-arms-trade demonstrations in Soho Square and barbed comments about "merchants of death", I draw satisfaction from having helped to bolster the defence capabilities of Britain's friends and allies in a tense region the stability of which is very much in our own national interest. At the same time the equipment and services we are supplying are generating employment and industrial technology on a major scale at home, and with the stimulus of the Al Yamamah aircraft deal with Saudi Arabia about to come.

Meanwhile it is back to refresher classes in our rusty Arabic for Grania and me as we prepare for our next post in Algiers. Our destination was to have been Libya, but in the light of my role there in the period preceding the overthrow of the monarchy it seems more prudent to try my hand amid France's toxic post-imperial legacy in North Africa rather than Britain's. The defence sales work brings a final flourish when I find myself deputed to take the commander of the Saudi internal security forces on the town in London. The evening's entertainment involves a performance of *The Pirates of Penzance* at Drury Lane, followed by dinner at the Savoy Grill. In the interval of the operetta, armed with the regulation orange juice, I ask the general if he is enjoying the show. "Very much," comes the reply, "but where are the parrots?"

Algeria
1984-1987

The overnight ferry from Marseille rounds the headland into Algiers' sheltered harbour in the light of a grey January dawn. Once the celebrated lair of a fearsome Barbary corsair fleet, for more than two hundred years the scourge of Europe's shipping and coastlines, the steeply rising shoreline of the city with its buttressing row of handsome, if shabby, arches presents a curiously familiar aspect. "It looks like Brighton's seafront or Eastbourne," I remark to my companion at the ship's rail, an English businessman whom I had met at a dinner the previous evening with our Consul-General in Marseille, David Gladstone. "Just so," comes the reply. "When the French developed the capital of their new Algerian province around its historic *casbah* over a century ago, they engaged the eminent Victorian engineer, Sir Morton Peto, to design the harbour below the town's cliff-face. The imposing waterfront he created was repeated at various towns along England's south coast."

I come ashore to a courteous welcome from the Foreign Ministry's Head of Protocol, M Baba Ali, a name that reveals his Ottoman Turkish ancestry. Indeed, as I shall soon discover, Algerian society, two decades after the country's release through a savage war of independence from the smothering grasp of France, is still rent with intercommunal tensions – Arabs, Berbers, Moors and Turks – the origins of which reach back through centuries of successive occupations. Here is a country where vendettas and bitter memories endure; a new nation constantly ill at ease with itself.

Ghardaia Oasis, Algeria – from a pen and ink sketch by Grania Munro

My deputy, Mark Gowlland, brings me up the Mustapha hill to the residence, known as Emerald Park, a tall and elegant mansion set in spacious gardens and built a century ago to serve as a social club and library for a stylish community which chose to escape from the winter smog of Britain's 19th-century cities in search of a milder clime in French North Africa. Some took up permanent residence, though the winter rainfall on Algeria's exposed and stormy coast is said to exceed that of Manchester. They even had their own hotel, the St George, still in operation on a neighbouring hill replete with its decorative Moorish tiles and tropical gardens. The production of tiles in traditional patterns has recently been resumed by a local ceramicist, Bou Mehdi; the dusty workshop where he is training young Algerians in this historic craft is good to find.

Notable among these Victorian winter migrants were a fashionable painter with the curious name of Augustus Egg, who lies buried in the nearby British cemetery, and one Karl Marx, who exchanged his earnest studies in the Reading Room of the British Museum for the handsome salons of Emerald Park. Indeed one of his first published treatises of social protest concerned the harsh rural conditions endured by the Berber peasants of the Kabylie Mountains to the east of Algiers, a physically beautiful yet rugged and feuding environment which, as I soon find, has hardly changed. Bought by a wealthy French merchant, the house had a further burst of historical prominence during the Second World War when it was briefly used as a headquarters by an obstructive General de Gaulle, following the landing in November 1942 of American and British forces in Operation Torch which prompted the vacillating Vichy regime under Admiral Darlan and General Giraud to turn its coat towards the Allied cause. The house was eventually reacquired by the British government after Algeria's hard-won independence and the forced exodus of France's *pied noir* population.

The house is however in a run-down state; its restoration will prove a rewarding challenge for me and for Grania when she comes out in a few weeks time – a case of the old Diplomatic Service maxim, "Pack and follow". It is run, more or less, by Ahmed, the Kabyle butler of long service complete with waxed moustache, heavily accented French and, like most older-generation Algerians, no Arabic. Ever willing he is nevertheless a confirmed procrastinator – "*Oui, oui, toute a l'heure, madame…*". Yet we become very fond of him. The small domestic staff that he supervises turn out to be congenitally light-fingered, a legacy we suspect of years of social deprivation, civil war and now a political system confined within the crude trammels of Marxist socialism. Like the traditional chatelaine, Grania is obliged to carry about with her the keys to every storeroom and cupboard. An infestation of bedbugs soon obliges us to decamp with the boys into an hotel while the local ICI representative fumigates the place with some magic preparation. It seems to work. The spacious grounds are the pride and joy of the roguish Ahmed Khoja, who lives crammed into the tiny gatehouse along with innumerable members of his extended family. A dilapidated outhouse on the cliff that rises at the back of the residence provides an ideal studio for Grania. The housing shortage in Algiers is indeed acute; according to Amari, our taciturn driver, many families have to sleep in shifts in the shambles of the old *casbah* and the crowded tenements of the French era.

* * * * *

By fortunate chance an early opportunity occurs for me to present my letters of appointment to President Chadli Ben Jadid, Algeria's Head of State. This is a formal ceremony which, given the secretive style of Algeria's military-run revolutionary government ("not so much a country with an army, as an army with a country", as an Algerian academic once puts it to me), provides a rare opportunity for a top-level discussion on the matters that connect two countries. In reality, after an initial flourish through the import of natural gas and cooperation in Algeria's hasty programme to establish a state-owned heavy industrial base, the relationship over the two decades since independence has been conducted pretty much at arm's length. During the vicious war that brought terrorism, political turmoil and even military mutiny to France, Britain, with all her own preoccupations elsewhere across the Arab world, sought to stand aside. The leading role which Algeria subsequently built up for herself within the anti-western Non-aligned Movement and among radical groups in Africa, as well as her choice of the Soviet Union as a major partner in her economic development, left little room for a close association. Moreover for all the poisoned legacy of rancour Algeria has remained very much dominated by her commercial links with France.

Recently however attitudes have started to shift as President Chadli has sought to dilute the rigid socialist dogmas of his more radical predecessors, and has acknowledged the value of previously suppressed Berber culture. Algeria has moreover gained credit in the west for having successfully brokered the release of the American hostages from their prolonged captivity in the US embassy in Tehran. There are faint stirrings of popular protest too. From the security of mosque pulpits preachers have begun tentatively to challenge the secular and self-serving governance of the military elite. Even the tired socialist slogans that adorn public places have been defaced; some bright wag has altered a prominent public exhortation in Algiers – *le travail et la rigueur pour garantir l'avenir* (work and discipline to guarantee the future) – to …*le travail à la rigueur…*, in other words "work if you feel like it". To Britain's advantage the new mood has brought a move to develop the teaching of English alongside Arabic and French and to send students in considerable numbers on higher education courses in British universities (a source of some French *chagrin*). There is also a growing liaison between us on the military front.

The audience with the President turns out to be a relaxed and affable affair, a welcome contrast to the gritty session which my predecessor had recorded with the late President Boumédienne. We speak mainly in Arabic, a tongue with which the President appears, like many of his contemporaries from the days of French rule, not to be completely at home. By coincidence a new Irish ambassador, actually resident in Malta and for whose detailed relations with the Algerians we have responsibility, is also presenting his credentials on this occasion, leading to some confusion when both of us claim to represent parts of that divided island. The presentation ceremony is traditionally followed by a session with press and television when each envoy is invited to speak about the objectives of his mission in Algeria. My attempt to say my piece in a rusty Arabic seems to confound some of those present, but brings interesting repercussions when I subsequently learn that the President apparently takes the opportunity of the Council of Ministers meeting the next day to chide his government colleagues with the remark that the British ambassador has better Arabic than several of them.

* * * * *

Grania's arrival after a couple of months brings order to the residence. It is a rich compensation to sit out on its wide veranda on a warm Mediterranean evening watching through the tall palms ships at anchor below in the Bay of Algiers as the plangent recital of the evening call to prayer echoes out of the minarets around the city's hills. The transport by air of our saluki dog is less congenial. Arrangements are made for him to come out in April in the cargo hold of the thrice weekly Air Algérie flight from Heathrow. We drive out to Maison Blanche airport to find no sign of a dog. As we reach home empty-handed the telephone rings. It is the kennel back in Kent with an apologetic tale of how the saluki, duly caged and sedated for the journey, awoke as he was about to be loaded onto the aircraft and somehow forced apart the wire frame of his cage. He then galloped off into the airfield in the gathering dusk, while all landings had to be suspended until he was rounded up. We agree to try again next month once he has settled down, and to administer a double dose of sedative.

Come mid-May we are on the point of collecting him when the telephone rings once again. Unbelievably the dog has repeated his Houdini-like escape from the Air Algérie flight, causing a second dusk closure of Heathrow. Goodness knows what it will cost us should the airport authority seek damages. We decide to have another go in June. This time the dreaded telephone call comes more promptly. Yes, the dog, now incarcerated in an iron chest, was successfully loaded. But the pilot then decided the aircraft was overladen. Something had to be left behind. It turned out to be a choice between the saluki or a large consignment of whisky, ordered by the government for the celebration of Algeria's forthcoming National Day. No question about it; the dog and his chest were offloaded. It is becoming clear that the saluki is not meant to come to Algeria. But we give it one more try, and arrange to despatch him, iron chest and all, as baggage accompanying our twin sons when they fly out for their summer school holidays in July.

We forget however to warn the boys. Arriving at the check-in desk at Heathrow they are startled to find their baggage augmented by the massive iron chest containing the anaesthetised animal. Things are further complicated when the Air Algérie captain turns up at the desk and asks what the chest contains. "*Pas ce chien!*", he expostulates, on learning the contents. "Three times I have failed to take off because of that dog. It's not flying with me." Eventually he is persuaded to have one more attempt. This time there is no telephone call and we collect the boys before going round to the cargo shed..., only to find no sign of the kennel, and no record either. It is incomprehensible. Around midnight there is a message from Air Algérie to ask if we are expecting a dog, and if so please could we collect it? Apparently the huge chest has been bumping its way around the luggage carousel for the past three hours. Off to the airport we go, and heave the great box into the car, hoping its occupant has survived. Back home we find a key and unlock the door. An outraged saluki steps through, gives one crisp bark at the family and stalks out of the room. Being an Arab hound however he thrives in Algeria and does his bit to control our plague of feral cats and rats.

The episode has an inevitable sequel. For it turns out next day that, having agreed to carry the dog, the airline remembers that foodstuffs packed in dry ice and live animals are not permitted to fly in the same hold. In consequence the decision is taken to offload a large consignment of fresh and frozen foods. By regrettable coincidence this happens to be the order from Sainsbury's which is intended to keep the staff of our embassy in groceries for the next six months. After sitting through a hot July night on the apron at Heathrow it is all unfit for consumption. The ambassador and his dog are far from popular.

* * * * *

Indeed provisioning turns out to be a constant headache in Algeria's sclerotic economy. Despite a fertile coastal region the country's state farms are inefficient, while food imports are organised in erratic fashion by official monopolies. In consequence the state-run supermarkets can go for weeks at a time without such basic items as meat, eggs, milk or even the couscous grain and chickpeas which make up the nation's staple. A primitive and manually operated ice-cream-making machine supplied by the Foreign Office turns out to require quantities of salt, a commodity rarely obtainable in Algiers; the nearest supply that Grania succeeds in identifying is said to come by caravan across the Sahara from ancient mines near Timbuktu. We spend many an Islamic weekend of Thursday and Friday driving out to the foothills of the spectacular Atlas range on foraging expeditions. On one occasion high up on a pass over the mountains we come upon a peasant sitting before a tray of eggs. We scoop up the lot and return home in triumph only to find they are all hard-boiled. Even the remnants of Algeria's once vaunted wines are not easy to obtain. The great vineyards that once sustained every Frenchman's *verre de rouge* are derelict, as are the handsome farmhouses of the fugitive owners, surrounded by the humble cabins of peasants who now occupy these demesnes. It reminds me of the abandoned great houses of former Anglo-Irish landlords in the west of Ireland and the Italian farmsteads now standing ruined amid the hills of Libya. There is a further complication, for full bottles of local red or rosé can only be bought at the vineyards in exchange for empty bottles, so the newcomer has somehow to arm himself with a stock of these. Quality too has deteriorated in Algeria's abstemious environment; two or three glasses are enough to produce a memorable head next day. All in all the acres of vines are treated as another unwelcome French legacy; much of the unsold product is said to be disposed of as industrial alcohol in barter deals with the Soviet Union.

There are open-air food markets in the city selling tired vegetables and fruit alongside flyblown and bloodstained horsemeat. Those in nearby villages are better furnished, and excellent fish can be found in the restaurants of coastal fishing villages. Grania favours a friendly market stall at Draria, a few miles outside Algiers. By curious coincidence her father worked for naval intelligence in the imposing turreted chateau nearby during part of the Second World War, when it was an outpost of the Bletchley Park code-breaking set-up. Forewarned of uncertain food supply she has taken the precaution of going on a restaurateurs' butchering and catering course, involving dawn parades at London's Smithfield meat market, before coming out to Algiers. This turns out to have been provident as on more than one occasion when we have a dearth of fresh meat she sets off into the city's hinterland in search of a sheep from a local abattoir, then brings the carcase home and butchers it from scratch to feed us and our guests for the next week or so; indeed there are times when a posting in Algeria seems more like an expedition than a diplomatic mission. There is even an heroic occasion when, having invited some members of the embassy to join our Christmas dinner, Grania ends up cooking it while standing in gumboots in raw sewage that has burst through the floor of our subterranean kitchen – an experience far removed from commonly held images of the sybaritic life of an ambassador's wife.

* * * * *

There is plenty for the embassy to do in building up a relationship with an Algeria that carries considerable weight on the African and Middle East scene and is gaining new prosperity from her massive Saharan reserves of oil and gas. Post-independence ties with the Soviet bloc are being slowly loosened – as the Algerian joke goes "we signal to the left but turn to the right". Yet there remains a sinister ingredient within their system. Algerians are regarded with respect but little affection among their fellow Arabs; not for nothing has this militant country been called the Prussia of North Africa. Moreover in a fashion reminiscent of Stalinist Russia officials can suddenly find themselves airbrushed out of the cast. This threat of removal of identity has its inhibiting effect on the bureaucrats with whom we do our business. One day I telephone the Foreign Ministry to speak with the obliging official in charge of relations with western states, only to be told that there is no one of that name in the ministry. When I insist that we saw each other only a few days previously, I am politely told that I must be mistaken as they have never heard of him. Such is the unfortunate man's rustication that I never meet him again; goodness knows what line he overstepped or which senior colleague in the Party he offended. Another time I find myself discreetly invited to lunch one day by a leading figure from the early days of independence with long service as a minister and then as ambassador to

London. For no evident reason he has been banished to his small apartment and denied outside contact; yet he will some years later be reinstated as Prime Minister. As the experienced French ambassador, François Scheer, puts it, everything in Algeria requires careful decoding.

We diplomats too are watched, albeit in pretty clumsy fashion. Ahmed, the butler, tells us he is required to go to the intelligence people every so often to report on whom we have had to the house. We have some fun providing him with red herrings to relate. Our somewhat taciturn Berber driver, Amari, whom we have fondly assumed to have no word of English, startles Grania and me out of our complacency during a long day's drive with Jim Whittell of the British Council to visit the university in Constantine by cutting short an animated discussion between us about a large bird circling above us over the high plateau. "*C'est un aigle.*" Well, there we are – with remorse I recall the scores of politically sensitive conversations he has silently overheard in the back of that limousine.

The irrepressible Swedish ambassador, Jean-Christophe Oberg, reputedly the *enfant terrible* of his country's Diplomatic Service, is tickled to find that his telephone account, an invoice which tends to bear little relation to reality, carries, through some happy clerical oversight, full details of when his calls have been tapped. We get an amusing first-hand illustration of Algeria's copious surveillance apparatus through the visit of a British army officer invited out to advise on the demolition of munitions. He is accommodated in the government-owned Aurassi hotel, a monstrous and ill-founded modern edifice that dominates the city heights. On his first morning he is met there by an Algerian officer who quickly takes him behind the reception desk into a chamber where he is greeted by the chaotic sight of a row of military personnel wearing headphones and attempting to listen in to the conversations throughout the hotel's bedrooms. The floor is ankle-deep in tapes. Says the Algerian officer, "We are glad you can help us. Here you see our problem." The visitor's hasty explanation that there must be a mistake as he deals with munitions leads his shocked Algerian guide to ask if he is not the "Russian signals expert", before escorting him rapidly back to the lobby with the request to say nothing of his experience to the ordnance officers who are due to collect him.

The moment comes when I even find myself turned into a diplomatic non-person. One afternoon in 1986 I am summoned to the Foreign Ministry to be told, albeit politely, that the Algerians have decided to freeze their relations with my embassy in retaliation for the action of my government in breaking off relations with Syria. This British decision has followed the uncovering in the nick of time of a Syrian-engineered plot to blow up an Israeli airliner about to fly out of London. My forceful remonstrations at this unjustified treatment are met with the excuse that the Syrians have asked the Algerians, as a close ally in the radical Arab camp, to show their sympathy by expelling me, but the Algerians have gone for the lesser expedient of sending me to Coventry – or rather to Limoges as they put it, using the French equivalent. (Subsequent research reveals that the two towns gained this accolade back in the 17th century when their remote locations earned them the reputation of being respectively the most unpopular military garrisons to which recalcitrant British and French officers were often posted.) On the way back to the office I feel a touch of regret, in a bout of *esprit de l'escalier*, not to have reacted yet more vehemently to the unwarranted action the Algerians have sprung upon me; it would have achieved no purpose however. In the event, and in a nice twist of irony, the ministry finds itself unable to carry out its sentence with full rigour as Britain happens at this time to hold the presidency of the European Union; accordingly they are obliged to continue to include me in the diplomatic round wearing this alternative hat.

It is all a bit of a charade. My consequential ostracism by certain Arab members of the diplomatic community is soon breached when, at a reception to mark Algeria's hosting of some Non-aligned or African jamboree, none other than the representative of Palestine, a member of Jerusalem's prominent Dajani clan, makes a point of coming up to embrace me in front of his startled colleagues. We are as it happens good friends; I have recently helped to arrange for his wife to have medical treatment in London, and his uncle was our embassy's legal adviser when I was in Tripoli twenty years earlier. It is endearing how personal links can transcend politics in the Arab world. By contrast the American air raid from bases in Britain on Col. Qaddafi's home in Tripoli in the same month as the El Al bomb attempt induces no Algerian reaction; the Libyan leader – "that mad dreamer" as one minister describes him to me – has succeeded in getting up Algerian noses with incursions over their mutual desert frontier and by forming a military pact with Morocco with whom Algeria is permanently at odds. Our next test occurs when the offer of our spacious grounds for the annual diplomatic charity bazaar is threatened with a bomb scare. At least we succeed in holding a lively reception for the Queen's Birthday, complete with Chris Barber and his Jazzmen to play for us and plenty of good English ale flown in from Fullers, the brewery adjoining our house in London.

* * * * *

My cold-shouldering does however afford an opportunity to explore the further reaches of this huge country. Its variety is astonishing; the lush valleys and snow-covered high peaks of the mountains of Kabylia, sheltering isolated Berber communities with their traditional enamel artwork; the upland plains of the Atlas range carpeted during the brief weeks of spring with wild flowers in a vivid tapestry of reds and blues before merging into the desert's sands; the wealth of well-preserved cities from the Roman and Byzantine eras such as Timgad, Djemila, the great legion garrison at Lambaesis, and Hippo – now Annaba – where St Augustine died in the fifth century, fulminating against the esoteric Arian heresy of the invading Vandals. A favourite outing for us on the Friday weekend is west along the coast to the Roman ports of Tipasa, overlooked by the tomb of Cleopatra's royal daughter deep inside a massive conical pyramid, and Cherchell, rich in classical mosaics. An engaging example of the way Algerians connect with their land's turbulent history is afforded to Grania when, reacting to graffiti scrawled on the wall of the tunnel that runs within Cleopatra's pyramid, she utters a protest about vandals. "*Non, madame,*" comes the guide's pedantic correction, "*c'est moderne.*" The historic city of Constantine, the scene of a desperate local resistance to France's long campaign of imperial occupation in the mid-19th century, sits perched precariously above its rocky gorge; to the west Oran has its great fortress built by Spanish invaders four hundred years ago, and Tlemcen, another historic centre of resistance to French conquest under the legendary Emir Abdel Qader who ended his days in romantic exile in Damascus, has a rich inheritance of early Islamic architecture.

Algiers too has its fascinating corners. Sometimes seen as the model for the elegant coastal capital of Celesteville in Jean de Brunhoff's children's stories of Babar the Elephant, its now dilapidated French apartment blocks in the art déco style contrast with palatial Moorish villas and the crumbling warren of the old *casbah*, the setting for the iconic 1960s film, *The Battle of Algiers,* which chronicled the bloody confrontation in 1957 between French paratroops and Algerian insurgents within its steep and narrow alleys. On the drive out to Tipasa one passes through Zeralda, where the "paras" had their barracks. The final evacuation back to France in 1962 of these toughened troops was accompanied by the belting out of Edith Piaf's haunting song, *Non, je ne regrette rien*, in a gesture of defiance against independent Algeria and also President de Gaulle, who had recognised that a weary France no longer had the will to resist the ferocious insurrection. For its part Algerians' sentiment towards their French heritage remains ambivalent. One example is provided by the state of neglect in which we find the significant collection of French Impressionist paintings and sculptures, left behind on France's evacuation 25 years ago to deteriorate under the leaking roofs of the city's old Fine Arts Museum. An educational game we sometimes play with the twins is to ask them to spot the several Rodins among the unlabelled bronze and marble figures crowded into the sculpture hall.

Swimming off Algeria's rocky Mediterranean coastline can be rough and treacherous, quite unlike the gentle beaches of Libya's desert shore to the east. Somehow this seems in character with the nation's temperament – as our boys find when they nobly swim out to rescue an Algerian woman who has got into difficulties. Having hauled her back to shore through the breakers they find themselves upbraided by her husband for having dared to touch his wife; perhaps he would have rather seen her drown. Lesson one – never take Algerians for granted. Down south there is the allure of the infinite Sahara, rich in oil and gas and with its intriguing population of veiled Touareg nomads, a hardy offshoot of the Berber race renowned for their skills in metalwork. Its barren mountains reveal a trove of prehistoric cave paintings. There are scattered Arab oases like El Oued and Touggourt, seat of the Tijani, one of the most powerful of the Maghreb's many Sufi movements; and above all Ghardaia, where the Berber Mozabites have created an irrigated Shangri-la with an intimate style of domestic architecture that had its influence on the modern French School of Le Corbusier. Of the neighbours Tunisia to the east offers visitors a smiling contrast to Algeria's grudging face. We drive across the hills for a family holiday in Tunis, with its fine classical heritage, colourful bazaars and well-ordered beaches. The attractive village of Sidi bou Said next to the ruins of Carthage is drowsy with the scent of young cannabis smokers. Yet there is a harsher side to President Bourguiba's benevolent autocracy; this is not a regime to be trifled with and Tunisians are careful to stay in line. Morocco on the other hand is off limits for us owing to an angry stand-off with Algeria over Moroccan military occupation of the former Spanish colony of Western Sahara; Algeria has chosen to give shelter and support to the refugees of the territory's national resistance movement, Polisario.

For all their rich history however the Algerians do little to make the occasional visitor welcome, with down-at-heel hotels and no tourism infrastructure. A high point in our own wanderings is an expedition with colleagues down to the oasis of Djanet to explore the spectacular plateau of the Tassili range with its wealth of rock art and then travel across the towering sand dunes of the deep Sahara. We are joined once again by Malcolm Davidson, the archaeologist friend who came on our similar desert journey in Libya twenty years earlier. The variety of rock paintings and carvings of human figures and their wild animal prey, some dating back more than eight thousand years, is astonishing; one's appreciation is further enhanced by the drama of the trail to reach them deep in the sandstone clefts. Our dashing Touareg guide insists that we surround our sleeping spaces on the ground each night with stones to discourage snakes and scorpions from disturbing us; not the most comforting recommendation for a good night's sleep, but it seems to work. One evening we find we have made our camp over the site of the underground burrows of a family of gerbils – or to be exact over the area these very hygienic rodents have set aside for their latrine. The indignant residents soon oblige us to go elsewhere.

The Touareg has brought along with him an exotic figure, one Esther Lamandier, a young woman who has earned an award-winning reputation in France as a singer of mediaeval Jewish Andalusian ballads. To hear her rich notes on a starry desert night in the echoing confines of a deep Tassili gorge is a thrilling and evocative experience. When our expedition stops for a break in the heat of the day he loses no time in disappearing with Esther into a swiftly erected bivouac for an amorous and energetic interlude while we relax somewhat pruriently in the shade of the only acacia tree for miles around, revelling in the sounds of the birds and the bees that it harbours while a dark resin, used by the nomads as writing ink, suppurates from its bark. In a minor act of pedantic vandalism Malcolm cannot resist getting out the runes of the Touaregs' obsolete Berber alphabet, Tifinagh, which we had assembled on our Libyan trip years before, so as to incise with it Kilroy's traditional epigram on a nearby rock face for the next pedagogic tourist who may pass.

* * * * *

We get few British travellers to Algeria. Those who do come are usually trying to make a cross-Sahara passage to Nigeria or other points in West Africa. With the constant threat of blinding sandstorms this can be a perilous journey for the motorist, producing headaches for our small consular staff to handle and not helped by the fact that they could well arise well over a thousand miles away beyond the last desert outpost at Tamanrasset. One celebrated episode, which fortunately occurred during the time of my predecessor, was the disappearance in the desert of Mrs Thatcher's son, Mark, who was taking part in the annual Paris to Dakar rally accompanied by a French paramour. Seeing his mother's intense distress the Algerians obligingly mobilised their air force to mount a wide search. The evident gratitude of the Prime Minister and her husband when Mark Thatcher and his companion were discovered some way off the rally route was not apparently shared by a less grateful Mark, who some suspected had deliberately been seeking his own romantic interlude.

The consul's role is not an easy one, particularly when faced with the not always reasonable complaints of travellers in some kind of trouble. The predicament is not new; a century and a half ago the eccentric English wanderer Charles Doughty, setting off on his solitary travels among the bedouin of Arabia Deserta, excoriated the consul in Damascus, who had rejected his exorbitant request for assistance in arranging safe passage, saying "his was no charge in any such matter. He had as much regard of me if I took such dangerous ways, as of his old hat." I have some sympathy with the consul, though we aim nowadays to be less abrupt. We face some similarly reckless cases however. In one instance a man and his wife decide to drive in an open car in high summer across the Sahara, aiming for Nigeria. Somewhere far to the south the woman dies of heatstroke. The husband shows little concern and is impatient to drive on, leaving his wife's corpse for us to deal with. We can only guess at his motives, as the consul flies off to distant Tamanrasset to sort things out. Yet more tragic is the instance of a young motorcyclist attempting the same route who loses the main piste in a prolonged sandstorm. Some days later his body is found by nomads, lying beside his machine only a short distance from the track. In a courageous show of human endurance the doomed man has kept a diary during the three days it takes him to die; the desperate narrative trails off into nothing on the final page. A party of young students from Britain, embarking on an adventurous crossing of the Sahara in jeeps and led by my old schoolmaster, finds a more congenial refuge camped out in our garden for several days while we cajole the ever suspicious authorities into releasing their walkie-talkie radios which have been promptly confiscated. Grania keeps them going on couscous. One unwary British couple, emigrating by yacht to New Zealand, have to take refuge in Oran in a storm. Unfortunately the Algerian customs discover a rifle concealed below decks and insist on arresting the pair. It takes us weeks of negotiation before they are released to continue their voyage, on payment of a massive fine. For it emerges that the scale for such financial penalties is calculated on the bizarre basis of the value of the form of transport in which the illicit goods arrived. They would have done better to have attempted their odyssey on bicycles.

Our most dramatic consular case however involves a young student who has opted to spend his time traversing the Sahara on foot from southern Tunisia right across Algeria to Morocco, and in summer too. This is a madcap scheme from the outset. The first we get to hear of it is when a letter reaches me in Algiers from his mother, a Mrs Barnet in north London, telling us of his trip and asking if we can make a search for him as she is worried not to have heard from her son since he crossed the Tunisian border into Algeria a couple of weeks ago. This we tell her is hardly surprising as there are few settlements in the southern Sahara and little chance of a postal service. A check we make with the Algerian gendarmerie confirms that he did enter the country as she says. They undertake to have their desert patrols keep an eye open for our wanderer. A fortnight later a more reproachful letter comes from the mother, insisting we look for her missing son. I try to explain that given the vast wastes he has entered this is the proverbial case of the needle in the haystack. The Algerians agree to redouble their limited search capability but come up with a blank; I have to warn the lady that, given the foolhardy nature of the adventure, she may have to prepare herself for the worst. To her credit Mrs Barnet does not give up readily; her next step is to get her Member of Parliament to take up the case with the Foreign Office. The Algerian authorities are making a real effort to help. But news is there none, and we have to conclude after six weeks or so the lad is unlikely to have survived.

An extraordinary sequel follows. Our vice-consul, John McManus, takes a short break with some friends to visit the spectacular Hoggar Mountains in the wastes around Tamanrasset. Driving through the stony landscape he spots a solitary figure with backpack some way ahead of them. It turns out to be a grizzled and heavily sunburnt young European, doggedly marching towards Tam. "Are you Barnet?" John calls out. Unbelievably it turns out to be so. "Well, write to your mother. She is very worried," says John sharply, and drives on. Henry Morton Stanley could not have done better in his celebrated search for Dr Livingstone a century earlier. We quickly pass the glad news back to the mother, who is over the moon about the effectiveness of the British Consular Service. She sends on to us a copy of the letter her son writes about his arduous traverse of the desert, involving days without food or water, and a final collapse in delirium in a rocky gorge where he was found and given shelter and survival by passing Touareg tribesmen. Once restored however and with heroic determination he resumed his trek, happening upon the consul within striking distance of civilisation. The letter ends with the laconic information that he would be carrying on to Oran as he had left his bicycle there and would ride it back across France to London. What unconquerable spirit! The only blot occurs when he has his pocket picked in Tamanrasset, whereupon we readily help him on his way.

* * * * *

Every few years the Foreign Ministry, in an attempt perhaps to offset its customary offhand treatment of a large diplomatic rent-a-corps, arranges an extensive tour for ambassadors and their spouses to one of the more remote parts of the country.

An outing shortly before our arrival had involved a wild boar shoot in the Kabylie Mountains. Apparently the wildlife suffered little damage though one or two ambassadors were winged in the *grande battue*. One such tour to the southern Sahara fifteen years before had been recorded by our then ambassador, Ronald Burroughs, as most notable for the hilarious presence of his Spanish colleague, a much-decorated Franquisto general, who had insisted on dragging a heavy locked trunk behind him at every stop. Intrigued speculation as to its possible contents included a collection of gorgeous spare uniforms and medals; some suggested it might be his wife.

In the winter of 1985 the corps is treated to a week's visit to distant Tamanrasset and the Hoggar Mountains. The tour leader is the indefatigable Head of Protocol, Baba Ali. A motley expedition on this scale requires considerable preparation. The Ministry's advance party finds Tamanrasset's only hotel a disaster area with no sheets or curtains or even water. In decisive Algerian fashion the manager is promptly sacked, the few guests are turned out, and the hotel repainted and put in order. Only the loo seats fail to arrive in time.

The tour keeps us on the move with visits to local development projects, including a somewhat hopeful rainwater dam being constructed in the desert by army reservists under an engineer captain, decked out like Wyatt Earp, and a reafforestation scheme where the wife of the Canadian ambassador creates a diversion by snapping a branch of a cabbage-like tree, the sap of which sprinkles the East German ambassador who had sought a nap in its scanty shade. It turns out that this is a highly toxic tree reported to cause blindness; Baba Ali leaps forward to sponge the somnolent envoy down. These visitations are interspersed with cross-country forays through the fascinating sandstone and black basalt moonscape of the Hoggar. In a straggling column we clamber up to a high plateau on which the valiant Père de Foucauld built a bare hermitage back in 1905 in order to live among the Touareg, in whose cause he later lost his life. His vigil is still kept by three White Fathers, one of whom has spent 30 years in this lonely eyrie. "We are all social climbers," mutters someone. The Pakistani ambassador, near to cardiac arrest, finds on reaching the top that the promised refreshments have stayed down below. The Swiss proffers glucose tablets.

Back at Tam Touareg tribesmen have been assembled to give a picturesque display of raiding and racing on their handsome white Mehari camels. The stuff for their flowing robes, luminous with blue indigo thread, comes from Kano, down in northern Nigeria; "a vagrant people", snorts the Nigerian ambassador, a coastal Yoruba who is finding the desert rather a strain. The Arabs among us are thoroughly at home, not least on finding classical Arabic alive and well in mid-Sahara in contrast to the corrupted patois of the coast. The Albanian, whom one rarely notices, achieves momentary prominence by becoming stuck in a camel saddle, narrowly avoiding embarrassing injury. The large African contingent stays grumpily in the shade. An evening display of dancing by Touaregs, bearing muzzle loaders, ends dramatically with a gun going off near a spot to which, in the dark, the Zimbabwean has retired at the call of nature. Veteran as he is of bush warfare and eight-years detention at Ian Smith's pleasure, Ambassador Nkomo's rapid exit is dramatic. The high point of the evening's entertainment is a performance by a shrouded lady introduced as the world's leading Touareg singer. Her dirge is hardly lively, but she knows her show business, having as accompanists all the female members of her family down to the newest born. Some twenty of these shapes crouch around her in the sand, alternately humming and breastfeeding their infants. It would make a sensation at the Hammersmith Odeon.

✳ ✳ ✳ ✳ ✳

The hesitation which Algerians face over links with foreign diplomats means that we have little social contact outside formal engagements at which we hesitantly dig our fingers (of the right hand) into whole carcases of roasted sheep; one gets to know where to pluck the more succulent bits. Indeed it is rare that Grania and I spend an evening with an Algerian family – a memorable exception is a delicious couscous meal at the home of the Mozabite Berber Minister of Culture and his wife. An intriguing female lawyer of French origin, Maître Marie-Claude Radjewski, who had defended Algeria's first President, Ahmed Ben Bella, at his trial following his capture by the French during the war, throws stylish dinner parties, slightly spoilt when on one occasion we are all subsequently urged to have rabies injections as one of her salukis, which had been around the kitchen during the evening, had since contracted this fell disease. My predecessor sought to break into Algerian society with sessions of Scottish dancing. One of his most enthusiastic recruits is a delightful young woman, handicapped however by having lost both her legs when planting a grenade in a café, frequented by French patrons, during the war's bombing campaign. By chance two gendarmes entered just as she was about to make her hasty exit; in an extreme act of sacrifice she sat tight to avoid raising suspicion and lost her limbs in the ensuing explosion. They were indeed bitter years.

We diplomats are thus thrown very much on each other's resources for our social round and the exchange of information that is a staple of our profession. There are all sorts among us; Algeria's prominence in the politics

170

of the Third World means that nearly every corner has its representation. As one would expect, the Frenchman plays a leading part within the western community. Among these the Finn is noted for giving dinners at which he vainly claims to get his own back on the Algerian guests who fail to appear by leaving their places at table vacant. The pointless result is that the rest of us have to shout across adjacent voids in order to conduct conversation. His very Finnish dining table is made of glass, which provides agreeable diversion as one peers through to see if any couples are playing footsie. The Turk, a keen gardener, manages to kill himself by sawing off the branch of a tree on which he is sitting. The Italian, a Sicilian nobleman, turns up his toes and is seen out at an impressive mass in the great basilica of Notre Dame d'Afrique which looks across from its headland towards mother France. A Colombian ambassador is suddenly appointed, apparently in the hope of coffee sales. Having difficulty getting his bearings he finds accommodation in the dilapidated Aurassi Hotel. By lucky chance he is quite a handyman, and sets himself, for want of anything else to do, to putting his suite in order. A few weeks on the manager comes to regret that the suite is needed for a delegation but there is an identical suite free on the floor above. Obligingly the ambassador moves upstairs and sets about repairing the utilities in his new abode. It is not long before another move is suggested by the wily manager; only then does the penny start to drop...

The Chinese decide to cut a welcome dash by opening a restaurant with fare flown in from Beijing. It is not long however before even they find their rice and spices impounded by Algeria's socialist bureaucracy. The Chinese ambassador invites us to a lavish dinner of traditional delicacies with each successive course described on a menu sheet. In the middle of the night I wake to what feels like a heart attack; could it have been those suspect pickled mushrooms? Shakily I go to get out our mycological reference book and look up the variety of fungus written on the menu card; "NOT EDIBLE" I read in bold capitals. Mercifully Grania had skipped that course. The evening produces another curious experience when my Chinese colleague admires the jacket I am wearing. "Very good Manchester," he comments. When I say it is corduroy he explains that in China the material is always called after England's former capital of cloth – a quaint relic of 19th-century imperial mercantilism.

For all radical Algeria's close ties with Russia the Soviet ambassador comes across as a figure of fun. An old-style Party apparatchik from Kiev he appears to speak no language other than Ukrainian and is rarely seen outside his fortress of an embassy compound, invariably accompanied by a harassed-looking young subordinate – known to us as "life support" – who acts as his shepherd and interpreter. The ambassador's moment in the limelight comes on an evening when, in a rare gesture of diplomatic hospitality, the Foreign Ministry arranges a special showing for the diplomatic corps of an award-winning Italian cinematic rendering of *La Traviata*. As we assemble in a decrepit downtown cinema, the ambassador and his family find prominent seats near to the screen. "Life support" is placed on his chief's left, next to his good ear. Our appreciation of what promises to be a special event is much diminished by the audible drone of this unfortunate lackey, who evidently has some Italian, interpreting every line of the opera's libretto into Ukrainian for his stolid master's ear.

One of the corps' main uses for the Algerian government is to be paraded along a red carpet at the airport on the frequent occasions when some African or eastern potentate pays a ceremonial visit. The arrival of the youthful new president of Ghana, Flight Lieutenant Jerry Rawlings, fresh from his *coup d'état* in Accra, is particularly memorable as he emerges in air force fatigues with a revolver stuck in one webbing anklet. Somehow his Algerian hosts manage to prevail on him to leave his armament behind when he graces a state reception that evening.

* * * * *

Our embassy is backed up by a small and somewhat beleaguered British community, consisting mainly of language teachers, a swelling team of business folk, the odd press stringer, a few wives of Algerian husbands met at college in Britain, and a clutch of Christian missionaries. The monthly open-house evenings we hold at our residence help us keep in touch. I contrive however to get across the worthy missionary group when, in my role as chairman of the council that runs the long-established British church adjacent to the residence, I feel obliged, having had my knuckles rapped by no less than the Minister of Religious Affairs, to ask them to desist from trying to convert Algerian Muslims. For apostasy remains ever a sensitive issue in Islamic eyes. My interdiction brings one of the more evangelical among them to storm out of a meeting having denounced me as anti-Christ, an epithet which, in my broad-church way, I had not expected to earn. Our chaplain, Adrian Pollard, inevitably known as Christian Ade, moves on after a year; the Anglican bishop, a mystic ex-Copt based in Cairo, insists that we trust in the Lord to find us a replacement, and somehow He does. There is however a hiatus during which several of us in turn try our hand at holding services. On one notable Friday I manage to challenge the very foundation of Judeo-Christian creation theology, when, in reading from the book of Genesis the account of the Fall in the Garden of Eden, I chance to misquote the Almighty as asking Adam "Who are you?" instead of where he is hiding. Mercifully the small congregation slumbers on unaware of the heresy.

The church itself has a long history, and contains a fascinating series of memorials commemorating the experiences of some of the hundreds of Britons taken captive by Algerian corsairs and held in onerous bondage unless converting to Islam during the three centuries when the city states of Barbary from Tripoli to Morocco raided European shipping and coastal towns as far away as Cornwall, Ireland and even Iceland. Successive British and other European monarchs from the early 17th century alternated short-lived treaties of peace with the Ottoman rulers of the "Warlike State of Algiers" with regular naval bombardments and payment of ransom, while the luckless British consuls occasionally found themselves put in chains. The legendary attacks of the Algerine raiders were finally brought to a close with the ferocious naval engagement of the city by an Anglo-Dutch fleet commanded by Lord Exmouth in 1816. Our library contains a copy of a polemical history of these dismal conflicts written by one of my Victorian predecessors, Sir Robert Playfair, under the title *The Scourge of Christendom*.

* * * * *

Our relationship with Algeria is now developing in encouraging fashion, in such diverse fields as higher education, consultancy and construction, and financial services. We have a useful dialogue going on Middle East and African issues, as well as on the politics of oil and gas production, a significant sector where British producers are discussing joint exploration with Algeria's heavyweight oil enterprise, Sonatrach. All this activity generates visits by ministers in both directions. I bring the Commerce Minister to London, where to my embarrassment he is kept waiting by Alan Clark, Minister for Trade, who, arrogant as ever, apparently likes to put counterparts from "Bongo-Bongoland" in their place. Our new association reaches a peak with an invitation to President Ben Jadid to pay a State Visit to London, the first of its kind. Received initially with enthusiasm, the invitation is however kyboshed when the country's disgraced first president, Ahmed Ben Bella, in comfortable exile in France, decides, no doubt deliberately, to cross the Channel and hold a hostile press conference in London, something the French have prudently forbidden him to do on their territory. In the paranoid atmosphere of Algerian politics Britain takes the blame.

Among visitors coming the other way the Agriculture Minister, John Gummer, taking a break from bovine disease at home, has a keen eye for antiquity. His hosts take us to the eastern uplands to see the Roman city of Djemila, with its splendid street lined with the remains of temples and markets; the two-hundred-mile return drive in the dark down the narrow gorges of the Atlas range remains a death-defying memory. A Foreign Office minister, Richard Luce, comes out for talks. He is about to fly on to Morocco when it turns out that the only flight for three days, on Saudi Airlines, has taken off early with the pilot refusing to wait for his VIP passenger. The long road journey is out of the question as antagonism has closed the border. We eventually get the Luces' on their way by a roundabout route next day. When I mention the awkward affair to my good friend the Saudi ambassador, he takes the captain's action up with Riyadh; apparently the discourtesy gets to the ears of King Fahd, who ordains that the pilot, an American, shall forfeit one month's salary – an autocratic yet appreciated gesture.

The Liberal Democrats send out David Steel, accompanied by the jazz-playing Earl of Winchelsea and a Mr Dunk, in a gesture of moral support for the guerrillas of the Polisario Front, as they wage a dogged resistance to Morocco's occupation of their Western Sahara homeland from desert camps down in the south-west. An Air Marshal who presides over the Commonwealth War Graves Commission comes to inspect the World War II cemeteries scattered around western Algeria. The Commission has recently moved its headquarters out of London to Maidenhead; I dare to suggest that with a bit of imagination they could have gone a few miles further up the Thames to Wargrave. As elsewhere in North Africa, the graves are beautifully tended by local gardeners, much to the appreciation of relatives for whom group tours are starting to be organised. The cemetery in Algiers lies right next to the German one; my German colleague willingly agrees the time has come to demolish the wall that separates them.

We get our ration of Royal visitors too. The Duke of Edinburgh, as President of the World Wildlife Fund, arrives with fellow members of its board to see how the dwindling population of Barbary apes, living in defiles in the coastal Atlas, are faring. I am warned by London to ensure that no outriders whatsoever are attached to Prince Philip's motorcade. Apparently the noise of their sirens has been known to bring on a fit of royal wrath. The Algerians, much attached to formal ceremony, are incredulous. It is only when I plead that my very career could be at risk if the instruction is not observed that they reluctantly agree to leave the motorcyclists behind. Predictably however all does not go smoothly. A heavy landing at Algiers airport by the royal flight aircraft with the Duke at the controls brings a rude comment from the control tower that is quickly retracted when the pilot identifies himself. We drive out some fifty miles into the mountains at the break of dawn, only to discover that our willing hosts in the Ministry of the Environment have overlooked the fact that the apes do not like to stir from sleep until the sun penetrates their rocky lairs. The waiters in the coffee house at the foot of the gorge tell us we have several hours to wait before this happens. Something must be done. I hit on the device of sending waiters up the gorge banging tin trays. Mercifully this racket induces a few soporific simian heads to peer out from their brushwood hides. We decide that honour is satisfied; the beasts are alive and well. The return drive brings near disaster however. Our motorcade of smart limousines from the presidential fleet, minus outriders thank goodness, reaches a remote level crossing just as the gates descend and a rare goods train ambles into view. As ill luck will have it, two traffic patrolmen on motorcycles who happen along the highway are clearly puzzled to find an unescorted presidential convoy stuck at the crossing. There is much revving of engines as they peer in at the Duke and the Minister in the lead car. I half expect an exasperated Prince Philip to take off into the *bled* with myself in apologetic pursuit. After an interminable interval the train clears the crossing and we shake off our cops. For his part the Duke seems unperturbed; I sometimes suspect that courtiers tend to overreact to the moods of their royal masters.

The Duke of Gloucester, himself a qualified architect, stays with us for several days, leading a mission of eminent consultants and contractors. He is a delightful guest, and Ahmed is carefully schooled by the valet and the detective in the art of boiling the breakfast egg (of which for once we have a stock) for precisely four-and-a-quarter minutes. Prince Richard reveals a neat turn of humour. During the delegation's ritual round of calls on Algerian ministers we find ourselves being lectured interminably (in French which I then have to translate) by the grudging Minister of Hydraulics on the alleged shortcomings of British consultants. As with relief we all make our exit, the Duke, whose eyelids have been drooping, puts it just right – "I think he praised us with faint dams." A good, if risqué, farming story he subsequently tries on the unsmiling Agriculture Minister falls completely flat. This is not a land for jokes.

His hosts arrange a flight down to the oasis of Ghardaia, famous for its traditional Berber architecture. We know from personal experience that the only hospice, the Abu Rustum, is infested with bedbugs. Grania prudently gives the detective and valet a short course in how to avoid being eaten all night; take a damp bar of soap, quickly turn back the sheets, and impale the little vermin on the wet surface before they can hop away. It is quite an art, but effective.

On reaching Ghardaia we are welcomed beneath date palms in an irrigated garden, a delightful setting. Prince Richard, who shuns stimulants, declines the coffee and is offered instead camel or sheep's milk. "Ewe or non-ewe," comes his happy quip, impossible to turn into Arabic. Then on to the hotel by way of the bustling market and ornate mud-brick mosques. We foregather in the Prince's suite to await the evening's entertainment, which is to include the seductive dancing of women of the Ouled Nail tribe, who for so long formed a romantic fantasy for remote French army garrisons. Suddenly the door bursts open and in rush the valet and detective, each brandishing a bar of damp soap. Pulling back the covers on the bed they enthusiastically set about attacking the sheet. "Got that one?" "There's another." To his astonished master the valet tries to explain their irruption. "Excuse us, Your Royal Highness, but Mrs Munro has shown us how to catch your bedbugs. Mind that one there!" Their energetic performance over, the pair make for the door, triumphantly clutching their speckled soap bars. Says the Private Secretary, "The servants' hall at Kensington Palace will never be the same again."

＊ ＊ ＊ ＊ ＊

As everywhere in the Arab world the intractable issues of Palestine and Arab-Israeli confrontation are never far below the surface. Expelled from their base in war-torn Lebanon, the Palestine Liberation Organisation under its hyperactive leader Yasser Arafat has found a new perch in neighbouring Tunisia. We have a chance to take stock of our policy in the region in a meeting of our Arab-world ambassadors. This is held in the elegant surroundings of the British Embassy Residence at Carthage. The mansion, a gem of a relic from an earlier pro-consular era, is a fascinating combination of old Moorish palace and classical Georgian villa. The walls of the huge saloon are incongruously clad from ceiling to floor with traditional ceramic tiles; the pastiche effect is distracting to say the least.

Tensions over Palestine reach a new peak when, in response to terrorist strikes by militant factions, the Israelis retaliate in September 1985 with a devastating air attack on the PLO's headquarters just outside Tunis. Shortly before this we in Algiers are caught up in the drama of the hijacking by Lebanese Shi'a militants, presumably with Iranian complicity, of TWA Flight 847 in an ultimately successful bid to secure the release of a large number of Shi'as from southern Lebanon taken captive following Israel's recent invasion of Lebanon to put a stop to PLO border aggressions. Over the first forty-eight hours of what becomes a sixteen-day marathon the aircraft shuttles twice between Beirut and Algiers, ending up stranded at Beirut airport having failed to make it to Tehran. On the two brief stopovers here Algerian negotiators succeed in securing the release of most passengers, except for some thirty-five American males and the exhausted flight crew. Among those released is the celebrated Greek singer, Demis Roussos, whom the hijackers have threatened to kill. Two of the stewardesses are British. The hijackers have already shown themselves prepared to use violence, having shot and dumped an American sailor on their first stop in Beirut.

While the aircraft is on the ground at Algiers airport on the afternoon of the second day, surrounded so we assume by Algerian guards and with crucial negotiations under way, I get a call in my office from our Military Attaché, Sam Coleridge, a delightfully cavalier Guards officer, formerly with the Special Air Services, who makes a speciality of getting into scrapes. One of his recent exploits has involved masquerading, happily undetected, as a Russian officer in order to observe an Algerian military exercise. Sam has gone to the airport to keep in touch with developments in the tense talks under way between the Algerians and the terrorists. It comes as a shock therefore to hear him say that by a roundabout route he is in fact standing under the hijacked plane in an isolated corner of the airfield; moreover he has taken Sarah, our young vice-consul, with him. With no one about and no limit to his audacity Sam reminds me that he was previously head of the SAS anti-hijack team at Hereford, and claims he can recover the aircraft single-handed if only I give the word. My sharp prohibition of such an act of derring-do brings a crestfallen Sam back home. Shades of the episode of Ronald Biggs and the Royal Navy in Rio; it seems to be my lot to spoil the fun of our armed forces.

* * * * *

The poisoned fallout from Palestine casts its long shadow over us in more personal fashion a few months later when our daughter Joanna, who is on a year's Arabic study at Bir Zeit University in the occupied West Bank, becomes directly caught up in a confrontation between the Israeli military and protesting students. The first Grania and I hear of the fracas is from the evening BBC news on the car radio; there are reports of fatalities and several wounded among the students. A nervous couple of days follow as there is no means of communication between Algeria and Israel; technically they are at war. To our relief a message then comes from our Consul-General in Jerusalem, Paddy de Courcy-Ireland, to say Joanna is safe. As it happens she is due to pay us a brief visit soon after. Acquiring a through air ticket from Tel Aviv to Algiers via Zurich proves quite a test, but with the help of a peacenik Israeli travel agent she manages it. Approaching Algiers however Joanna discovers that of her two passports the crucial one which does not contain Israeli immigration stamps must have been retained by the official who had put her through a third-degree search at Tel Aviv airport before sending her on her way with a "hope you get into Algeria alright." With presence of mind she clips a vaccination certificate over the pages bearing Hebrew marks and hopes for the best with a lovely smile for the grim-faced immigration officer. It does the trick. "Welcome to Algeria, mademoiselle," says he as he stamps her entry.

It turns out that Joanna and her colleague from Durham University spent a dangerous few hours, mostly under their beds, as bullets flew around the Bir Zeit campus. It had been a frightening experience; some Israeli soldiers had evidently been out of control, firing live rounds among the students, wounding a number of them. From her refuge Joanna had however contrived to record the vivid sounds of battle. Despite being searched on her departure from Tel Aviv airport she has through an artful ruse managed to smuggle the tape out undetected. To her credit and furnished with a fresh passport she returns to Palestine and resumes her studies. It is not long however before another confrontation occurs and the university is shut down by the Israelis. There is a curious sequel to her adventures when her missing passport subsequently turns up among a bunch, handed over to the Foreign Office at the insistence of Mrs Thatcher, after Israel's security outfit has been discovered to have purloined a quantity of British passports.

* * * * *

More than three years have passed and the time is nearing for a move, both in career terms and for the family's sake. Having laboured long to dictate in a stilted French my communications with the Algerian government, I have even managed to pass the Foreign Office's advanced interpreters exam, and gratifyingly with higher marks than my colleague in Paris. Our twin boys, with us for the school summer holidays, have discovered the *English language hour*, a new and little-patronised request programme on Algerian Radio, complete with its DJ, Mustapha. They ring in to ask for something to be played. Delighted to have someone on air with a genuine request Mustapha asks how long we have all been in Algeria. Luke's unguarded reply says much; "We have a year to go…".

I have also had a run-in with Algeria's rough and ready medical service. A chest infection sends me to Dr Djijelli, a specialist at the old colonial Mustapha Hospital. In pouring rain he leads me round the sprawling campus looking for an electrocardiogram machine in working order. Eventually he spies a line of dripping patients outside a hut. "This looks promising," says the doctor as he knocks at the door. It is opened by a figure in a grubby white coat and with a bristling waxed moustache. I am invited straight in and onto a battered trolley beside a machine that has ominous-looking wires coming out of it. The technician connects me up and threads two wires into a wall socket just behind my head. He turns a switch; nothing happens. With a standard French imprecation he gives the machine a blow; still nothing. "Ambassadeur," he says, "kindly hold these two wires into the socket while you are lying there." Nervously I oblige, to the fizzing sound of sparks. Fitfully the machine starts to churn out paper. "*Trés bien*," says my friend. "Now, ambassadeur, I shall tell you the story of the battle of Dien Bien Phu."

And the old soldier is off, with much gesticulation and simulation of cannon fire, on a vivid account of how his regiment, the Tirailleurs Algériens, had been part of the large French Army contingent some 16,000 strong, which was surrounded and routed in 1954 in the isolated valley of Dien Bien Phu in Indo-China by an overwhelming force of Viet Minh independence fighters under General Giap. The experience of this catastrophic defeat of a French force, including several Algerian units, by guerrilla troops not only hastened France's withdrawal from her colonial empire in South-East Asia; it also provided a spark to ignite Algerian national resistance to French rule later that year. Meanwhile, on my rickety trolley, I am the captive audience for a dramatic narrative of death and destruction. Not a moment too soon the machine stops. Armed with a roll of graph paper I set out to find Dr Djijelli. He looks at the printed sheet and its erratic trace in disbelief, and asks what happened. Told about the naked wires and the battle story, he gives a shrug, tears up the cardiogram, takes a cursory X-ray, diagnoses pneumonia and prescribes a hefty dose of antibiotics. He will treat me at home, as the risk of cross-infection in the Mustapha is too great. Three weeks later I find myself evacuated back to the Brompton Hospital where they pronounce me on the road to recovery; the admirable Dr Djijelli's rudimentary treatment has worked.

I find I am not the only one to experience the hit or miss character of the Mustapha Hospital. The Indian head of the United Nations mission goes there for a routine medical check and duly sends the certificate of test results back to his headquarters. Several weeks later he is alarmed to receive a letter from the administration in New York letting him know that his sex change has been recorded. He had evidently been handed the results sheet for a pregnant Algerian lady. Such is the UN's bureaucracy that he is not at all sure he can get the verdict reversed.

* * * * *

In the wake of her Soviet mentor a Marxist Algeria is taking important if hesitant steps towards political and economic liberalisation – *décrispation* is the French term they have adopted for the process. But there is an elephant in the room here whose presence is not yet fully apparent – a growing groundswell of extremist Islamist sentiment among a youthful population, poised to vent their frustration at the meagre product of years of closely regulated state socialism from which only a military caste and a self-perpetuating political elite are seen to have derived benefit. It is a portent of years of savage sectarian strife to come. Indeed a small group of Islamist fanatics has already taken to an outlawed existence in the hills of the lower Atlas behind the capital. For its part the government is tying itself in theological knots in an effort to reconcile Islamic tradition with the norms of a modern society. Aids to the control of a runaway birth rate are proving particularly contentious; the state-controlled press even runs articles extolling the practice of *coitus interruptus* by the Prophet Muhammad.

Yet this tormented country is also one of real potential. Behind the straitjacket of outdated political dogma and an overblown bureaucracy Algeria is rich in mineral resources and well endowed with human talent, together with a fascinating history and striking natural beauty. These contradictions prompt me to entitle my farewell despatch to the Foreign Secretary "The Barbary Fig", the French name for that fruit from arid lands we call a prickly pear. One has to get past the sharp spines of its skin to find the sweet flesh within.

Foreign Office
1987-1989

Surtout n'ayez pas trop de zèle

Charles-Maurice de Talleyrand-Périgord

So it's back to the Foreign Office after the briefest of homecomings. As I climb the familiar and well-worn steps in the great courtyard, one of its resident pigeons drops a generous deposit square on my shoulder. "Absit omen," I mutter as I head for one of the scarce washrooms.

With the imposing title of Deputy Under-Secretary of State I find myself responsible for overseeing policy towards the whole of Africa and the Middle East, a vast parish yet familiar ground. What strikes me is how little has the furniture, let alone the architecture, of these unsettled regions, or for that matter Britain"s significant involvement, moved during the eight-year interval since I last engaged with their affairs. The Thatcher years have seen a restoration of Britain's prestige and self-confidence on the foreign stage, though the objectives of our policy continue to give priority to parochial concerns such as national defence and security and economic prosperity within the framework of our European and other alliances rather than to issues of more universal benefit. The mindset is still conditioned to a large degree by recent history, including the time warp of a global Cold War rivalry with the Soviet bloc and a preoccupation with the legacy of post-imperial responsibilities. Meanwhile the states of Africa continue to suffer the tensions of post-colonial and intertribal readjustment under a succession of self-perpetuating, and often violent, political autocracies – a series of percussion caps ever threatening to ignite. At least the 1979 settlement in

Rhodesia/Zimbabwe appears to be holding, albeit under a leadership with strong nationalist credentials. White Power continues to assert its supremacy in South Africa however, in the face of growing international economic and political calls to dismantle the apparatus of apartheid. The choices for action here are proving particularly acute for the Conservative government of Margaret Thatcher with her right-wing instincts. We have our own doubts within the Office about the efficacy of swingeing economic sanctions for which there is considerable public and media pressure; these are unlikely to prove more than gesture diplomacy. But the Prime Minister's resistance looks more emotionally based.

The Middle East meanwhile continues to present a major powder train. The inflammatory issue of Palestine, and the endemic suspicions of western designs which this cancerous issue fosters, is gaining reinforcement from the populist and seductive message of an historic and culturally distinct Muslim identity, the force of which we saw unleashed across the region following Iran's Islamic Revolution of 1979. Violent confrontations continue to be the order of the day between Arabs and Jews in both Israel and the occupied lands of Palestine. To the east Iran and Iraq are still exhausting themselves in all-out combat with suicidal attacks across dense minefields, accompanied by the use of long-range missiles and even poison gas, for many years prohibited as a weapon of war. The threat to the stability of the whole area and its crucial source of oil supply to the world has however given a stimulus to the restoration of our close ties, in defence as well as business, with the Arab states of the Gulf. Our improved standing among the Gulf's dynastic regimes is confirmed with a visit to Saudi Arabia for talks on security. We nearly come unstuck however when the heir to the wealthy sheikhdom of Qatar risks expulsion by the Ministry of Defence from an officer cadet course at Sandhurst on grounds of incompetence, or perhaps corpulence. With an eye to a potentially valuable future relationship with this gas-rich mini-state we just manage to pre-empt shooting ourselves in the foot.

An insidious erosion is however becoming apparent in the authority of the Foreign Office itself. Mrs Thatcher's appropriation of the main levers of government has seen 10 Downing Street arrogating to itself a growing oversight of foreign policy through a secretariat under the astute Charles Powell, himself seconded from the Diplomatic Service. The days are passing when Prime Ministers like Macmillan, Wilson or Callaghan were content to delegate the lead in overseas policy to tried and trusted Foreign

Secretaries. Perhaps Lord Carrington during the first Thatcher years had been the last to enjoy such independence. Geoffrey Howe, I now find, faces a constant tussle to have his way; as proposals for action on issues great and small, notably in connection with relations with continental Europe or with South Africa's repressive regime, are regularly challenged from across the road, the despondent word goes round – "our cock will not fight". Yet it is Howe who, summarily supplanted as Foreign Secretary two years on, will subsequently accompany his abrupt resignation from government office with a bitter speech that administers a deadly wound to his leader's inspirational but increasingly obdurate rule.

* * * * *

The Prime Minister's personal sensitivity over Britain's standing across the world is played upon by the more nationalist sections of the tabloid press. *The Sun* newspaper, priding itself on its pugnacious five-line editorial comments, has a particular hold over her. I get an early taste of this tendency towards knee-jerk overreaction when No. 10 adopts a fit of indignation at a summary demand by Nigeria's military regime that we move our visa office in Lagos to somewhere less close to the military headquarters. The request is of course unreasonable and to be resisted. But *The Sun* chooses to make a meal of what is essentially a minor issue and uses the episode for a characteristic round of Africa-bashing This easily ignites the Prime Ministerial fuse, and we find ourselves harried to create a row when a cooler approach would have had a better chance. Soon afterwards I head for Lagos to try get strained relations back on track. For such a wealthy oil-producing country it strikes me as a run-down and chaotic city with an alarming crime rate. Lively Nigerians deserve better government. Opposition is however firmly suppressed, as I find when I pass an entertaining evening with former president Obasanjo, dining off boiled chicken at his farm outside Lagos as torrential rain drips through the ceiling.

Margaret Thatcher's instinctive distaste for Africa's politics is brought to bear on the far more significant question of how to handle South Africa's apartheid regime and the possible application of economic sanctions. As popular unrest increases, there is growing public pressure for the imposition of such penalties on the part of domestic opinion in Britain and elsewhere across the English-speaking world, notably in the United States with her large black population. The issue is producing deep divisions among members of the Commonwealth, a successful institution which certain of our present leaders are however starting to regard as more of a distraction and impediment to British overseas policy. In the Netherlands too, the cradle of the Afrikaaner community, public outrage has led to minor acts of sabotage against banks which continue to operate in South Africa. The arguments for the institution of trade sanctions under UN auspices hold a certain attraction, but may have perhaps more to do with moral censure than with the prospect of effective and persuasive damage to the country's powerful economy. Whatever the case however it is clear that the Prime Minister, mindful of substantial British business interests and prepared to regard South Africa's regime as an outpost against the spread of Soviet influence in Africa, is not prepared to entertain the idea.

So our attention focuses on the discouragement of foreign partners whose close relations with South Africa are helping to sustain the regime. It is no surprise to find a French hand here with the discreet supply of equipment to the security forces. Another player maintaining strong business connections is Japan. This brings me to Tokyo, my first taste of the far Orient, via a refuelling stop at Anchorage in an Arctic Alaska where everyone appears to live off a diet of unappetising jerked beef. The historic British Embassy compound is a haven in the heart of this hectic city, not unlike its elegant counterpart in Tehran. I give a talk on British policy in Africa and have a series of courteous and not particularly productive meetings in the Foreign Ministry. For Japan, whose imperial traditions never extended to Africa, her economic and commercial interests tend to come first. My companion from our embassy has the bright suggestion that, should our discussions start to flag, we introduce a bit of levity by bringing in the topic of elections. My doing so is succeeded by a period of hilarious distraction as our hosts elaborate at length on the subject, with the linguistic substitution of "r" for "l" each time the key word is enounced. With difficulty I keep a straight face. The long flight back across the Pacific to a stopover for talks in Washington takes a whole day. It comes as a shock on arrival to find that, having crossed the Date Line, I start the same day over again.

It is becoming evident however that, even without economic sanctions, the apartheid regime in South Africa is not going to survive. An early trip to Cape Town, Johannesburg and Pretoria for meetings across the political spectrum from right-wing Afrikaaner diehards to white liberals and black left-wing opposition reveals that under the pressures of political and economic isolation many are looking for a way out of the dead end of repression and white supremacy within which the intransigent President P.W. Botha has confined his country. Faced with international ostracism South Africa can no longer bear the growing cost in military, and also human, terms of open conflict against the Marxist regime in neighbouring Angola and a guerrilla war in Namibia. It is horrifying to see the desperate conditions in which hundreds of black families are forced to eke out a resentful existence under tattered plastic shelter in the notorious Kayelitsa camp on the Cape Flats, where my tour in the company of relief workers is shadowed by two hefty policemen with full holsters and black shades. The elegant setting of the famous Barlow winery in nearby Stellenbosch presents a stark contrast to the camp's depravity.

✳ ✳ ✳ ✳ ✳

Angola with her valuable oil revenues, yet ruined by civil war and sustained with Soviet and Cuban support, has become a new focus of American and British diplomacy, involving a close liaison with my experienced US counterpart, Chester Crocker, in London and in Washington. At the Eaton Square home of the right-wing Conservative politician, Julian Amery, I have a surreptitious meeting with Jonas Savimbi, leader of the South African-backed anti-Marxist rebellion from bases in the south of the country. Awkwardly kitted out in suit and tie and carrying his trademark knobkerrie stick the portly guerrilla shows no spirit of compromise with the government in Luanda. The repercussions across the continent of Angola's militant posture bring me on visits to a number of key African states. In Senegal there is a rare chance to take a boat out to the offshore island of Goree. Notorious for its history as a major depot for the transit of black slaves to the plantations of the New World on the "middle passage", it has become an idyllic refuge for some of Europe's sybarites; we lunch in enchanted floral surroundings with an expatriate member of the Gilbey family. Zaire too, still the vast and corrupt fief of Joseph Mobutu, takes up much attention. On one visit I take a battered and overladen ferry across the broad Congo River to the tinpot court of President Sassou Nguesso of the Congo Republic in Brazzaville. In the mist of a tropical morning the shining river, some mile-wide at this point, belies its bloodstained history. At the presidential residence I find a guard of honour decked out in vaudeville French military uniforms. Brazzaville brings memories of a visit many years earlier en route to Southern Rhodesia for the school holidays. During a brief refuelling stop by the BOAC Hermes aircraft I had my first encounter with French culture in the shape of a delicious *baba au rhum* and never forgot the experience.

On this occasion my Sabena flight from Brussels to Johannesburg via Kinshasa brings its own drama. Among the passengers is a contingent of Afrikaaner families returning to South Africa after a visit to their original homeland in Flanders. Almost alone among African states Zaire maintains links with South Africa's apartheid regime. In the middle of the night there is perturbation in the row behind my seat. It turns out that the elderly Afrikaaner sitting there has died. The cabin crew lay him out in the aisle beside me; this is all I need for catching a nap before we get to Kinshasa. Now comes a dilemma. For should the Zairian authorities, on inspecting the aircraft, discover a mortality, they are likely to insist on the defunct being unloaded. Yet to leave Grandad behind in darkest Africa is the last thing his grieving Boer relatives can accept. Everyone is getting more and more upset.

I come up with a cunning plan; the steward and I haul the corpse back into its seat, shielded by my copy of The Times grasped between its hands. The more it stiffens the better. With considerable relief I disembark at Kinshasa in the early hours. While clearing through the airport I hear the aircraft take off for the south. The ruse must have worked.

* * * * *

I am fortunate to have Lynda Chalker as the Minister of State responsible for Africa. She takes a real interest in the affairs of the continent and is held in high regard among the leaders of the numerous British Commonwealth states in Africa – to some she is "Mother Africa". There are interesting developments in train, as the first post-independence generation of leaders, enclosed within a dogmatic attachment to single party and statist systems of government, starts to leave the scene. In many cases their successors are showing a welcome readiness to experiment with more pluralist and transparent polities. President Mugabe too is continuing so far to demonstrate, on the surface at least, a commitment to uphold the multiracial independence constitution for Zimbabwe that was agreed in Lancaster House eight years earlier. All this we seek to encourage, although our ready assumption that greater transparency in governance and the liberalisation of the media will help to mitigate endemic peculation at senior levels is starting to look premature. Uganda under the recently established President Museveni is one of the first states to turn her back on years of misrule and murderous tyranny. She is also making a bold effort to educate her population about the incipient scourge of the AIDS pandemic that is taking its tragic hold on Africa, while other states persist in self-denial or just blame the west.

Entebbe turns out to be off the airlines' map, Uganda's national carrier having collapsed some while back. The High Commission in Nairobi come up with a light aircraft with a jolly Kenyan pilot for the final leg. As we bump our way over Kenya's lush green hillsides with their prosperous coffee plantations, it is disconcerting to see that almost every instrument in the cockpit has a sticker over it saying "inoperative". Still we get there eventually, to find the airport still bears the scars of the sensational airborne assault eleven years earlier by Israeli paratroops to release some 140 hostages held there by the infamous Idi Amin following the hijacking by Palestinian terrorists of an Air France flight bound for Paris from Tel Aviv. The terminal building has its bullet marks and broken windows yet, while the wrecked remnants of Uganda's Soviet-supplied air force litter the tarmac. The country's sorry and lawless state is reinforced when I find that the staff of our recently re-established High Commission in Kampala cannot leave their homes or offices without an armed escort of Royal Military Police, an ominous foretaste of things to come elsewhere in Africa. My visit coincides with the annual Queen's Birthday reception, an occasion marked by a good spirit of reconnection with Ugandans after the horrors and the isolation of past times. Jolly music is provided by musicians of the Ugandan Army, oddly clad in green denims and shiny new gumboots. I get a warm welcome from President Museveni when I call on him in the faded elegance of the former colonial governor's residence beside Lake Victoria in Entebbe. His plans to liberalise and restore his country's shattered economy certainly merit our support. At least Uganda is a fertile land, though riven by tribal and religious rivalries that date a long way back.

Similar moves to unshackle political and economic life are becoming evident elsewhere – in Tanzania and in Zambia. A visit to Zimbabwe to chair a policy meeting of our ambassadors in southern Africa, is followed by contacts in South Africa where cracks are at last becoming evident in the edifice of Afrikaanerdom, and on to mountainous Swaziland, former British protectorate and an oasis of peace where the high point in the diplomatic calendar turns out to be attendance at the annual parade of nubile virgins from among whom the monarch chooses a new wife. The final stop is Maputo, Mozambique's Indian Ocean capital where a socialist President Chissano is, with some Soviet support, wrestling to consolidate control of a sprawling former Portuguese colony in the face of a determined guerrilla resistance backed in clandestine fashion by South Africa's apartheid regime together with right-wing elements in the United States. With an armed escort I follow a railway line leading on to Zimbabwe, which is being repaired with British help in the face of frequent sabotage, and stop at a large plantation growing pineapples for export and recently brought back to life by the carpet-bagging British entrepreneur, "Tiny" Rowlands, who somehow contrives to ingratiate himself profitably with both saints and sinners among Africa's leaders. Back in run-down Maputo I find Chissano readily appreciative of the aid support he is receiving from Britain. This leads on to his coming with his wife on an official visit to London when Grania and I find ourselves acting as their hosts for a theatre evening. In its wisdom the government's hospitality organisation sends us off to see the musical "High Society", a jolly enough show yet a bizarre choice for a president who has yet to shed his Marxist credentials. *Verb. sap.* – perhaps that is the point…

* * * * *

Meanwhile things are as active as ever in the other wing of my parish, the Middle East. With the United States obsessed with isolating Iran in retaliation for the two years until 1981 spent as hostages by the staff of the American embassy in Tehran, the pressures we try to apply through the Security Council in New York for a ceasefire in the interminable war with Iraq are pointed mainly at Tehran, regarded, not always justly as I see it, as the principal villain. Iraq's ruthless leader, Saddam Hussein, to whom it turns out the Americans are slipping military intelligence on the sly, gets away with little more than reproof for his pitiless persecution of his own people, including an atrocious exercise in ethnic cleansing among the Kurdish population in the north. This operation, known as the Anfal campaign after one of the books of the Qur'an, involves the transportation and subsequent mass murder of many thousands of Kurds, as well as involving iniquitous aerial attacks with poison gas; regrettably for lack of corroborative verification beyond the reports of western journalists we remain at the time unconvinced of its scale. The gas weapon is also being used in attempts to stem mass assaults over Iraq's southern borders by fanatical troops of Iran's Revolutionary Guards. When I summon in the Iraqi ambassador, Mashat, a hapless apparatchik of a tyrannical regime, to register Britain's outrage at these breaches of well-established international conventions, he ripostes with a defiant argument that Winston Churchill would not have hesitated to employ such a weapon had Nazi Germany invaded Britain. "Nonsense," I tell him; and then, recalling boyhood bus journeys to school in Sussex in the early years of the Second World War with my rudimentary gas mask to hand in its case, I just wonder... My official protest does at least make the front page of *The Times* next day.

We have other bones to pick with the Iraqis, not least over their ingenious and persistent efforts to get round the strict prohibition we have applied to the supply of weaponry by direct investment in heavy industry in the Midlands to manufacture materials they claim are for petrochemical plant but which could well have military application. This operation ultimately turns out to be connected with a science-fiction project for a long-range "supergun", and will later be the subject of a tedious and inconclusive official enquiry. Mashat endeavours to cover tracks with warm hospitality towards the minister responsible for the Middle East, the clever if conceited David Mellor, and myself at a dinner in his fashionable Kensington embassy (which happens to have been the former home of an uncle of mine until it received a hit during a German air raid in the war). The smart dinner service brings a sinister echo of the past as the plates still bear the royal crown and a golden monogram *"F"* for King Faisal, murdered in the revolution of thirty years ago. The ambassador follows this up with a lunch *à deux* in a fashionable Lebanese restaurant in Mayfair's Shepherd Market – the atmosphere is strained though the fare is delicious. I am brought up short a few weeks later however when we learn from the Metropolitan Police that an Iraqi, resident in London, had recently died in suspicious circumstances from food poisoning in the street outside the very same restaurant after lunching there with the ambassador. There had been two other guests who had just arrived from Baghdad and had flown out again that very afternoon. No one at the restaurant, and least of all the ambassador, was able to explain how the tragedy could have happened...

It is however our relationship – or rather non-relationship – with a paranoid Iran that affords the greater preoccupation. Formal diplomatic links between us have been suspended ever since my time as head of the Middle East Department eight years ago. The skeleton mission which the Iranians maintain in London under the surprising aegis of Saudi Arabia is headed by a pleasant young official, Akunzadeh Basti, who is clearly under instructions from a militant Tehran to make a meal of any issue that crops up with the British imperialists. We start with a fierce complaint of police brutality against a junior Iranian consular official who is caught red-handed attempting to nick a pair of socks from a clothing store in Manchester. To make his point, Basti brings the employee round to the Foreign Office, where, in my imposing first-floor room and under the forbidding gaze of a bushy-bearded 19th-century Qajar Shah in full regalia whose full-length portrait adorns the wall, he has him drop his trousers to reveal the alleged bruises. I get him to cover up again swiftly lest my well-brought-up personal assistant should happen to pop her head around the door.

Iranian gunboat attacks on tankers carrying Iraqi and Kuwaiti crude oil down the Gulf under Royal Navy protection, a latter-day instance of gunboat diplomacy, constitute a more serious bone of contention. The search for a formula to halt Iran's bitter and interminable war with Iraq brings me with David Mellor to a meeting of the UN Security Council in New York and on to Washington to compare ideas with the Americans. We begin badly at the National Security Agency there when the minister throws a childish tantrum at having to be searched; all very trying. The visit does however allow a break for me to make a quick round of long-lost American relatives, cousins Flo in the snowy woods of Connecticut and Hodding Carter, formerly White House spokesman for President Jimmy Carter (no relation), at his elegant period home in Alexandria. Then it is back to London on British Airways' notorious "Red Eye Special", with a short and sleepless night writing up an account of our talks for the Foreign Secretary and straight into the hothouse of the Office on arrival.

A tentative restoration in 1988 of our full relations with Iran is terminated after only a few months by an uncovenanted crisis stirred up by the high-profile objections of Iran's theocratic regime to the publication in Britain of the prize-winning blockbuster novel, *The Satanic Verses* by Salman Rushdie, on grounds of blasphemy against Islam. There is a strong presumption that the furore across much of the Islamic world over the narrative's offensive connection of the Prophet Muhammad with certain heretical texts, leading to attacks on bookshops and culminating in Ayatollah Khomeini's infamous *fatwa* calling for the author's assassination, has much to do with political opportunism within an unsettled Iran. At the same time however it marks the reawakening of a populist and radical religious consciousness that is starting to transcend national boundaries within the Islamic world, fuelled by an ever-latent sense of political and also cultural resentment over western influence. While there is no case for apology over publication of this provocative, yet indifferent, book, I manage through a fortunate personal connection to limit damage by getting the agreement of the publishers to hold back on a scheduled paperback edition in the interest of wider security. But the storm gathers pace, culminating in yet another abrupt rupture to our relations with the Islamic Republic and the withdrawal of all diplomatic staff on both sides. I bid Basti a protocol farewell at Heathrow airport. Curiously enough we get on rather well, despite all our fraught exchanges; we shall find ourselves having an amicable reunion at a Red Cross conference in Geneva ten years on.

There is no denying that the tempestuous reaction from radical sections of the Muslim community abroad, and in Britain too, has caught us off guard. The helpful Omani ambassador tells me that he and his Arab colleagues in the London Diplomatic Corps are surprised that we appear not to have seen the storm signals, as *The Satanic Verses* has for several weeks past formed a fulminating staple of the Friday sermons in mosques across the country. Surely, he says, we, as in his own land, keep a close eye on the messages of our imams, and presumably on the content of Sunday-morning sermons in churches too? I am lost for words, while he clearly finds my denial hard to credit. (Cut to ancient church in rural village, where venerable rector, preaching to a scanty and somnolent congregation, is flattered to spy an unfamiliar figure in shabby raincoat in the rearmost pew taking copious notes with a pencil stub). The ambassador's query does however prompt me to enquire of the security folk whether they had spotted any portents of the tempest to come; none at all, is the response. Clearly the era of benign neglect of Islam as a political force has to come to an end.

August 1988 brings a rancorous acceptance of a United Nations ceasefire resolution by both belligerents, slowly worn down by massive war casualties, Scud missile raids on their respective capitals and, a final straw for Iran, the, possibly accidental, shooting down of an Iran Air civilian jet over the Gulf by an American warship, the USS *Vincennes*. The antagonists have nothing to show for eight years of conflict but economic impoverishment and mass slaughter. Meanwhile concern that the Iraqi Embassy in London may once again be up to no good brings me out to Baghdad to see the Foreign Minister, Tariq Aziz. He receives me and our ambassador, Terry Clark, in the pseudo-military uniform that Saddam Hussein obliges all his ministers to wear. It is a frosty and unproductive encounter, marginally offset by a friendly dinner that evening with one of his senior officials. Unknown to the outside world their pathological leader has just unleashed his genocidal campaign of mass extermination against his Kurdish population. Baghdad itself has a depressing and furtive feeling; the historic British Embassy building, a relic of former authority and now somewhat worse for wear, stands out in its extensive compound on the bank of the Tigris; it will be a long time before, in the words of one of its most famous native sons, Sindbad the Sailor, Baghdad is once again the "City of Peace".

* * * * *

These same years of ferment across the Middle East see significant developments in the perennial search for a settlement between Israel and the factions that represent the inhabitants of the Palestinian territories. The issue is brought back sharply to international attention by the outbreak in early 1988 of a popular uprising among the Palestinian population, increasingly frustrated at the political and economic stalemate resulting from Israel's obdurate occupation. This upheaval, known in Arabic as the *intifada* with its mixture of pacific and violent resistance, combines with the excessive brutality with which the Israeli military attempts to suppress it to receive unprecedented visual publicity in the international media. It prompts a surge of renewed diplomacy, particularly on the part of moderate Arab leaders like Saudi Arabia's King Fahd, and also from Washington and London, to calm the situation and find a way out of a dangerous confrontation on the basis of the well-worn formula of "land for peace". Liberal supporters of Israel among the Jewish community in Britain with whom I keep in touch, such as Lord Goodman and Greville Janner, do their helpful bit to urge moderation on Tel Aviv. The levers of influence are complicated by the facts that Egypt finds herself relegated to the sidelines by other Arabs for having made her separate peace with Israel following the Camp David Accords ten years earlier and has since renounced her territorial claim to the Gaza strip, while King Hussein's Jordan, now courted by the Americans as a partner for an autonomous Palestinian entity, has chosen to distance herself from a political association with the West Bank and Jerusalem.

The *intifada* opens the way for the Palestinian leader, Yasser Arafat, based in Tunis, to stake a unilateral claim to statehood. In a crucial move of reconciliation he has at last recognised Israel's right to exist, though a newly emerging Islamist hard core calling itself Hamas remains implacably opposed. The pressure from Arab states for this concession during a summit conference held in Algiers is confirmed to me by contacts in the Algerian Foreign Ministry on a return visit to my old stamping ground. Arafat has moreover made an historic repudiation of terrorism on the part of the Palestine Liberation Organisation. That this significant declaration puts Israel on an awkward spot is brought home soon afterwards on a visit to Washington. During my call on Tom Dines, the chief executive of AIPAC, America's most influential pro-Israel lobbying organisation, we are interrupted by a telephone call from Tel Aviv. At the other end it turns out to be none other than Israel's hard-line Prime Minister, Yitzhak Shamir, who is clearly twisting Dines' arm to go out and discourage George Schultz, the Secretary of State, from building on this unwelcome step forward which opens the way to American acceptance of an independent Palestinian entity alongside Israel, anathema to expansionist Zionists. To his credit Dines maintains that the repudiation of terrorism needs to be seen as a *fait accompli*, but his response cuts little ice with his irate interlocutor. He replaces the handset with a resigned expression that says much.

* * * * *

A trip is needed through this fractured landscape to see for myself how the scenery is changing. Taking along the young official responsible for the Arab-Israel desk we start in Cairo, more dusty and frenzied than ever, and where the grand hallways and lofty saloons of the historic British embassy residence close to the Nile afford an oasis of calm. There are still shades of Lord Cromer's vice-royalty, and of Mountolive, the quintessential ambassador in Lawrence Durrell's *Alexandria Quartet*. As everywhere in Egypt's famously bloated bureaucracy the personnel in the Foreign Ministry across the river push paper around to little effect while real policy is handled by the minister and his personal staff in quite another building. Osama al-Baz, President Mubarak's foreign policy adviser, makes it clear to me that, while regrettably she remains ostracised by fellow Arabs, Egypt is focusing her attention to good effect on the recovery of territory in Sinai and the development of diplomatic links with Israel. I benefit from a product of this cooperation the next day when we take the newly established daily flight from Cairo to Tel Aviv on a battered Boeing. The other passengers are mainly Israeli tourists, blazing a trail to see Egypt's historic heritage. Significantly however there appear to be no Egyptian tourists availing themselves of the reverse trip.

My first ever visit to Israel is a mixed experience. This is a complexed and restless society, where good Jewish jokes are offset by insipid menus. (Why is it that the strict *kosher* diet is so tasteless whereas the Muslims' closely regulated *halal* fare can be delectable?) My meetings with a broad range of opinion among parliamentarians in the Knesset and officials in the Foreign Ministry contrast tentative support for a peace settlement with outright disregard in right-wing quarters for the worsening predicament of the Palestinians under occupation. It is encouraging however to encounter more liberal figures such as Yossi Beilin who seem committed to work for a solution; the army general commanding the West Bank, Ephraim Sneh, whom I meet in West Jerusalem's historic King David Hotel, also shows a genuine understanding of the frustration felt by Palestinians under occupation. Indeed the upheaval of the *intifada* is perhaps being succeeded by a period for reflection on both sides, which could be propitious.

In Jerusalem we cross over to the Palestinian side of the equation. The embassy driver drops the two of us off at a favourite hostelry, the American Colony, a fine old building of honey-coloured stone not far outside the great Damascus Gate of the Old City. It is owned by the Vestey family, descendants of Swedish Protestants who migrated to Jerusalem from the United States at the start of the century in the vain hope of witnessing the Second Coming. Crossing the forecourt where the walls are festooned with bright geraniums we enter the hotel lobby to find a hive of activity with arc lights blazing, people bustling, thick cables all over the floor and cameras focused on a low settee beyond the reception desk where a smart couple are seated. They look vaguely familiar; yes, believe it or not, here are two of Hollywood's grandees, Peter Ustinov and Lauren Bacall. We have interrupted the middle of a filming sequence. Before we can beat a retreat one of the directors catches us and insists we go right ahead and check in at the desk while they carry on filming. For, as he charmingly puts it, with our tropical suits, dilapidated luggage and regulation Whitehall briefcases we are the living image of how two British civil servants would have looked on arriving at the hotel back in the mid-1930s, which is when the film they are making is set. In other words two anachronisms from Central Casting... I am not sure whether to be flattered or offended; am I really caught in a half-century's time warp? We have become involuntary extras in a film of Agatha Christie's crime novel, *Appointment with Death*, which draws on her time in Palestine with her archaeologist husband, Max Mallowan.

It is a pleasure to wander again after an interval of some thirty years through old Jerusalem's bustling alleys and to experience the muddle of feuding Christian confessions within the hallowed Holy Sepulchre, relic of the mediaeval Crusades. A new experience is to be able to walk right around the old walls of a city that had been divided by a barbed wire frontier when I last visited from the Jordanian side before the 1967 War, and to pass through the historic Jaffa Gate towards the quarter that is home to ultra-orthodox Jews with the men clad in the black frock coats and broad-brimmed hats of Poland's 19th-century *shtetl*. Our meetings with Palestinian figures in the West Bank and Gaza over the next couple of days confirm the restrictions under which they are obliged to live, and which have fuelled the *intifada*. Bir Zeit University, where our daughter Joanna had her brush with the Israeli army, still operates under the shadow of closure, while the spawning Jewish settlements we find around Jerusalem, in Hebron and in defiant trailer homes along Gaza's barren frontier with Egypt, no longer a land of citrus groves, present a provocative challenge to the crowded and resentful Palestinian refugee camps. A sense of despair is palpable; unforeseen at the time, it will take the side effects of an inter-Arab war, the Gulf War, three years later to break the logjam of negotiation.

With a certain sense of relief we walk across the old Allenby Bridge over the river into tidy Jordan, where a car takes us on up the hills to Amman. I go with our ambassador, John Coles, to call on King Hussein who receives us with his customary courtesy. His relationship with Britain remains close and he is frequently to be found in his house in Kensington's "embassy row". Frustrated at finding the proposals of the Reagan administration in Washington for a Palestinian autonomy on the West Bank under Jordanian sovereignty continually blocked by Israel's right-wing leadership and by talk of decanting the Palestinian population eastward across the River Jordan, the King has recently taken a bold step to reverse the whole political scene by turning his back on Jordan's long-standing claim to the West Bank. This leaves Arafat's PLO, stuck in beleaguered exile in Tunis, with a nominal responsibility. The King's main regional preoccupation now is support for Saddam Hussein's Iraq, at open war with Iran and dependent, much to Jordan's economic benefit, on the long trans-desert road haul from the Red Sea port of Aqaba for her supply lifeline. Our visit to the Royal Palace produces an unexpected contact with the past, when it turns out that the King's secretary escorting us is none other than the young son of the sheikh of the Howeitat bedouin who had been allotted to be my *rafiq*, or companion, during my Arabic-language sojourn in their tents all those years ago. We greet each other as old friends.

* * * * *

The turbulent Middle East region can always be relied upon to produce plenty of activity back in the Foreign Office. It strikes me that I have come on stream at the wrong time. The more senior one becomes, the longer the hours one works – eleven or twelve-hour-days are now the rule, whereas I seem to remember that back in the 50s when I joined the show it was the reverse; one's superiors were rarely at their desks after 6, while we juniors toiled on in the "Third Room". Perhaps the post-war world was a less complicated place. One issue that continues to preoccupy, and frustrate, us is how to obtain the release, alive and without payment of any form of ransom, of three British subjects. Terry Waite, special representative of the Archbishop of Canterbury, John McCarthy, a TV journalist and Brian Keenan, a teacher, have been held for long months somewhere in Lebanon and presumably in grim conditions by a shadowy Shi'a guerrilla group, Islamic Jihad. Terry Waite's captivity has gained a particularly high media profile as a result of his earlier success in negotiating the release of hostages held in Iran and in Libya. He had however become an object of suspicion among radical groups on account of an imprudent association with Colonel Oliver North, a maverick player in President Reagan's fanciful exercise to sell weaponry to a boycotted Iran for the benefit of the anti-communist Contra group in Nicaragua. In an endeavour to carry things forward I take to lunch in the elegant Pall Mall surroundings of the Travellers Club Walid

197

Jumblatt, the influential leader of Lebanon's Druze community in their mountain fastness, under whose nominal protection Waite was operating when he made contact in early 1987 with Islamic Jihad to discuss the hostages and was himself taken captive by them. Jumblatt claims to be unable to find any trace of Waite's whereabouts, and moreover to have warned Waite of the risks he was taking and the assumption that his powerful reputation would ensure his inviolability. With Lebanon in a state of civil war and under partial Israeli occupation Jumblatt sees little prospect of early rescue or release for the captives, though he does give an undertaking to keep trying. Ariel Sharon, Israel's former Minister of Defence who was obliged to resign following his complicity in the appalling massacre by right-wing Lebanese Christian militia of Palestinian families in Beirut's Sabra and Chatila refugee camps, also turns up in London only to find that no minister is prepared to see him. The lot falls to me; his dismissive views on Palestinian rights make for an uncongenial encounter.

We also have two State Visits by Arab monarchs, the first by King Fahd of Saudi Arabia and a year later King Hassan of Morocco. There is protocol galore, with the ritual yet worthwhile mix of ceremonial, official banquets, exchanges of honours and gifts, all interspersed with political discussions. Both leaders bring large suites with them, greatly exceeding the accommodation on offer at the Palace. The genial King Fahd is escorted by a teenage son, Prince Abdul Aziz, without whose propitious company the King is said not to travel. The Moroccan monarch's visit however presents the greater challenge to our diplomacy. The press, ever on the lookout for sensation, have recalled the notorious occasion during the Queen's visit to Morocco some years earlier when King Hassan, an autocrat with a reputation for poor timekeeping, gave an open-air lunch in honour of his guest and then kept her waiting out in the heat for a considerable period before turning up himself. At the time the British tabloid journalists accompanying the royal party made quite a meal of this discourtesy. They hasten to resurrect it now for their readers, and relish the prospect of similar lapses of strict protocol on the present occasion.

As it happens the King, possibly forewarned of this media minefield, keeps pretty well to schedule, and arrives at the Lord Mayor's ceremonial banquet in the Guildhall no later than dignity might allow, though some of us waiting there are holding our breath. But certain newspapers must still have a go at the visitor. Unsurprisingly it is *The Sun* that tops the list with an offensive banner headline to greet the King's arrival in London that reads "The Desert Prat". Fortunately the allusion means nothing to the visitors. But an ingenious, if disingenuous, scheme is hatched that, should there come a query from the Moroccan suite, it should be deflected as involving a flattering reference to a much-respected General Prat who led British forces in the victorious North African campaign in World War II.

* * * * *

One of my most agreeable duties is to attend upon the Queen when she receives foreign envoys from countries in my African parish who are newly appointed to the Court of St James. Leaving a desk awash with papers in mid-morning, I struggle into my dark-blue diplomatic uniform, considerably let out since it was first tailored in Savile Row thirty years earlier, and, complete with gilt sword and a hat crowned with white ostrich plumes, set off for Buckingham Palace. These are relaxed and friendly occasions preceded by a few minutes private talk about the country concerned. The occasional regal opinion on certain political figures before the envoy is ushered in always comes as a tonic. The audiences are informal with easy chat, sometimes in French; the Queen's knowledge of foreign parts, and particularly of her Commonwealth countries, is impressive. After the audience it is customary for the envoy to give a reception, either back at his embassy or in some smart hotel. After putting in an appearance at one of these functions, I am waiting in full fig at the door of the Carlton Tower for my car when an American voice says in my ear, "Say, could you call me a cab?" I turn, hand upon sword hilt, as the startled hotel guest, who has not unreasonably taken me for the commissionaire, withdraws with nervous apologies.

The first prize in this diplomatic burlesque goes however to the High Commissioner for Swaziland, who parades at the Palace on a freezing January morning in his national dress. Unfortunately this involves a naked torso above a loincloth of lion's pelt and with other leonine appurtenances and bright if sketchy prints of cloth attached to the outer limbs, all topped off with a large feather in his hair. The characteristic warmth of the Queen's greeting helps to offset an all-too-chilly saloon. But there is a further ordeal to come, for, as protocol requires, whereas foreign ambassadors are driven to and from their audience in an open carriage and pair, Commonwealth

High Commissioners are entitled to a grander equipage of an open landau and four. The Swazi High Commission, whither the envoy is returning to hold his reception, happens to be in a narrow street somewhere behind Harrods. At the best of times it is not easy to find a parking space for a simple car in that popular district. So a carriage and four horses present the coachman with a considerably greater problem. The result is that we all end up a block or two away from our destination, obliging the half-frozen High Commissioner and me to take a stroll together down Pont Street in our contrasting costumes and to the evident astonishment of bystanders. "I guess they're making a film, dear," says a passing American to his startled wife. "Not at all; quite normal," I am tempted to reply.

* * * * *

Two hectic years have somehow flown by and the desert beckons again. For the moment there is something of a lull in the tensions that have been engaging us around Africa and the Middle East, though this probably has as much to do with plain exhaustion on the part of the protagonists as with any diplomatic initiatives. Soviet Russian forces are finally being withdrawn from Afghanistan in the face of a determined Afghan insurgency with some material support from the USA and the UK – sowing seeds however of troubles to come. Even South Africa's apartheid regime is running out of road. My first choice has been the embassy in Saudi Arabia, and so it turns out. It is familiar territory, and our long-standing relations with the Kingdom are acquiring new substance after a period in the doldrums, as I have discovered on a recent visit to Riyadh to discuss the security threat from Iran. There will be plenty to keep us busy. So it is back to Arabic refresher lessons for Grania and me. But first we seize the chance to take a month in Central Africa to see the work of a British aid charity of which I am a trustee.

African Interlude
Spring 1989

Ex Africa semper aliquid novi

Pliny the Elder

E ight o'clock on a crisp and clear African morning finds Grania and me landing at Harare's international airport that has seen better days. We are embarking on a tour of institutions which have support from the Beit Trust, a British charity of which I am a trustee. The trust was established ninety years ago under the will of Alfred Beit, a friend and associate of Cecil Rhodes and an honourable figure among the "Randlords" who developed the diamond and gold resources of South Africa in the high time of British imperialism during the late Victorian era. To his credit he left a large portion of his personal fortune in trust "for the benefit of the people" of the two Rhodesia territories, which had recently come under British rule as Europe's major powers sought to divide central Africa among themselves. Over the subsequent years the Trust, from a base in England and with an office in Harare and a network of local correspondents throughout the area, has developed into a substantial benefactor in the fields of health, disability, education and also wildlife conservation in what are now the independent Commonwealth states of Zimbabwe, Zambia and Malawi. Each year one of the British trustees, bringing their experience of the region or in the Trust's specialist fields of activity, makes an extensive tour to report on the Trust's operations, ranging from buildings and equipment for mission hospitals and schools, many in remote locations and reached over rough roads, to scholarships abroad for higher university degrees.

This is what brings us to Africa towards the end of a southern summer of heavy but welcome rains, with an energetic itinerary that will cover the Trust's activities in a Zimbabwe that is still enjoying a post-independence phase of best behaviour and prosperity, oblivious to the social disintegration and economic catastrophe that will engulf her within a decade; a run-down Zambia still stagnating within the dogmas of Kenneth Kaunda's stale and corrupted state socialism; and a scenic and ever cheerful Malawi that has to watch her step under her authoritarian life President, the nonagenarian Dr Hastings Banda. All in all quite a mix. There are tentative signs of political progression towards more democratic and transparent governance in some corners of this vast continent, though how the benefits of this transformation will be distributed has yet to be seen. All three countries are moreover starting to suffer the decimating scourge of the AIDS virus for which no treatment is yet known; a culture of promiscuity is not helping things.

＊ ＊ ＊ ＊ ＊

Our tour around the three territories is made in the company of the Trust's representative in Harare, Bruce Fieldsend, a former Rhodes Scholar who was previously headmaster of Peterhouse, one of Zimbabwe's foremost secondary schools which has benefited much from the Trust's grants over the years. The visit also coincides with the presence in the area of our twin boys who are undertaking a gap year as assistant teachers, James at Box 2, a Marist Brothers mission school below Zomba's tropical mountain in Malawi and Luke at Ruzawi, a preparatory school in the tobacco-growing uplands to the east of Harare. We take an African break with them in the Hwange game reserve and the magnificent Victoria Falls where construction of the elegant old hotel was funded by the Beit Trust back in 1914 to facilitate tourism. Zimbabwe's Rhodesian time warp is brought home to me when woken early by the clanking arrival at the adjacent station of the night train from Bulawayo, still hauled by one of the same monster Beyer Garrett articulated steam locomotives, on the footplate of which as schoolboys my brother Neil and I once worked a happy shift as assistant firemen over the same route nearly forty years ago.

Harare and Bulawayo are still prosperous and well-tended cities where suburban bungalows with their tin roofs and cool *stoep* verandas sit under a canopy of vivid flame trees on streets wide enough to turn a team of oxen, as first decreed by Cecil Rhodes himself. Robert Mugabe, who has recently taken over the presidency from the engagingly named Canaan Banana (subsequently imprisoned on a charge of sodomy), is firmly installed in Harare's elegant old Government House. Sir Humphrey Gibbs, now the Trust's local chairman, sat out four beleaguered and defiant years here as the Queen's representative following Ian Smith's rebellious declaration of unilateral independence in 1965. Back in my schoolboy days a group of us got into gubernatorial hot water for ripping the billiard table's precious baize cloth in a riotous game of billiard fives – I suspect it still awaits repair.

Yet there is a sinister undercurrent; the period following independence ten years ago has seen an armed protest movement among the minority Matabele tribe in the south ruthlessly suppressed with North Korean help. We get a taste of the tensions this savage campaign provoked when we fly down to a wildlife conservancy's primitive airstrip far into the bush of the southern Lowveldt. With the land no longer suitable for cattle ranching local farmers have restocked with wild game, including the black rhino, a beast which the Trust is now engaged in protecting from near extinction through poaching to meet an oriental appetite for the supposed aphrodisiac qualities of its horn, compounded by a belief on the part of tribesmen in the Yemen in its talismanic properties for the handles of their ornate daggers. Ranch buildings where we stop for a night are surrounded by high-security fences, an effective if rudimentary defence against attack by intruders. On the way to visit a mission school in the heart of resentful Matabeleland our car is held at a police checkpoint. In the boot the constable finds Grania's shooting stick. "What is this?" he asks, examining it with curiosity. "A shooting stick," she replies, and instantly wishes she had not uttered. For the officer's suspicions are immediately aroused. "How does it shoot?" comes the question, accompanied by frank disbelief that it is just an object for perching on. It takes a good spell of patient explanation and demonstration before we are allowed to proceed.

The mission school, when we reach it deep in the *bundu*, is an inspiring sight with cheerful pupils and dedicated teachers operating in buildings that have certainly seen better days, a state of affairs that the Trust can help to remedy. Indeed it is a humbling experience to witness the devotion which those working in mission hospitals and schools, often in the most primitive conditions, bring to their vocation. I am reminded of a conversation I had a few months earlier with President Mugabe when I found myself his host at a Foreign Office lunch in his honour during an official visit he was paying to Britain. Asked by him whether I have personal connections with Zimbabwe, my mention of the Trust catches his attention. "As far as I am concerned," he says, "the Beit Trust has a free hand in my country." "How so, Mr. President?" "If it were not for the Trust, I would not be President. You see, it was a Beit Trust bursary that paid for my secondary education." Well...; but the pledge has always been honoured.

* * * * *

A bone-jarring ride from the Falls to Lusaka over one of Zambia's potholed highways takes all day plus a bent wheel rim that a wayside mechanic sorts out with the aid of a mallet, Africa's standard repair tool; MMBA, as I have heard wearied aid workers chant as the bush rolls by – miles and miles of bloody Africa. Yet the valiant mission hospitals and schools where we stop along the way are heartening to see. We eventually reach Lilayi game lodge just outside the city on the farm of Peter Miller, one of the Trust's three local correspondents who give generous time to travelling around the country keeping an eye on our projects. Sadly Peter is later to die in one of Zambia's all too frequent road accidents; another Trust correspondent John Harvey and his wife Lorna will also lose their lives, murdered in cold blood at their farmhouse by three members of the South African guerrilla movement who appeared to have borne a grudge. Lorna's father, Sir Stewart Gore-Browne, was a legendary and enlightened figure who created back in the 1920s a grandiose English country mansion and estate beside a marshy lake in Zambia's remote north-east, miles from the nearest European settlement and which he ruled with benevolent autocracy. This African idyll is now a deserted monument to a colonial dream.

For all its stylish government buildings and suburbs bright with flowering trees Lusaka has a sad look. A spanking new high-rise block, built with Chinese funds, serves as headquarters of the sole political party. Before it stands a fine statue of an African holding out between his hands a severed link of chains; the caption on the plinth reads "Liberty". Below it someone is said to have scrawled, "You people will break anything". Not a happy place, but we have an encouraging and convivial get-together with a group of Zambians – administrators, business people, medics and academics – all players in their country's future who have undertaken postgraduate studies at British universities under the Trust's auspices. The evening has been organised by my cousin, Theodore Bull, who has made his life in Africa, at first in Rhodesia/Zimbabwe until he was kicked out by Ian Smith's regime for his liberal views, and then in Zambia where his wife, the daughter of a Barotse chieftain, is a minister in the Kaunda government.

We carry on northwards stopping at a succession of clinics and colleges where the Trust may be able to help improve the facilities. The Great North Road up to the Copperbelt is every bit as dilapidated as elsewhere; locals joke that if you see someone driving in a straight line along a highway, he must be drunk. Petrol stations are few and far between. When predictably we run out of fuel, succour turns up in the shape of a pickup truck that turns out to be driven by no less than the Minister of Mines. He is returning from a wedding and has his daughters, all in their finery, in the open back along with a full jerrican. Without hesitation he empties this into our tank while Grania presses packets of Polo peppermints she providentially keeps to hand on the delighted girls. We go our ways in warm friendship. There is a generous heart inside Africa.

The once prosperous towns of the Copperbelt turn out to be in a run-down state with the nationalised mines almost at a standstill. The Barclays Bank rest house where we put up has intermittent electricity and *nshima* maize porridge on the menu. One of our purposes is to renew a connection with the local Copperbelt University. Our call on the dean, an impressive individual who turns out to have studied in Britain through one of the Trust's postgraduate fellowships, produces a plan to modernise the library. While we sit facing him in his darkening office as dusk gathers outside, I detect a growing uneasiness on the dean's part. Making our way out along a covered walkway we are struck by shafts of strong beams from the setting sun; in the dark stairwell it appears that one of these continues to attach itself to me. Investigation reveals that a torch which I have in my trouser pocket has switched itself on and throughout our meeting has been shining out of my loins through the lightweight material. The dean's discomfort is accounted for; it must have been a transfixing experience for him to see his beneficent visitor so intriguingly illuminated.

* * * * *

Impoverished and secluded Malawi, strung along the western side of its great lake, is as bustling and friendly as ever. "What have you brought for me?" enquires a roguish customs official at Lilongwe's smart new airport as he starts to open our suitcases. "Funds for new schools," we reply – not quite the answer he was hoping for. The autocratic Dr Banda is never far away as his ancient face adorns the cloths that enclose the ample posteriors of most women. There is still no television station and foreign visitors must conform to a sober code of appearance that derives from his strict Scottish Presbyterian upbringing; no long hair for men and full-length skirts for women – hardly the hippie trail. The smart administrative capital has been built with aid funds from South Africa in return for recognition of its discreditable apartheid regime by the quirky ruler of this diminutive Central African state. In a battered hire car we drive for several hundreds of miles between the hot plains of the Shire valley in the south and the rolling green uplands of the north. This is a beautiful and fertile land, though again the roads are in poor repair. In places they have been washed away by heavy rains; on our way across the Viphya range in central Malawi we are blocked by a large bus that has become bogged in the deep mud. We join its passengers to make a work party to dig it out, and then fall flat on our faces trying to heave our own car through the glutinous red earth. A good rinsing is required at the mission school which is our next port of call before we can get down to business.

For a good part of its route the highway from Lilongwe down to the former colonial capital, Blantyre, acts as the frontier between Malawi and its neighbour, Mozambique, a country torn apart by an interminable civil war since achieving independence from Portugal. It is a strange experience to see the lands on the Malawian verge crowded with the tidy mud huts and maize patches of hundreds of refugees from the ruined and deserted villages just across the road where the people fear to tread for risk of guerrilla bands and landmines. The scene brings home the artificiality of Africa's colonial boundaries. In Blantyre the Trust is funding improvements to the old colonial hospital and the restoration of the handsome Presbyterian cathedral built a century ago in red brick by Scottish missionaries. Another project involves the restoration of the great white elephant of an Anglican cathedral, impractically sited a century earlier by missionaries, anxious to escape the lethal scourge of blackwater fever, on the inaccessible Likoma island off the Mozambique shore of Lake Malawi, well out of reach of its flock yet of a scale comparable to Winchester's great basilica. At Karonga at the lake's northern tip there is a chance to visit one of the most far-flung cemeteries of the Commonwealth War Graves Commission, where lie buried British colonial troops killed in the campaign against German forces in Tanganyika during the First World War. Its tidy garden remains a monument to a remote corner of empire.

We make our way north along the shore of Lake Malawi by a succession of isolated mission hospitals and schools that receive support from the Trust through construction or repair of clinics, operating theatres, staff houses, classrooms, even boreholes and generators. The southern section is the home of the Yao, one of the few Muslim tribes in central Africa. They were converted by Omani Arab slave traders from Zanzibar on whose behalf they raided other tribes. It was to put an end to this dark trade in the name of Christianity that David Livingstone and other Scottish missionaries chose to risk their lives in the area a century ago. Today the Yao make their living from lake fish which they dry on sun-baked trays; the pungent smell carries far along the road. It is a treat to stop for a night at the stylish Club Makakolo lodge on the lakeshore.

The evening brings however a sinister touch of President Banda's ubiquitous surveillance machine. With the Fieldsends and also James, who has joined us from the Marist school nearby at Zomba, we turn up at the dining room and are asked to wait while a special table is prepared for us. This turns out to be against a wall on which hangs a splendid stuffed buffalo's head; a hunting trophy we assume. In the middle of a convivial meal with plenty of disrespectful chat about the way things go under the Banda regime Grania suddenly hushes us. "There's a clicking noise coming out of that buffalo," she says, looking up at the wall above us. "Nonsense!" we all claim and carry on with the gossip. But soon she stops us again. Yes, that could be a scratching sound coming out of the beast's jaw. I also know from experience in Algeria that Grania's security antennae are exceptionally acute; it is not for nothing that she is the daughter of a former naval intelligence officer. "I'm off to investigate," she says. "I'll head for the ladies down by the service door and take a peek into the kitchen as I go by." Bag in hand and setting off across the restaurant she turns through the service door, only to be bundled rapidly back through it by a waiter who points the way to the ladies. In due course Grania returns to our table with a look of triumph. "I was right; I just had time to see there's a man standing on a table right behind this wall with his head through it. He's replacing a recording tape." So no one is above suspicion in today's Malawi, least of all perhaps a long-established foreign charity. We retire soon to bed in our chalets by the moonlit lakeside, somewhat shaken by the experience, yet knowing that in its limited way the Trust is able to provide real help to the people of this lively and attractive country.

Saudi Arabia (at peace)
1989-1990

Now slowly moves the shadow of the rock,
And cools parched bodies in a weary land.
'No God but God' they cry – I cannot mock
Their absolute assurance of his hand
Outstretched to bless. They clearer see
Than the ungainly camel, or the hills
Ringed round the Prophet's tomb – their certainty
Allah to praise, whether he saves or kills.

From *Medina* by Raymond Blackburn

A couple of weeks of a crash refresher course in Arabic and Grania and I find ourselves in mid-July on a Saudia flight bound for Riyadh. A short stopover in Jedda serves to remind us of the cultural frontier we have crossed as Grania is shunted off into a separate female waiting room from which I manage to extricate her to catch the onward leg. Arriving in Riyadh's palatial new airport in the small hours we find a friendly welcome from the Foreign Ministry's protocol officer and my deputy, Derek Plumbly, (who by happy chance was briefly a bachelor tenant in our Chiswick home when he first joined the Service). Despite the hour the heat is quite something. This is to be our home for the next four years, and with a full-scale war thrown in.

Riyadh has come a long way since the dusty and drab town I knew only six years ago. Gaudy new villas sprawl over the baked stony plateau, new

209

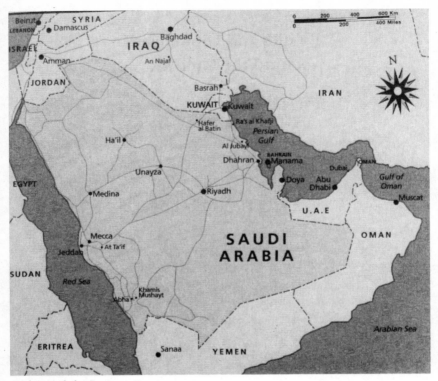

Arabia and the Levant

highways form a grid between smart high-rise hotels, shopping malls and office blocks, domed palaces out of the Arabian Nights and set in lush landscapes accommodate King Fahd and other senior princes, while the mud-walled warren of the old town with its bustling souk markets behind the old fort and "Chop Square", as irreverent expatriates call the place of public execution, is gradually being torn down and replaced with stylish replicas built with modern materials. Even the handsome salukis that used to stray about the town in search of prey have disappeared – into the cooking pots, some say, of the teams of Korean construction workers that have arrived to build the new metropolis. With the Kingdom now producing a massive quarter of the world's oil consumption the stagnation of the early 1980s has been succeeded by a boom. This is evident in the form of impressive new ministries to house a growing bureaucracy; outstanding among these temples of government are the Interior Ministry, designed in

210

the shape of a vast flying saucer, and the Foreign Ministry, a clinical white fortress designed by a Dane in which I am regularly to lose my way among its labyrinth of courtyards and Kafkaesque corridors. Never was Ariadne's ball of string more called for to navigate one's way out.

For the Diplomatic Corps too life has changed with the recent transfer of all foreign embassies up from their former exile in Jedda into a new diplomatic quarter on the rim of the deep Wadi Hanifa ravine to the west of the city. Each country has been invited to create its own homes and offices in a style that will combine national architectural confection with the discreet privacy that goes with Saudi Arabia's secluded Islamic traditions. The whole area is surrounded by an earth rampart on the crest of which some bright planner has placed obstacles for physical exercise; unsurprisingly few diplomats choose to take advantage of these gymnastic facilities in Riyadh's unrelenting temperatures. The British contribution to this international architectural festival involves shuttered windows piercing blank walls of the mellow local sandstone, well contrived on the whole and set amid a pleasant garden landscape. For such a large and busy mission however space is tight; apparently Mrs Thatcher has decreed that it is time Britain turned her back on the imposing embassies of the past. Our comfortable residence, for all its state-of-the-art electronics and cooling systems, turns out to afford quite inadequate space for the hospitality we need to offer; we shall have to do something about this. At least it is a relief to find that our diplomatic haven is out of bounds to the bothersome religious police, or *mutawwa*, who so eagerly patrol the city to ensure no public and provocative display of female flesh, nor non-observance of the regular prayer times.

* * * * *

I plunge into the round of visits to senior figures – key Al Saud princes who hold the central reins of government, as well as other ministers and leading business folk. It is striking to be reminded of the particular value which members of the ruling family continue to place on the close historical relationship between our two nations, going right back to Britain's support for the resistance of Amir Abdul Aziz to the rival Al Rashid clan of Ha'il, which took the part of the Ottoman Turks in the First World War, and for his subsequent consolidation of Al Saud authority culminating in the foundation of the Kingdom in the early 1930s. I reconnect with Prince

Sultan, full brother of King Fahd and the long-serving Minister of Defence, with whom I had dealings during my last spell here, and with Prince Saud al-Faisal, the Foreign Minister whose experience and wisdom amid the upheavals of Arab world affairs are so widely respected. Little do I suspect that our partnership during the Kuwait crisis a year later will have us living almost in each other's pockets. Another important call is on Crown Prince Abdullah who, despite a heavy stammer uncommon in an Arabic speaker, is an imposing and popular figure with family connections to the bedouin community and known to hold strong views over Palestine. Prince Abdullah heads the National Guard, in the Valhalla-like headquarters of which on the outskirts of Riyadh I used to find myself negotiating contracts in interminable night-long sessions in my Ministry of Defence spell.

It being high summer many personalities have decamped for the Red Sea coast. Meetings thus involve early starts on the shuttle down to Jedda on Saudia's Tristar aircraft that are starting to show their age. There is however comfort to be drawn from the Qur'an's sonorous invocation of a safe journey that precedes take-off, and the hour and a half flight gives a useful opportunity to make contacts, provided of course that one's neighbour is not invisible within a black *abaya*. Passengers are welcomed with a traditional cup of bitter cardomum-laced coffee, together with a ripe date to be placed between one's front teeth to sweeten the beverage as it passes through – it takes time to master the art. You never quite know whether the flight will be straightforward. On one morning a couple of religious busybodies take it into their heads that it is ungodly to have men and women travelling in close proximity. So they insist on rearranging the seating in mid-flight, moving all females into the front and forcing all males into the rear of the plane, regardless of what class they have paid to travel. Meanwhile the pilot strives to keep the jumbo on an even keel while this game of general post takes place in mid-air.

Jedda is now a stylish city with its handsome new corniche interspersed with bizarrely ornamented roundabouts and lined with hotels and cafes, and mosques too of inspiring Islamic design. Downtown gleaming headquarters of banks and trading houses, created by some of the world's leading architects, contrast with the vibrant and dilapidated warren of the handsome old town that dates from the Ottoman era, its tall and shuttered buildings built of blocks of whitened coral and adorned with the intricate wooden lattices of their oriel windows. It is an inspiration to wander through its vibrant alleys where stalls offer everything from colourful garments to exotic spices and antique metalwork. One can even find increasingly rare Maria Theresa thalers, the handsome and historic coinage from another era. The city itself has however become a traffic nightmare.

The high point of this marathon of diplomatic protocol is the ceremony of presentation of my credentials to the King. This takes place one warm evening in Jedda in the magnificent royal palace that spans an offshore island, reclaimed from the seabed and girdled with palms. As I set out in an official convoy, bolstered by members of the embassy staff, from our villa in the compound occupied by our Consulate-General, I spot one of them has brought along the latest issue of *Private Eye* which, I happen to recall, contains a disrespectful item on the Saudi royal family. Here's a hostage to fortune; what if there is a security search on our arrival? The offending journal gets stuffed away in a hip pocket and we hope for the best.

King Fahd is known for being a nightbird and likes to hold his audiences well after the late-evening *'Ishaa* prayers. His custom, as I have been warned, is to open with a thoughtful if prolonged commentary on issues of mutual political or social interest, to be heard out in respectful silence, and then to invite response and discussion of particular business between us. Interruption earns no points, but the homily merits close attention. It is an advantage to be able to follow his well-crafted Arabic, as this often reveals points of emphasis which would be lost in translation. (How truthful is the French adage – *Les traductions sont comme les femmes; quand elles sont belles elles ne sont pas fidèles, et quand elles sont fidèles elles ne sont pas belles...*). On this first occasion the genuine attachment of the Al Saud dynasty to its near century of close friendship with Britain – a privileged position which we have sometimes tended to discount – comes across strongly, with particular emphasis on defence, economic development and education. During the critical times that are to follow, I shall find myself developing a healthy respect for the committed, yet ever-cautious and subtle, course which this elderly yet outward-looking autocrat pursues in steering his wealthy, pious and ultra-conservative nation through the shoals of regional turbulence and religious bigotry towards a greater integration with the modern world – or, as some have put it less charitably, dragging it forward into the fifteenth century. Come to think of it, that is exactly where we are, according to the Islamic calendar.

* * * * *

A bout of high-profile diplomacy is not long in coming. King Fahd has worthily engaged his country in hosting a conference in Ta'if, an historic town high up in the mountains of the Hejaz above Mecca, aimed at ending once and for all the twenty-five-year agony of Lebanon's civil war. The arrangements are elaborate in order to ensure that the surviving, if by now antique, members of Lebanon's rump parliament who have been bidden to attend, many from a voluntary exile, lack for nothing in the way of creature comforts and specialist medical attention to keep them alive. With the help of Morocco, Algeria and the Arab League Prince Saud has skilfully brought this geriatric assortment of politicians, so long steeped in an inter-confessional enmity in which neighbouring states have lent a ready hand, towards a precarious settlement. This now needs to be bolstered with early endorsement by the UN Security Council in New York.

As it happens only three of the five Permanent Members of the Council, the Americans, French and ourselves, have diplomatic relations with Saudi Arabia; the two Communist members, the Soviet Union and China, are still regarded as godless and thus beyond the Pale. The three of us are soon brought into close consultations on the shape of a Security Council resolution. These culminate in an urgent late-night summons to Ta'if. I scramble onto an early flight from Riyadh and find myself deposited, along with my French colleague, in a run-down old hostelry some distance from the spanking new Sheraton hotel where the meetings are being held. It all turns into one of those diverting experiences that can enliven the routines of diplomacy. On arrival I find myself lodged in a poky and insalubrious room; only later do I realise that the policeman whom the Saudis have deputed to be my "minder" has appropriated the more commodious suite intended for me. The hotel's aged owner, with whom the Frenchman and I while away much of the day, turns out to be a fascinating relic of the days of the old Hejaz. Having enlisted as a lad in the service of Sharif Hussein in Mecca he had accompanied Emir Faisal, partner and protégé of Lawrence of Arabia, during his brief spell as Hashemite ruler over Syria following the Arab campaign of World War I, until kicked out by the French and moved across by Britain to the throne of Iraq. The old fellow had then switched allegiance to the Al Saud and had accompanied King Abdul Aziz's son, Faisal, on a groundbreaking visit to London in the early 1920s. He cannot believe his luck in having the chance to taunt the representatives of both Britain and France over their nations' arbitrary carve-up of the Ottoman provinces under the ill-omened Sykes-Picot Agreement and the controversial Balfour Declaration on a Jewish homeland in Palestine. We are caught in a fascinating time warp.

We three western envoys find ourselves closeted that evening in detailed textual discussions with Prince Saud and his fellow panellists. Language proves a bit of a challenge as the American deputy ambassador has no Arabic or French, the Frenchman no Arabic, the Algerian Foreign Minister little English and the Moroccan none at all. The Arab League's impressive Lakhdar Ibrahimi, together with Prince Saud, is luckily conversant in all three tongues, but it is still a polyglot Babel. We get there in the end, thankful we have not had to cope with Russian and Chinese to boot. But my real test is to come. Returning late to a dimly lit hotel room, and of course with not a drop of the hard stuff for sustenance, I try to activate a telephone connection to our mission in New York. The telephone service of the Azizia Hotel turns out to be as ancient as its owner. Its exchange, faintly audible and manned by a semi-literate Sudanese night porter with no comprehension of the crucial web of telecommunications of which he has become the nerve centre, is quite unable to raise either New York or London. At my end the obstacles are no less, as the obsolete handset is located at the opposite wall to the room's only working lamp. The only way to make notes is to spreadeagle myself across a carpet strewn with pomegranate pips. The wallpaper appears to carry a selection of female names and telephone numbers; for all the results I am getting in pursuit of diplomacy I might as well call one of those. Eventually by relaying messages much of the night via our offices in Riyadh and Jedda I manage to get my report through. All in all a revealing, and entertaining, lesson in life behind the electronic façade of Saudi Arabia's Magic Kingdom.

* * * * *

We soon pick up the rhythm of life in this singular and pious country where activity stops for prayer five times a day and discussion is sprinkled with sagacious Arabic proverbs. The Saudis give considerable weight to their close and long-standing links with Britain, in regional affairs, in security, commerce, education and in practical administration. In consequence the expatriate British community, now some 30,000 strong and spread across the subcontinent between the three centres of Jedda, Riyadh and the oil-producing Eastern Province on the Gulf shore, is one of the largest outside the English-speaking world. It is important for us to keep in touch with them, as later events will prove. I find myself giving regular talks to their active business groups. Indeed the promotion of Britain's important trading relationship forms a major part of the embassy's work; there is an incessant stream of visiting business missions. In one bizarre episode I get a letter from a well-known bell foundry in London enquiring whether Saudi Arabia, with her reputation for piety, has church bells in need of repair or replacement; I reply with a gentle reminder that no peals are rung in a minaret.

For all the cultural differences with their Saudi hosts our expatriates keep a lively social life going on their comfortable compounds despite the strict local codes of behaviour and dress, especially where females are concerned, the clumsy defacing with black felt-tip of any female flesh depicted in imported magazines, and the prohibitions on women driving and on alcohol. It is no accident to find how the well-stocked supermarkets tend to group on adjacent shelves the basic ingredients for concocting a home brew. Among the expatriate highlights are the annual Remembrance Day concerts when we all belt out "Land of Hope and Glory" with patriotic fervour, and with other foreigners happily joining in.

Christian worship presents a challenge in this puritanical Islamic nation where the prevalence of the revivalist Wahhabi school of theology and the custodianship of Islam's two most holy shrines, at Mecca and Medina, reinforce a prejudice against other faiths. In practice senior members of the Al Saud regime are inclined to adopt a pragmatic approach, but feel constrained by a powerful clerical establishment. In consequence we find ourselves indulging in a form of "catacomb" worship, with Anglican services held discreetly on Fridays – the Muslim day of rest – in the community hall on the embassy compound, and with a tacit undertaking that we shall not court any publicity. Unhappily this dictates a limit on the numbers we invite to participate and the exclusion of dedicated members of other Protestant confessions who feel bereft of Christian comfort, a situation that inevitably gets me into hot water with certain evangelical circles back home. Moreover there is no cleric to lead our services apart from the good Bishop Brown of Cyprus and the Gulf, who gets smuggled into Saudi Arabia every few months in the guise of a teacher, with the authorities turning a helpful blind eye.

Relief comes unexpectedly in the shape of Tola Roberts, a Nigerian lecturer in dentistry at Riyadh's King Saud University up the road, who turns up at church one Friday and reveals himself to be an ordained priest on the side. A blessing from heaven indeed; duly empowered by the diocese I conduct an ecclesiastical induction in the armchair comfort of our sitting room. Christmas is marked with a merry evening of carols and a disrespectful embassy pantomime production. The news of the award of a "K" in the New Year Honours gives us both a great shot in the arm. It brings a call from a newspaper in Aberdeen, the Granite City my father's family left a century ago to try their luck over the border.

Our first Boxing Day brings a sudden summons to see King Fahd. As I enter a gilded audience chamber in Riyadh's Al Yamamah Palace I find the King flanked by his brothers Crown Prince Abdullah and Defence Minister Prince Sultan. What can be afoot? Am I about to get a Christmas headwashing? To my relief it turns out that I am bidden for a relaxed review of our defence cooperation. After a while the Crown Prince rises to leave, just as an attendant is bringing us a tray with glasses of the King's favourite carrot juice and a single glass of milk. At a call from the King, "Abdullah, come back. You haven't drunk your milk," his brother stops to oblige. King Fahd turns to me; "I always make sure Abdullah drinks his milk," he says contentedly. An intimate glimpse of brotherly affection between two of the world's most powerful septuagenarians.

* * * * *

The surrounding desert with its high dunes and sandstone escarpments, eroded into towering shapes, affords a great playground. In our 4x4s we practise desert-driving skills and explore cavernous canyons. There are memorable nights under the sparkling desert firmament. Just to the north of Riyadh lies Al Dira'iya, the old 18th-century capital of the Al Saud, its ornate mud-brick palaces abandoned and in ruins ever since the town was razed by the Egyptian military expedition led by Ibrahim Pasha back in 1816 to punish the Al Saud and their fanatical Wahhabi tribesmen for their puritanical desecration of the shrines of Mecca and Medina. After spring rains there are rare truffles the size of potatoes to be gathered from below the desert's crust. On one camping trip, for which Grania concocts a delicious confection of pasties containing truffles sent over to us by one of

217

the King's sons and with a touch of illicit bacon added, our party comes to a bedouin settlement where hawks are trained for hunting expeditions. These fierce raptors can sell for tens of thousands of dollars. Having been rash enough to admire one handsome bird, what should happen but a few days later its owner turns up at our gate in Riyadh with a falcon he wants to present to us. Daunted at the prospect of taking in such a rapacious creature, said to consume a rabbit each day, I manage politely to divert the gift to the home of the unsuspecting Swiss ambassador, who had also been on the trip. He makes the mistake of accepting the bird. For good order's sake we decide to put up a notice at our gate saying "No hawkers".

Riyadh has a handsome new zoo. It turns out that its visitors, being unaccustomed to seeing wild animals in captivity, are in two minds whether they are meant to admire the fauna or to throw stones at it. The vigilantes of the religious police are also soon on the scene with a virtuous decree that the sexes must be kept apart and the monkeys must have their private parts covered; just another headache for the curators. Some Saudis keep private menageries on their "farms" outside the city. One of them proudly shows us an ostrich which he has just brought back from Sudan; he grumbles that the airline made him buy a first-class seat for it. His lion has recently escaped...

Riyadh's crumbling souks are another wonderland, the rows of shops crammed with dazzling gold jewellery, antique silver ornaments and eastern garments. Some of the carpet stalls have interesting tribal rugs from Afghanistan, where the ongoing war against Soviet occupation has introduced stylised symbols of tanks, helicopters and missiles into the traditional designs. There is a hospitable welcome from Saudi friends among the country's prosperous merchant families from cosmopolitan Jedda across to the oil-rich Gulf coast, and within the Al Saud clan as well – an agreeable contrast to Algeria's inhibited society. Family weddings, albeit carefully segregated, involve night-long high jinks for the women guests, with music and dancing till break of day, while their menfolk briefly assemble to salute the groom with a ceremonial cup of bitter coffee before departing to solitary bed. Visitors from the UK with their own contacts in the Kingdom help introduce us to various circles within this many-sided yet very private society – a cousin, Paul Webber, who trains racehorses, opens doors to the racing crowd with their lavishly appointed stables down at the Equestrian Club; Keith Middlemas from Sussex University does the same with a well-funded, if somewhat orthodox, academic scene; David Sulzberger, a specialist in Islamic art, brings us into contact with a lively, if subterranean, creative community, while Grania finds herself drawn into an intensive and surprisingly emancipated feminine environment. With a group of Saudi women, who in their seclusion seek to express their aspirations through painting, she organises an exhibition of their works in our Riyadh home, together with some of her own. The initiative turns out a great success, though it does lead to my receiving a no more than ritual rap on the knuckles from the protocol people for what some in authority appear to regard as an incautious step towards female liberation. Prince Abdullah bin Faisal, known as AFT, who was educated in Britain and is in charge of the flourishing new industrial city of Jubail on the Gulf coast, becomes a particular friend; there are enjoyable evenings of barbecued Nejdi sheep with half-tamed Arab horses to ride out at his "farm" amid the desert sands. The milk from his camels is sweet and refreshing, but one needs to go carefully for it tends to "revisit" you later. The British Council under Clive Smith, an old friend from Tripoli days and with a special interest in the Kingdom's prehistoric heritage that is starting to be revealed, runs an active cultural programme. Grania takes on work there advising young Saudi women students on educational courses in Britain.

It is not long however before we encounter a more sombre side to the Kingdom. A Deputy Interior Minister, known for his liberal outlook, invites us to dine with his family in their stylish modern villa. There turns out however to be a purpose to the evening. After a delicious repast we find ourselves sat in front of a television to watch a series of "confessions" in Arabic by a succession of nervous young men. They are Shi'as of Saudi and Kuwaiti nationality, convicted of the attempted sabotage a few months earlier at Iranian instigation of petrochemical installations at Jubail. Most of them now face public execution, and are being paraded on television for the public's education. We sit out the programme with diplomatic courtesy, but the ghoulish display takes the shine off the party. Justice in accordance with *shari'a* law has its harsh side.

* * * * *

The confident state of relations between Britain and the Kingdom brings business visitors galore. Much time is spent in setting up these visits and in providing hospitality. We have hardly settled in to the residence when Charles Denman, an old friend and leading figure on the Middle East business scene, turns up. His first evening with us produces a drama when a large rat hops over his foot in the drawing room. With his help Grania succeeds in corralling it for the night to await a more professional solution in the morning. Ministers succeed one another thick and fast from London to be led through official guest houses and five-star hotels in Jedda, Riyadh and over to Dammam and Al Khobar on the Gulf coast, in pursuit of the King and other peripatetic Saudi personalities. Soon comes the first of many visits by the Foreign Secretary, Douglas Hurd, one of the last of a generation of holders of that office to succeed in retaining authority over the conduct of Britain's foreign policy in the face of a progressive takeover by 10 Downing Street. Ideas are shared over a deteriorating scene in Palestine as well as in Iraq with Prince Saud, followed by a late session with King Fahd on his island retreat on the Red Sea coast.

Tom King, the Defence Secretary and an old friend from Cambridge days, arrives to carry forward with Prince Sultan and the King Britain's support for the Saudi Air Force and the industrial investment programme that goes with it. With Crown Prince Abdullah we discuss Britain's close involvement with the National Guard, and also seek his intercession with Iraq's bloodthirsty president to spare a British journalist, accused of spying, from execution. Help is willingly given, but the sentence goes ahead. There is a banquet lunch in Tom's honour. These can be curious affairs as the custom is to rush through the successive courses of delicious fare with one's plate being removed by an attentive waiter almost as soon as one has got a fork into the first mouthful. A predecessor of mine, James Craig, claims the record is ten courses served and removed within 25 minutes. I assume that what is taken away is enjoyed at greater leisure by the hungry attendants. When I ask the significance of the two glasses of rich-looking milk before me, Prince Sultan explains that one comes from a grazing camel and the other from a camel on heat, a subtle lactic distinction. There is a minor domestic drama when a waiter at the lunch I give in return at home, finding himself squeezed between the table and the wall, manages to pour most of the contents of a pot of scalding coffee down the front of Prince Sultan's pristine white *thobe*. Fortunately the Prince takes it all in good part and an awkward diplomatic incident is avoided. Seeking, as a diplomat always should, to turn the mishap to advantage I persuade Tom King to press on his return to Whitehall for funds to enlarge our inadequate dining space. Tom duly works his magic and within weeks builders are on site to construct a spacious extension which the new residence should have had from the start. A war later on is to give us the chance to make further improvements.

Other early visitors include "C", the anonymous head of Britain's overseas intelligence service, who comes to compare notes on developments in Saddam Hussein's unpredictable rule over Iraq with his Saudi counterpart, Prince Turki, a son of the respected and modernising King Faisal who was assassinated by a relative back in 1975. We all set off from Riyadh one stormy morning in a VIP Hercules of the Saudi Air Force to see the King who is on one of his desert circuits among the bedouin at Hafr Al-Batin near the northern border with Kuwait. Arriving at this remote location the pilot circles around trying to make a safe landing through a swirling sandstorm. I spot what looks like the end of the runway between sandhills. "But we don't know which end," says Prince Turki dryly, and tells the pilot to abort the attempt at landing and return to Riyadh. Things don't always turn out as planned in the Kingdom; we call it the "botheration factor". The Secretary of State for Wales, Peter Walker, also turns up, looking to increase the number of Saudi students at Welsh universities. I take him to see the jovial Minister for Higher Education who greets his visitor in a tongue that is certainly not Arabic. When it turns out to be Welsh there are red faces for all his visitors from the Principality, none of whom is familiar with the national tongue. Game and set to the minister; it emerges that he obtained a doctorate at Aberystwyth.

A visit by the Chairman of the BBC, Marmaduke Hussey, turns into quite an adventure. His enthusiastic hosts in the Ministry of Information, keen to give him a taste of the Kingdom's modern infrastructure, arrange one hot morning for us to witness progress on Jedda's new seaport where a dramatic skyscraper of a control tower is nearing completion. On arrival we find ourselves invited to step into an open metal basket in order to be hoisted some 250 feet into the air suspended by a single cable from the arm of a distant remote tower crane. Confidence is not increased when we discover that the Taiwanese workman who will accompany us has no means of communication with the crane's operator in his distant eyrie. Never one to decline a challenge, Duke Hussey insists we both climb in. There follows a vertiginous experience as we are hoisted into the sky and swung around the top of the tower on our frail-looking wire. I start to wonder whether the Foreign Office's risk insurance will cover this escapade, though at least it is cooler up here than on the ground. Safely returned to *terra firma* we are taken on to the pilot-training school operated by Saudia and invited to have a go at flying one of their Boeing 747 simulators. Once again Hussey does not hesitate, but finds he cannot fit his iron leg, a legacy of gallant service in the Second World War, into the captain's seat. So I take over alongside the Deputy Information Minister, Shehab Jamjoom, while Duke is relegated to the engineer's jump seat behind. The exercise is remarkably realistic as I clumsily attempt a landing at Geneva in poor visibility. All kinds of warning klaxons are mixed with cries of distress from my companions as, jarred by sickening jolts, I contrive to bring the heavy aircraft down some way short of the runway, just avoiding ditching in the lake. I think I would like a simulator for Christmas; it has certainly been a morning to remember.

The most startling visit turns out to be one by the Trade Secretary, Nicholas Ridley, a figure known for his devotion to Margaret Thatcher's brand of right-wing conservatism. When I take him and his accompanying party of senior business folk to Dammam to call on Prince Mohammed, the Governor of the oil-rich Eastern Province and a son of King Fahd, the minister is presented, as is the custom, with a handsome curved sabre. As we drive away Nicholas Ridley tells me how he looks forward to displaying his prize at home, adding the curious enquiry whether its carved handle might be ivory. With a premonition of what may be coming next, I confirm this is probably so. The minister then comes out with the confession that this is awkward as he happens, as the former Secretary of State for the Environment, to have recently piloted through Parliament a conservation bill prohibiting the import of ivory into Britain; could I possibly arrange for some merchant in the souk to provide a certificate that the handle's material is plastic? Putting my job on the line I resist the idea. But I doubt it will be dropped, and so it turns out. The party goes on the next day to Jedda where ministerial pressure is promptly brought on our luckless Consul-General to oblige.

The visit has however an even more bizarre ingredient. It happens to coincide with the momentous news of the fall of the Berlin Wall with its prospect of the early reunification of the two halves of Germany. On learning this Nicholas Ridley works himself into an hysterical state. "This is dreadful. I must telephone Margaret immediately. I can already hear the jackboots marching down Whitehall. Ambassador, you must call me a press conference right away." Steady on, I say to myself; this is unreal. I point out that there is no point in calling in journalists; given Saudi Arabia's deliberate self-isolation from the world's media plus the absence of any significant press in her Eastern Province where we find ourselves, he would collect no more than a local hack who might not even know where Berlin was. With disbelief he mercifully drops the idea. An alarmist telephone call is still made to No. 10. Nicholas Ridley's emotional anti-German article in *The Spectator* soon after his return home brings an abrupt end to his long ministerial career.

* * * * *

In the spring Grania has suddenly to go into hospital. After an uncertain initial operation she is rescued by the skilful surgery of Professor James Lawrie in Riyadh's well-equipped military hospital. The Defence Minister, Prince Sultan, keeps in touch and generously waives all the charges for her treatment. Once she is up we take ourselves off for a brief recuperation in one of the vertiginous hilltop villages in the country behind Nice, a spectacular region we had explored on breaks from Algiers. Back in Riyadh our Arabic-speaking daughter, Joanna, comes out to work as a volunteer in the regional office of UNICEF, which is headed by Sabah al-Allawi, a member of a prominent Iraqi family and no friend of its present Ba'ath regime. Dining one evening with him and his Kurdish wife we have our first experience of *manna*, a white fungus delicacy, eaten as a sweetmeat, that grows along the branches of bushes in parts of northern Iraq and is reputed to have been the source of the Old Testament account of sustenance in the wilderness.

A minor crisis blows up when our Bangladeshi butler who supervises the running of the residence is suddenly arrested on a charge of trying to sell some of our precious stock of whisky. A man of long and loyal service this is hard to credit. It turns out however to be the case; the Saudis, in what is evidently a telephone intercept, – a practice we have always suspected – have overheard him being put under pressure by one of his compatriots. He is sentenced under *shari'a* law to be lashed and detained in prison. This is most awkward as storm clouds have begun to gather and we have many visitors; impossible to go to war without a butler. My irrepressible Yemeni driver, Ali, contrives to visit Mahmoud and comes back with a colourful account of the chastisement; he has counted with relish the weals on the back of the wretched man. Something must be done. I go on bended knee to the Deputy Governor of the city, Abdullah Beleihid, to plead to have my butler back; he is a good friend and obliges, a huge relief. Mahmoud, prostrating himself with contrition, is restored to us, just in time for the far greater crisis that is about to strike.

Ominous indications have been gathering of trouble brewing in Iraq. Saddam Hussein, the country's despotic and ruthless president, is finding himself, following the collapse of his long-running and costly war with Iran, in a tight economic corner, with massive debts for his arsenal of weaponry and with a restless, million-strong army on his hands. In a desperate search for more revenue he decides to turn up the screws on his wealthy and diminutive neighbour, Kuwait, a state no longer under British protection, over which Iraq has since Ottoman times made a spurious claim to sovereignty and with which she shares a rich trans-border oilfield. A hostile propaganda and diplomatic campaign is steadily built up, aimed at securing Arab sympathy for Iraq's predicament with allegations of Kuwaiti theft of Iraq's entitlement to crude, and backed up by sinister military manoeuvres in the vicinity of their frontier. An unsubtle response by the Kuwaitis to this crude blackmail, calling for early repayment of the $12 billion loaned to Iraq for the prosecution of the war with Iran, only serves to stoke up the tyrant's sense of grievance. Attempts by the Saudis and other Gulf Arabs to placate Saddam, if need be with offers of financial help, are brushed aside as Iraq's propaganda machine broadens its appeal to public opinion with invective alleging fresh conspiracy on the part of the western powers and Israel over the ever-sensitive nerve of Palestine. The campaign comes to a climax in an ill-tempered Arab summit convened by the Iraqis in Baghdad.

Despite this menacing background the Arab states, even the increasingly wary Saudis, cannot quite bring themselves to conceive of one Arab state attacking another. The stepping up of Iraq's diplomatic and military threats is on balance seen as an elaborate exercise in sabre-rattling. Following assurances of non-aggression given by Iraq's president to both the Egyptian and the Saudi leadership, a similarly hopeful view is taken in Whitehall and in Washington. My own misgivings ebb and flow as Saddam develops his elaborate game of cat and mouse. Grania has already returned to London to start our long-anticipated spell of summer leave; I am due to follow in a few days time. Growing doubts over whether I can afford to depart are reinforced when I find all this uncertainty shared by the shrewd Prince

Khaled al-Faisal, the governor of Asir, to whom I make a brief visit amid the spectacular mountains of his province down on the borders with Yemen. Here is a very different Saudi Arabia of cultivated hillside terraces overseen by traditional stone watchtowers and where tribesmen are clad in skirts of bright cloth, their heads adorned with wreaths fashioned out of the flowers of the area which wild bees turn into a famous honey. Groups of baboons squat beside the winding roads. My return to Riyadh's hot and dusty plateau coincides with a Saudi–hosted peace encounter between Iraq and Kuwait in Jedda on the first day of August. It comes as a rude shock to us all when Iraq's attendance at this last-minute piece of diplomatic theatre turns out to be no more than a smokescreen for the invasion of Kuwait by Iraqi forces that very night. The arch-despot has deluded himself that he can get away with seizing his neighbour with impunity while a divided world looks on.

Saudi Arabia (at war)
1990-1991

La guerre est une chose beaucoup trop sérieuse pour etre laissée aux militaires

De Talleyrand (encore)

I wake early on the second of August to the dramatic news that an airborne and armoured assault on Kuwait, 400 miles of desert away to the north, is in progress. The bedroom window looks across to the Iraqi Embassy, newly-built in a severe Arabian style; its diplomatic occupants are about to receive their marching orders. Initially caught off balance, as we all are, by Iraq's act of rash aggression, Saudi Arabia's ageing leadership takes a day or two to recover; its slow response is not helped by the fact that Saddam Hussein has chosen the height of hot summer to make his move, a period when senior Saudis, and Kuwaitis too, are normally taking a prolonged break in the more tolerable climes of Europe or the United States. Once rallied however no time is lost in mounting an impressive show of political resolve to cobble together an unprecedented Arab and international coalition, involving at its height no fewer than 37 countries, to work alongside its own forces in defending the Kingdom against the likelihood of an Iraqi incursion deeper into Arabia. Eventually it will act to drive the Iraqis out of Kuwaiti territory.

The leading role is taken, alongside the Saudis, by the United States, whose land, sea and air forces in the area will top out at around a half million, followed by Britain at nearly 50,000. Other major contingents will come from France, Egypt and even Syria, sweetened with the Egyptians by Saudi financial largesse. Financial contributions come from Japan and

226

Germany while other states fill in gaps here and there. The Saudis' smaller Gulf partners, seeing themselves too under a measure of threat, play their part with bases and troops. Crucially an enfeebled Soviet Union, on whose staunch support for his belligerency Saddam is no doubt counting, turns out to have no stomach for this contest and readily sits on the sidelines, bought off with an astute Saudi loan coupled with a long-awaited diplomatic recognition. For their part the Iraqis spare no effort to conjure up support from the usual suspects among the Arab world's radical constituency, plus Hashemite Jordan's King Hussein and in Africa too, by playing on the ever-raw nerve of western domination and suggesting that a pull-out from Kuwait should be linked to an Israeli withdrawal from occupied Palestinian lands. The Cold War may be behind us, yet the crisis has rapidly put the world at odds with itself once more.

For all of us life has been turned upside down overnight and some nine months of intense activity now lie ahead. It will be a constant challenge to keep up with – or preferably to stay ahead of – what has become a fast-moving drama and even to maintain an illusion of control. All the embassy's fronts burst into life as we are submerged in political assessments and exchanges with both London and with the Saudis, as well as with our American and European partners and a Kuwaiti government that finds itself decanted into a comfortable if nervous exile in a luxury hotel down in Ta'if on the Red Sea escarpment. On top of this come the reception and accommodation of ever-growing numbers of British forces, the management of a large and uneasy civilian community, an irruption of an intrusive and demanding British media into the Kingdom's sheltered society, and of course military and official visitors in an unending stream, all culminating after five months of military stand-off and Iraqi defiance in full-scale hostilities under the threat of ballistic missile attack. Yet we find ourselves taking the strain with a will and a shared sense of commitment to the task of putting a stop to Saddam Hussein's outright aggression. It is fascinating to see how such a crisis bonds individuals together with common purpose, leavened within the embassy by present laughter and an ever-ready attempt to look on the humorous side as we struggle to keep ahead of a fast-expanding game. Bob Regan, the Ministry of Defence representative, starts up an irreverent news-sheet, *Thunderbox*. When my personal assistant takes herself off, her welcome volunteer replacement is the cool-headed Lisa Jacobs, who provides indispensable support in the months to come. Ever looking as if she has just stepped out of a bandbox, she manages to break the hearts of several officers on the headquarters staff.

* * * * *

Events start to move at a hectic pace. Forget summer leave; here is an act of piracy that has to be challenged. After a week of intense diplomatic condemnation of Iraq's action, at the United Nations in New York and across much of the Arab world, an early offer of military help from the United States and Britain to counter growing signs of a threat to the Kingdom from Iraqi forces now collecting on its border with Kuwait is accepted by the King. With due prudence he and his Foreign Minister, Prince Saud, have first gone flat out to ensure they have a majority of Arab countries onside before risking inevitable public controversy over the presence of western and infidel forces on Arabia's holy ground. Divisions among participants in a suddenly convened Arab League meeting in Cairo boil over when a Kuwaiti delegate chucks a dinner plate at the Iraqi delegation. An unsolicited offer by an as yet unknown Osama bin Laden to defend the Kingdom with the cadre he has raised of Arab *mujahideen* fighters – a *jihadist* corps that will become known, and feared, under its banner of Al Qa'eda – following their victorious campaign against Soviet forces in Afghanistan is brushed aside, a rebuff that will bring its violent backlash in later years.

In bellicose mood Mrs Thatcher loses no time in authorising the despatch of an RAF Tornado squadron to the Kingdom. Conditioned as I am by spending much of the past thirty years implementing Britain's withdrawal from direct military engagement in the Arab world this abrupt reversal of hallowed policy takes my breath away. I recover it fast enough however when we are telephoned from London that very day by a senior RAF officer with the news that the aircraft will fly out tomorrow – where are they to go, please? It will take some fast footwork to get an immediate Saudi answer on this one. Suspecting that a measure of theatre is called for, I ask the defence attaché, Peter Sincock, and his air force colleague, John Ambler, to don their most splendid gold-braided uniforms and come right away to see the commander of the Saudi Air Force, General Beheiry. We find him already run off his feet with the alert of his own force and the arrival of shoals of American warplanes. With a nice touch of humour he complains that at present his main threat comes not from the Iraqis but from a mid-air collision. Could we not delay a bit? No way – I am up against an impatient Prime Ministerial deadline from London. After we reject the offer of an out-of-the-way parking lot near the border with Yemen he suggests the airbase at Tabuk, up near the Jordan frontier. As this still makes little patrolling sense I insist on a slot alongside US and Saudi aircraft already crowded on the vast airfield at Dhahran on the Gulf coast. The good general agrees to put our case urgently to Prince Sultan who gives his prompt clearance. Phew! We are over the first hurdle.

The Tornadoes' arrival, together with the despatch of Jaguar fighter aircraft and refuelling tankers to Seeb in Oman, brings with it the rapid establishment of a headquarters team in Riyadh, to work closely with the Saudi and American military and our embassy as the Kuwait situation develops. A good Saudi friend from a leading merchant family, Teymour Ali Reza, readily offers accommodation for the Dhahran aircrews on one of his compounds. Air Vice-Marshal Sandy Wilson comes out to take command of the RAF's cooperation with the Saudi and US military and with the embassy. An easy-going personality with the benefit of having known General Beheiry in the past we quickly get on to good working terms. Indeed I find my own previous army service and three years of secondment to the Ministry of Defence gives a boost to my credibility with our military commanders over the months ahead, as well as helping to decode all that military jargon. Sandy rapidly sets about arranging for additional facilities for the RAF in neighbouring Gulf states, where other western forces are starting to compete for bases in what my crisply effective and chain-smoking American colleague in Riyadh, Chas Freeman, is calling the world's largest military theme park. A joint visit to the first RAF units at Dhahran produces a photograph in the UK press of the two of us with eyes tilted skywards in Battle of Britain pose; the bow tie I happen to be sporting provokes some sartorial correspondence in *The Times*.

It is soon apparent that the defence shield so rapidly being mounted with air patrols is thin by comparison with Iraq's well-equipped air force. Moreover problems have arisen in aligning the RAF's cautious approach to engagement with Iraqi warplanes with the more gung-ho rules adopted by the Americans. By chance we learn that the maverick Alan Clark, a favourite of Mrs Thatcher and now a minister of state for defence, is due to make an unscheduled refuelling stop in Riyadh on an RAF transport flight while returning with a party of journalists from a visit elsewhere in the Gulf. With Sandy I extract him from his plane and take a wander in the dark through rows of parked American aircraft while we put the case for reinforcement and for sorting out the engagement tangle. Predictably Alan Clark jumps at the chance to make a mark at home, and not least to get up the nose of his boss, Tom King. A second Tornado squadron soon materialises in the Kingdom; another squadron is sent to neighbouring Bahrain. Our unauthorised encounter has a curious corollary when, amid the sensation caused by Alan Clark's publication a decade later of his scurrilous and rebarbative personal diaries, I appear to be the only British diplomat about whom he has a charitable word to say; what, several colleagues have wondered, can I possibly have done to deserve his benediction? Taking a ride north one morning with Sandy Wilson in his jet up to Tabuk where RAF ground-attack Tornadoes are to be based, I am surprised to find him asking the local governor to provide hotel accommodation for the aircrews, as I know their US counterparts on other airfields are existing in huts or even tents. The RAF do seem a bit featherbedded.

Sandy Wilson's reign is not however to last. By early autumn it is becoming clear that international political pressures on Iraq to withdraw from Kuwait, accompanied by swingeing economic sanctions, are getting nowhere. Opinion within the Saudi leadership, and shared by their major western partners, is shifting towards the option of international military action, or at least the threat of such, to dislodge the occupation under a permissive United Nations franchise. As one wag puts it in the House of Commons debate on going to war, if Kuwait had grown carrots, no one would have raised a hand to help her. But there is not just oil at stake; wider considerations of international security require this act of naked aggression to be countered.

The decision brings with it the despatch of substantial army contingents to the Kingdom, principally from the United States but also from Britain and France, to join already mobilised Saudi ground forces supported by troops from Egypt and Syria. As Sandy himself concedes, ground is not won by air power. The status of the French forces is to remain something of a headache right up to the last moment as their government continues to equivocate over outright opposition to Saddam Hussein – an each-way bet, we uncharitably suspect, against the eventuality of securing from the Iraqis some $10 billion worth of debts owed for sophisticated weaponry which

France has unwisely continued to sell them despite western embargoes during the long war with Iran. At one of our regular meetings of European Union ambassadors my tiresome French colleague in Riyadh, Jacques Bernière, has the nerve to brag that there are more French troops than British in the Kingdom. "But, Jacques," says the Italian softly, "we don't know which way they are facing…"

In Britain's case the reinforcement involves a full-scale armoured brigade – "The Desert Rats" – to be based around Jubail, where the modern port not far south of the Kuwait frontier and run by our good friend, Prince Abdullah bin Faisal, offers an ideal supply base. I arrange for its local logistics to be handled by the Kanoo trading house, whose record of support for Britain's presence in the Gulf goes right back to the campaigns of the First World War. It is a pleasant surprise to see the brigade led by Patrick Cordingley, whom I last knew in Benghazi twenty-five years ago. We now find ourselves together in a different desert. The Royal Navy's "stop and search" watch in the Gulf waters is also strengthened. To our surprise an Argentinian Navy frigate turns up in the Gulf, and asks to patrol with the British flotilla rather than the Americans; another hatchet from the Falklands War, ten years earlier, is thus happily buried. The army's arrival however produces a dogfight in Whitehall over command. Sandy Wilson is plainly keen to carry on. He has the support of Air Marshal Paddy Hine, the highly effective overall commander of UK forces who has his headquarters back at High Wycombe in Buckinghamshire but is now a frequent visitor to our parish. It is not to be however. In characteristic fashion Mrs Thatcher cuts through the wrangling with her personal preference for General Peter de la Billière, whose impressive military career has been spent mainly in the shadows of Special Forces Operations including earlier fighting experience in Oman. It turns out to be an inspired choice. Peter de la Billière is throughout the months ahead to enjoy a relationship of close and confident cooperation with both of the coalition's supreme commanders, the genial Sandhurst-trained Prince Khalid bin Sultan, heading up the Saudi and other Arab forces and ever ready to welcome his visitors with a brimming cup of cappuccino, and the American General Norman Schwarzkopf who has the charge of all western contingents, a larger-than-life individual, popular with his troops but of whose notorious short fuse his senior officers stand in considerable awe. Both commanders come to set store by Peter's wise advice on both strategy and tactics, as well as on the deployment of the British contribution to the coalition's motley force. For our part we hit it off right away. I willingly find myself becoming a main source of political advice to him and his staff, headed by another able airman, Ian Macfadyen, although I gather that this unofficial role does not entirely meet with approval back in the Ministry of Defence. Meanwhile a begrudging Sandy Wilson returns home.

* * * * *

The eruption into Saudi Arabia's sheltered and ultra-conservative Islamic society of thousands of western troops with their infidel ways inevitably leads to strains. One particular shock for Saudis is the sight of gun-toting American female soldiers steering pickup trucks around a country where custom dictates that women should not drive. Fired up by the foreign presence the religious police and other zealots become more intrusive than ever. One of the American women pilots who fly the huge Galaxy transport aircraft over from the United States tells Grania how she and her female co-pilot were refused radio contact for landing by the controller in the Riyadh airbase tower until she produced a male voice to handle the talk-down procedure. Fortunately the plane's loadmaster, a non-flier, was a man. In the interests of social harmony western troops are denied access to alcohol (nor will they find any substitute antifreeze in their desert vehicles). Peter de la Billière comments that he has never known an army with so few problems of discipline. Pork too is prohibited, though it is rumoured that hogmeat is still finding its way into the rations with the carcasses described as sheep with snouts. Christian worship needs to be discreet; we decide to reclassify army chaplains euphemistically as morale officers. Entertainment for off-duty troops is also a challenge in a country where theatre acts are a rarity and live music is still regarded by many as a profanity. Even the British community's morris dancing group has to leap about in the sanctuary of expatriate compounds. Sandy Wilson cannot believe his ears when I insist that visiting entertainment must be confined to male comedians and conjurors. But in the event the magician, Paul Daniels, minus his luscious assistant Debbie, turns out to be a great success with the lads, and that old trouper, "Lance Bombardier" Harry Secombe, has them in stitches. Harry proves a highly entertaining house guest for us. He flies back to Riyadh one evening from a turn aboard a ship in the Gulf patrol with a deep gash on his forehead. As Grania mops up the damage it turns out that the helicopter taking him out to the ship had made a sudden dive to sea level when an Iraqi missile radar appeared to have locked on to it. Harry's head had come into contact with the roof. "Must have been someone who didn't like *Songs of Praise*," is his laconic comment. The Americans make do with a visit by Bob Hope, to press flesh and be full of wisecracks. Saudi sensitivities are however offended when an American unit in Dammam goes a step too far with a local production of *The Best Little Whorehouse in Texas*.

Another problem arises with our military bands. Strangely we end up with no fewer than 19 regimental bands in country, as bandsmen have a dual role as stretcher-bearers in battle and there is every expectation that, in the event of hostilities, the Iraqis may unleash their illegal arsenal of chemical and biological weapons, bringing multiple coalition casualties. Bands need somewhere to practise however. When I raise our quandary with Prince Fahd bin Abdullah in the Defence Ministry, he helpfully suggests they blow away in some remote desert corner; the bedouin herdsmen are unlikely to be fussed. With the advent of Christmas and the prospect of conflict now imminent, it seems appropriate to turn our seasonal party into a "Waterloo Ball". Peter de la Billière offers a wide choice of bands to play for us. We choose the Scots Guards, complete with chamber group as well as the dance band, all in desert fatigues with Red Cross armbands. The evening is a lively one, if tinged with poignant anticipation of tests to come. At the close I thank the bandmaster warmly and ask to make some small donation. "Tonight we would normally be playing at the Savoy," he hints. "Well, sorry about that," I say, "but you are now on more active service." Only after the cheerful bandsmen have departed do we discover they had homed in on our clandestine beer supplies.

Our large community plays its part in providing amenities as the number of British troops swells. Expatriates in Jubail set up a canteen, others offer hospitality in their homes. Grania puts together a "treats for troops" scheme to collect books and videotapes, both in country and sent out from home by friends and by charities like "Listening Books". On one occasion as she and the wife of our consul in the Eastern Province drive up to Jubail to deliver a load her companion, who is heavily pregnant, shows signs of miscarrying. Diverting smartly to a medical corps forward hospital that has conveniently been set up in a local compound, known with typical army humour as Baldrick Lines, Grania asks the guard on the gate to find a

233

gynaecologist. Taken aback, he explains that a field hospital does not normally include this speciality. Help is found however and all is well. The scheme leads on to a well-intentioned project by the *Daily Star* inviting Women's Institutes around Britain to bake "battle cakes" from a somewhat dense fruitcake recipe and send them out by post via General de la Billière. The response is such that it soon overwhelms the RAF's supply flights to the point where cakes are starting to hamper the flow of essential military kit and even munitions. My own suggestion is to use the heavy cakes as a substitute for artillery shells when battle comes.

Meanwhile Nick and Anna Cocking bring over the colonels of the three regiments in the "Desert Rats" brigade for an afternoon of croquet, a civilised break from their preparation for war up on the Kuwait border. Observing that our troop buildup includes regiments with an Irish background, my Irish colleague, a good friend, asks if I could discreetly arrange for him to visit 'his' soldiers on the Kuwait border. We gladly fly him up on the Air Corps Islander. One of them, commanding the Royal Irish Hussars, turns out to be Arthur Denaro, who had organised the SAS live-rounds training exercise with my police guards that so startled my mother back in Rio de Janeiro twenty years ago.

* * * *

The management of morale and security among the 30,000-strong British community who face the possibility of being caught up in a military conflict is by no means an easy task. Reassurance becomes a first priority for us and we lose no time in activating our well-established system whereby individuals within each group across the country are appointed to act as volunteer wardens with responsibility for relaying advice or instructions sent out from the embassy and consulates. For all their initial sense of trepidation our expatriates are taking the onset of the crisis in steady fashion and without any significant rush for the exit. In any case it being high summer many families are home on leave. Their morale is not helped however by a temptation on the part of the British media, including the BBC on whose overseas service we must depend to carry our official messages of advice, to spice up the threat and our counsel too, provoking understandable alarm among relatives back home over the community's safety. I find myself having some sharp altercations in radio interviews over the limited scale of these risks, at least while a military stand-off lasts – Angela Rippon goes so far as to accuse me of a "cavalier" attitude towards the safety of British citizens. It is however clear to us, as to the Saudis, that a mass evacuation of foreign technicians would not only have a damaging effect on Saudi public morale but would seriously inhibit the functioning of key areas of the Kingdom's infrastructure, and medical services too. A careful balance needs to be struck here. Moreover we find ourselves acting as a bellwether for other European communities. The combative Spaniard fulminates in our meetings about the gutlessness of his small "*colonia*".

It does not help when the board of British Aerospace, the largest British contractor in the Kingdom with over 4,000 employees and families and with a crucial role in support of much of Saudi Arabia's Air Force, gets cold feet and presses me to order an evacuation of all British families. I manage to resist this course and hold the line that while it makes sense for those with children to take a spell out of the area, it is for individuals and firms to make such decisions. We thus avoid a mass exodus with all its wider impact on morale within the country; by and large members of our community prove robust, even when some come under long-range missile attack at a later stage, a development which through insufficient intelligence we have presumed to be unlikely. The installation by US forces of Patriot anti-missile batteries in Riyadh and Dammam provides some comfort. It provokes another jibe too – there are two things that are working in Saudi Arabia; Patriots and expatriates.

On our frequent trips to east and west from Riyadh to keep in touch it is reassuring to find a good spirit accompanied by a rash of truculent slogans on tee-shirts, such as "These colours don't run". The Riyadh community's annual Remembrance Day concert turns into a stirring occasion as everyone launches into a mighty rendering of "Land of Hope and Glory" that would outdo the last night of the Proms. In my Christmas talks to expatriates in the three main cities I stress the crucial role that many of them will be called upon to play in the event that the Kingdom finds itself at war. A bizarre warning message put out by the Saudis on how to recognise a gas attack by seeing birds fall out of trees and cars crashing into each other is greeted with the comment that it sounds like any normal day in the Kingdom. I sometimes take the Rolls across to the Gulf coast centres; with flag flying the ageing barouche seems to help morale among the community and with visiting media too. An armoured Range Rover is in due course supplied by London. There is near disaster when it suffers a blowout at speed on the desert motorway. Mercifully our back-up car manages to block the train of heavy trucks and military transports careering along behind. It is little comfort to be told subsequently by Land Rover that the vehicle is top heavy and should not exceed fifty miles an hour, hardly a practical speed for the distances we have to travel.

Embassies elsewhere in the Gulf face a similar dilemma. As for luckless British expatriates in Kuwait they have either been taken hostage into Iraq with some of the men staked out as human shields in locations regarded as potential military targets, or have gone into local hiding with the help of Kuwait's resistance. Our ambassador, Michael Weston, and the consul, Larry Banks, have defiantly volunteered to stay on, holed up in the diplomatic sanctuary of the embassy compound where for several months they live off tinned tuna and a vegetable patch. We somehow contrive to set up a faint radio link with them. Back home our daughter Joanna goes to work for a volunteer outfit that offers reassurance by telephone to distressed relatives of those held captive by the Iraqis. On a timely visit to London the good Prince AFT calls by and offers to cover all the outfit's telephone bills. The BBC does its bit with a daily radio programme sending personal messages of comfort to those in captivity or hiding. It is not always plain sailing however. One morning comes a vinegary recorded message from a wife accusing her husband of "consoling himself in captivity", adding ominously that what is sauce for the gander is sauce for the goose! Hardly words to perk up a prisoner's morale. Simon Wilson, the Vice-Consul, installs himself complete with Union Jack and solar topee at a remote border post with Kuwait to intercept some of the Britons who are attempting a risky dash for freedom across the desert. Not all make it; one poor man, captured by Iraqi troops, is shot. I am rung one night by Prince Mohammed bin Fahd, governor of the Eastern Province, with the news that two members of our community have been found wandering among pipelines near the Kuwait frontier and carrying binoculars. Their tale that they are on a birdwatching expedition strains Saudi credulity and they have been arrested as spies. How stupid can people be? Can't they see there is a war on? To my relief the Prince agrees to release them with a sharp admonishment.

With the New Year bringing a growing prospect of a battle in Kuwait and of Iraqi retaliation against the Kingdom (jokers are saying that Vera Lynn has been overheard gargling), we step up advice to send families out of possible danger while encouraging those with jobs to stay at their posts. Our plans for possible evacuation by road to centres more distant from a conflict are taking shape though numbers are going to present a challenge. The embassy has been re-equipped with a state-of-the-art communications system with the Foreign Office; techniques have come a long way since those nights of laborious arithmetical decryption back in Kuwait thirty years ago. For those who stay precautions now have to be put in hand against possible gas attack. Air-raid sirens are suddenly tested as we stick anti-blast tape over our windows and seal off "safe havens" in our homes. It brings back childhood recollections of the 1940s blitz. All of us in the embassy have to be trained in the donning of cumbersome anti-chemical warfare suits. A large consignment of gas masks is sent out from London to be distributed to members of the community in Riyadh and vulnerable centres on the Gulf. Each of the 10,000 masks we eventually issue has to be individually fitted, a marathon task made no easier when a number of British wives and daughters in Saudi families turns up, all shrouded in black *abayas*. Their males forbid the two army corporals, assigned to do the fitting, to touch their women. There is much giggling as Grania and other embassy ladies take over the delicate job. The Saudis too have started to issue gas masks; it is hoped that the long and hairy beards worn by zealots will serve as a filter. There is a report that the busy songbird market down in the souk has run out of canaries.

* * * * *

King Fahd and his ministers are showing an unflagging and single-minded determination in their endeavour to sustain the will of the Arab community, and of the world at large, to resist Iraq's act of naked piracy. A nation cushioned in prosperity and piety now finds itself at the core of a major storm, while, for all our direct engagement in the crisis, we outside contributors are satellites around the Kingdom's central pinion. A particular bitterness is manifested towards King Hussein of Jordan, and Yemen too for not coming off the fence over Iraqi aggression; the Al Saud harbour more than a suspicion that this equivocation is coloured by hopes of recovering lost territories along the Red Sea coast should Iraq go on to gain the upper hand over the Kingdom. In the case of Yemen, Saudi retaliation takes the form of summary expulsion of thousands of Yemeni workers, a move that produces a critical bread shortage when it emerges that many bakeries are run by Yemenis. Mercifully my excellent driver, Ali, is spared; I simply could not get by without him. At the same time Kuwaitis have been flooding in their thousands into the Kingdom seeking refuge; they find themselves hospitably housed in empty apartment buildings and even in five-star hotels which their unruly children soon turn into disaster zones.

The crisis has also unleashed calls for domestic reform, culminating in a bold, if premature, protest in Riyadh when a group of women take over the wheels of their cars and attempt to assert their right to drive. At the same time a powerful wave of opposition has arisen among religious conservatives, both in the Kingdom and beyond, to the idea of an association with the forces of infidel states, a heresy constantly exploited by Iraq's nimble propaganda machine. With opinion now shifting towards military action, the King finds himself obliged to spend as much time on retaining the support of his country's influential clerical establishment, occasionally with more than a grain of theological sophistry, as on shoring up, financially if need be, the political resolve of other key states, notably the Soviet Union, and even certain "Eurowimps". It is a help that the Iranians, having their own bones to pick with Iraq, are so far staying on the sidelines.

I find myself a constant visitor in the Foreign Ministry's labyrinth as we strive to sustain the basic trust between us that, for all our cultural differences, the crisis demands. As the impact of our military presence builds up one has constantly to keep half an eye on an Islamic dimension, dating back to AD 622 – incongruous perhaps but essential. A priority task is the negotiation of an agreement with the Saudis to protect the legal status of our troops in the Kingdom. With his fluent Arabic Derek Plumbly turns out to be tailor-made for this sensitive role. Visits to talk with the King and his ministers by Douglas Hurd and Tom King, as well as by senior military figures, play an important part in sustaining trust. We also get visits by Energy Secretary John Wakeham to discuss the Saudis' welcome steps to calm a nervous oil market, and Archie Hamilton, the Armed Forces Minister, whom I press to get some order into our military's chaotic local expenditure, if we are to qualify for the generous readiness of the Saudis to refund costs. On one of Tom King's visits I join him to see 7 Brigade rehearsing an armoured advance across the desert in their Chieftain tanks. It feels strangely familiar to be back in the commander's turret of a tank on the move, nearly forty years after engaging in similar manoeuvres over north Germany's Lüneburg Heath. Armoured warfare has hardly changed. At the Jubail supply base we get stuck in the lift of the port control tower and have to be hauled out manually – plainly an Iraqi gremlin at work.

With Douglas Hurd I fly down to Ta'if to find Kuwait's dejected ruling family perched in the isolated comfort of a Sheraton Hotel where we press a reluctant Sheikh Jaber al-Sabah to get out and tell the world. Meanwhile in Britain the summary dislodging by the Conservative Party of the King's trusted ally, Margaret Thatcher, in November comes as a rude shock to the Saudis. We happen to be back in London at this moment to attend a very special investiture by the Queen, and I use the opportunity to secure a personal letter from the Iron Lady's successor, John Major, assuring the King of his government's continuing commitment to the cause. A couple of days in the peace of the South Downs do much to refresh us. When I see King Fahd on my return he appears reassured, though time will tell. I have a job however to explain to a sceptical Crown Prince Abdullah how it is that under our vaunted democratic system a leader can be replaced without a public vote of endorsement; he has a point.

* * * * *

At very short notice comes news from the Foreign Office that the Prince and Princess of Wales propose to come out three days before Christmas to meet the troops. A welcome idea on the whole, but one which will test Saudi protocol, already under strain from an avalanche of coalition visitors. The presence of Prince Charles in the theatre of battle can certainly be turned to advantage, both as a morale booster for troops and for our community, and as a show of solidarity with the Saudis. But I have serious reservations about Princess Diana's coming with him. For one thing local protocol will require the laying on of a separate programme for her. More important however is the likelihood that, given her celebrity status, the British media here will go overboard with her glamorous feminine presence among active service formations in the desert, further complicating the efforts of the Saudi authorities to dampen conservative sentiment, already hypersensitive over the alliance with infidel forces. Moreover Iraq's agile propaganda machine will not hesitate to exploit the issue.

When I put these points to Peter de la Billière, and to Paddy Hine who happens to be on a visit, I find they have their own practical reservations on the security front. We agree to resist a visit by the Princess while welcoming that of the Prince of Wales. This is eventually accepted in London, but, as I soon gather on the grapevine, only after some sharp correspondence from one corner of St James' Palace. The refusal does not go down at all well with the Princess, who has apparently set her heart on coming out and finds herself sent off instead to Germany on a worthy errand to cheer up the families of RAF squadrons now in the Gulf. I suspect I have burnt my boats with her and so am little surprised to receive a cold shoulder when we meet in due course at the victory parade in the City of London. Only some while later does it emerge that among the officers present in the Kingdom at the time is one Captain James Hewitt of the Scots Guards. I shall have another encounter with the Princess's self-regard a few years later when she puts herself at odds with the Red Cross over landmine victims in Bosnia.

For its part the visit of the Prince of Wales is a boost for morale all round. When Peter and I fly early to Jubail to meet the Prince's aircraft we are greeted by the dramatic sight of pack-laden soldiers of 4 Brigade silhouetted in the first light of dawn as they disembark from trooping flights. Prince Mohammed, the governor in the Eastern Province, has also come early to greet Prince Charles with a cardomum-laced cup of Arabian coffee. We go on to a briefing with General Rupert Smith, who has taken command of the newly formed British division. Visits by the Prince to 7 Brigade are followed by a night on patrol with the Navy, a call on the RAF base in Dhahran, and then on to Riyadh to see the British headquarters and the coalition's air operations centre, a crowded tent encompassing a forest of dim computer screens monitored by a gallimaufry of radar specialists – Saudi, American, British, French and Canadian. As one US marine puts it, "Last month we had a visit from President Bush, but now we've got us a real VIP." The Saudis too pull out the stops. Talks with Crown Prince Abdullah are followed by a handsome banquet to which leading figures among our community are invited. A wink is also tipped to me that Prince Charles considers our decision over the Princess' presence to have been the right one.

✳ ✳ ✳ ✳

The New Year brings John Major out on an early visit to make his number with the King as well as to see our forces on the ground and to connect with Kuwait's leaders in exile. His evident concern to achieve maximum international support in the event of hostilities including the formal backing of the United Nations Security Council is in contrast to his predecessor's inclination to ride roughshod over such formalities, and strikes the right note with the Saudis; it is a relief to find No. 10 in step at last with the Foreign Office's more measured approach. Careful thought is also put into the sincere and genuine, yet characteristically modest, message of support he brings from home to the troops with whom he mixes; a contrast to the histrionics in which his predecessor would have indulged. It goes down well in a round of visits we make by helicopter to 4 Armoured Brigade, newly arrived from Germany, in their sand-dune camp near the Kuwait frontier, and to oil-streaked REME fitters in a busy tank workshop in Jubail. At sea the Navy put on an impressive review of their by now substantial Gulf flotilla, complemented by a brace of Australian Navy frigates, while airmen on the RAF base in Dhahran cheer him loud amid banners calling for Kate Adie, the BBC's veteran war correspondent. Spirits are high on the eve of battle. Up on the border I run into Adrian Pollard, our former chaplain in Algiers and now in the army, ministering to the Royal Fusiliers. We get him down to Riyadh for a break and to celebrate a eucharist for our Friday churchgoers.

* * * * *

January sees a tense mood as everyone holds their breath to see if Saddam Hussein will heed the deadline of 15 January, set by the United Nations Security Council for Iraq's withdrawal from Kuwait. The stream of visitors from London fills the house – Foreign Office, parliamentarians, military brass and even some think-tank wallahs – all taking the chance to check things out on the ground before civil flights cease, and calling for careful briefing and support from the embassy. Gerald Kaufman, the shadow foreign secretary and whom we last entertained in Rio days, gives a helpful assurance to Prince Saud of the Labour Opposition's support. One fear we all share is that Iraq will go for a partial withdrawal, holding on to Kuwait's northern oilfield while affording a pretext for the more lukewarm Arab participants to pull out of the coalition. In the event her intransigent and pugnacious ruler ignores this option. The die is effectively cast for war when his Foreign Minister, Tariq Aziz, comes out with a summary refusal to consider withdrawal at a crucial last-ditch meeting in Geneva with the American Secretary of State, James Baker, adding a threat to extend the conflict to Israel in another crude bid to enlist Arab support. Grania and I join with Saudi friends that fateful evening to witness on television Iraq's defiant response; it is a sombre moment, yet one now reinforced by a sense of shared commitment. As a Saudi officer wryly puts it, "We Arabs have a way of turning defeat into a virtue." A riddle starts to go the rounds – what did Saddam Hussein and his father have in common? Answer – neither knew when to withdraw…

The days now leading up to the deadline see the Saudi leadership putting prodigious effort into stemming an outbreak of cold feet and attempts at diplomatic mediation on the part of certain coalition partners as well as the Russians, the United Nations Secretary-General, and even certain appeasing British politicians too. I find myself in touch with Prince Saud and his officials on a daily basis, particularly over steps to thin out what remains of the British community without provoking a stampede. It is a relief to find our expatriates holding their nerve well; the consular and military staff devote much time to keeping in touch with up-to-date reassurance. We are still not being helped however by the BBC editors' incorrigible temptation to embroider our soothing words of broadcast advice on what precautions to take, nor by a premature French instruction to their community to leave. For their part the Americans are still hesitating to issue gas masks lest it induce panic. At the same time our plans are being laid with the Foreign Office for a full-scale evacuation should the possible eventuality of Iraqi attack with long-range missiles armed with chemical or biological warheads materialise.

Prince Saud does have one surprise up his sleeve when I get an urgent call one afternoon to the Foreign Ministry. While waiting there with Charles Hollis of our political section the chief of protocol suddenly brings in a devout-looking individual, clad in a white Arab robe and sporting a wispy beard, who he claims would be interested to meet me. While this gaunt figure starts to explain that he is on a visit from London to both Baghdad and to Riyadh on behalf of his Muslim community, I fumble to discover who he could be. Enlightenment comes in the form of a stage whisper from Charles; "It's Cat Stevens, ambassador." Well! What incongruous circumstances in which to meet one of our family's musical heroes, now a convert taking the name of Yusuf Islam, and in Saudi Arabia on an earnest mission to form a view on the theological legitimacy of a military alliance between Muslim forces and those of Britain and other infidel states. We are back to AD 622 again. Drawing on my all-too-slender familiarity with

Islamic history, I remind him of a battle at Badr, near Medina, when the Prophet Muhammad is reputed to have sought an alliance with a local Jewish tribe to defend his followers based in the city against a pagan force sent from Mecca; surely our alliance today faces a similar challenge to defend Kuwait. A touch of casuistry here perhaps, but the point appears to be taken.

* * * * *

We are also facing a vexing issue of access for a growing press contingent. There have been differences for some weeks with the Saudis over the presence of the British media. Press from all around the world are now gathering in strength in anticipation of a contest. I experience their voracious appetite for news at first hand when on a visit to Dammam the governor hands over two British technicians who have managed with a French colleague to make a bold break for freedom by cover of night in a small motorboat from where they were being held captive at a port construction site in Iraq, eventually making it through mined waters to a landfall just inside Saudi territory. At a press conference we lay on for the weary pair to tell their story to the crowds of journalists, the interrogation proves overwhelming. Still their drama is grist to our mill, and the fugitives are delighted to find themselves receiving a generous financial bounty from the Saudis as a reward for having escaped.

Long-standing Saudi prejudice over what they see as a distorted and often salacious approach towards the Kingdom by our media has however resulted in British journalists coming up against restrictions on visas by the Saudi Embassy in London, which is also alleging a pro-Iraqi bias in the reports on the BBC's influential Arabic Service. The problem has been eased through the intervention of one of the information ministers in Riyadh, Shehab Jamjoom, and also by the willingness of the Kingdom's ambassador in neighbouring Bahrain, Ghazi al-Gosaibi, later to be a very effective ambassador in London, to authorise entry visas. A BBC Panorama programme however on preparations for hostilities, which looks like containing material deliberately unflattering to Saudi culture, has not helped the image and London is becoming tetchy. Somehow I contrive with Prince Saud's help, and even a direct approach to the King, to find a way round the obstacles just in time for war. With only days to go before the ultimatum expires Prince AFT invites a large group of us to a *meshwi* out at his desert

243

camp where we partake of the delicious meat of the black-haired Nejdi sheep that form the staple of the bedouin's flocks. It is a cold winter night, near to freezing, and the sky is crystal clear. Soon it will be filled from the north with dust and the fiery tails of explosive missiles together with the dense smoke of oilfield fires as we face what Iraq's posturing ruler terms "the mother of all battles".

* * * * *

Peter de la Billière comes round on the evening of 16 January to let us know that following the expiry of the United Nations ultimatum the first wave of the coalition's air bombardment of military and infrastructure targets in Iraq and Kuwait will go in at first light: a massive armada of some 2,000 aircraft will be involved. We narrowly avert an awkward diplomatic hitch when a last-minute call from the Foreign Office warns us they have somehow overlooked the need to issue the formal Declaration of War which is a prerequisite to obtaining Saudi consent to our forces launching an attack from Saudi territory as required under our agreement – a legal technicality perhaps but an important one. Permission is now required that very night. With the help of his superb Arabic Derek Plumbly and I burn midnight oil to concoct a form of declaration in longhand for King Fahd, who, thanks to his preference for nocturnal lucubration, gives his assent just in time. Three a.m. brings a din over Riyadh as a succession of giant American B52 bombers and aerial tankers takes off for the north. Saudi and RAF Tornadoes are setting out from other bases on the same mission. For me there is a sense of relief that our months of phoney war are at an end and that action is at last in hand to reverse Saddam's act of international piracy and the brutality it is inflicting on the luckless Kuwaitis. Ian Macfadyen galvanises his morning briefing down at the British headquarters with Shakespeare's stirring lines by Henry V before Agincourt.

Iraq's retaliation is not slow in coming, taking the form the next night of a Scud ballistic missile aimed not at Saudi Arabia but at Israel in a high-stakes strategy on the part of Saddam Hussein to divide the Arab from the western elements in the coalition by provoking an Israeli counter-attack on Iraq. It takes heavy pressure by the Americans and the promise of a Patriot anti-missile defence around Tel Aviv, as well as dramatic sorties by US and British Special Forces deep into the Iraqi desert to seek out the elusive missile launchers, before Israel's right-wing government is persuaded to turn the other cheek. The second night brings the first salvo of Scuds on the towns of Dhahran, Dammam and Al Khobar on the Gulf coast. In Riyadh we have our baptism a night later when six missiles approaching the city are met by a morale-boosting, if only partially successful, barrage of fireworks from the Patriot batteries, at a sensational cost so we reckon of some $25 million. As the wags put it, once a Patriot has fired its missiles it becomes an expatriate. We all get our first taste of air-raid alarms; there will be plenty more to come over the next few weeks. Such is the speed of these Soviet-supplied rockets that we get only a couple of minutes warning before they arrive. The accuracy of the mathematical calculations made by the Iraqi technicians, who have succeeded in extending the range of these Russian weapons of mass terror by several hundred miles, is truly impressive. There is also the danger that, despite warnings given by James Baker at the Geneva meeting of serious retribution in the event of such material being used, the missiles may be carrying chemical or biological warheads which we know Iraq has been developing. So we take rapid shelter in the safe areas of homes and offices, while sharing muffled and nervous jokes through our gas masks. A walk across the embassy compound involves climbing laboriously into the all-enveloping and stifling chemical-weapons suit, though the temptation is to make a dash for it. The all-clear has to wait until a specialised unit, provided by the Czech army, has had the chance to test the air in the area of impact, a tedious but necessary process.

We keep an emergency telephone line open round the clock in the embassy to respond to calls from worried members of the community. The watch is shared by staff and those of our wives who are staying on. The morning after the first raid on Riyadh I am asked by the BBC's World Service for a message of advice to a jittery community. I suggest that everyone carries on as normally as possible while staying tuned to the radio broadcasts and generally "keeping your heads down". In the early hours of the following night, when Grania happens to be on duty on our "hot line", a call comes from a member of the community with a strong Indian accent who explains in worried tones that he and his family have since morning followed to the letter the ambassador's instruction to keep heads down. They are starting to get headaches however; is it now alright to "straighten up"? Grania gently assures him that this is quite in order. Later that night another call comes from a woman who says she can manage her gas mask but can't get her cat into her handbag. Another caller wants to know what to do with her parrot during a raid; all very human, and very British too.

The alarms now occur every four or five nights. The wardens are doing a great job in keeping what is left of our still large community calm. All civil flights to the Kingdom are suspended but the military manage to squeeze a small number who now want to get out onto returning trooping flights. It is a comfort to all when, to their credit, British Airways agree to open a special schedule out of danger's way into Jedda and also lower down the Gulf. The brunt of the Scud raids is being felt by expatriates in Dhahran and Al Khobar where a large number of them are employed in crucial roles by Aramco, the huge national oil enterprise, and also by British Aerospace in support of the Saudi Tornado force. David Lloyd and his small consular staff are having a tough time of it; the ever-resourceful Chris Wilton, who in more normal times heads our trade promotion work, goes down from Riyadh to support them. Grania and I take the desert road, now crowded with American military convoys, across to the Gulf coast to meet the community, including a visit to the British School that has stoutly contrived to stay open. We also have a chance to see off RAF Tornadoes from Dhahran's crowded airbase on their early morning patrol in Kuwait's skies. The middle of one lively Scud raid on Riyadh sees the arrival of a Royal Military Police team, sent out to protect our embassy against terrorist attack. The five-man party, led by Staff Sergeant Steve Brumpton, settles quickly into our house; they become firm friends as we spend a large part of the next six weeks in their vigilant company. In fact the only action they are to see is when one night one of the team obligingly shoots a tomcat that has been paying unwelcome attentions to a stray moggy, Scud, that has adopted us. The gunshot involves some explaining to the Diplomatic Quarter's sceptical police patrol.

* * * * *

The opening of the military campaign brings no let-up in the pressure of work; very much the contrary as we are now fully taken up with community and media matters, as well as keeping abreast of the conflict and setting plans with the Saudis and with London for the post-war security scene and for participation in the reconstruction of Kuwait. The interrupted nights do not help, compounded by Grania and I contracting a bout of pneumonia induced by the air-conditioning system in our safe room having been sealed off against a gas attack. An Irish doctor who is seeing out the war keeps us on our feet. Our own spirits are being bolstered by supportive messages from family and friends; one that particularly touches me comes out of the blue from Jack Turner, the sergeant in my tank troop during National Service nigh forty years ago; brought up in a Durham mining village with the evocative name of Pity Me, he joined the army rather than follow his family down the pit.

The large press contingent is becoming restless in its search for stories; the advent for the first time in war of instant telecommunications back to their journals and stations means that filtering measures employed in previous conflicts are no longer practicable. For the most part their reporting is supportive and allays Saudi misgivings, though a couple of London dailies, *The Independent* and, more surprising, *The Times*, are unable to resist negative comment on Saudi ways and on the performance of British forces too. We decide to go for the alternative course of maximum briefing material, no matter how trivial, in order to keep the editors' appetites fed. It seems to work. Prompted by a feisty Kuwaiti lady doctor, Fawzia McKinnon, and with our encouragement, a still shocked Kuwait leadership has been prevailed upon to set up its own media outfit. Another Kuwaiti, Ma'an Sanea, who runs a major business in the Kingdom, has succeeded in smuggling across the Kuwaiti border a copy of the nation's census, a crucial record which the Iraqis have sought to destroy. The main coalition commanders, led by the combative Norman Schwarzkopf with his homespun references to guys in white hats versus guys in black hats, give a briefing each evening under the arc lamps of the press centre in a downtown Riyadh hotel.

Back home Tom King is getting a bit edgy that we are stealing the media limelight, but there it is. We get a warning from the Foreign Office to keep an eye on a visit by Andrew Neil, the unpredictable editor of *The Sunday Times*; so he is diverted out of harm's way onto a day-long maritime patrol from Oman, far to the south, in an RAF Nimrod. I hold sessions with British journalists on the political background in the Kingdom as well as interviews with Saudi newspapers and TV. The score of Tom Lehrer's old ditty on the "Mushroom-Coloured Cloud" sits open on the grand piano in the house and catches the attention of the *Daily Express* correspondent. His light-hearted piece is repeated in an Australian paper, where it is seen by

Grania's sister Deirdre. The BBC's Kate Adie, shortly to be "embedded" with a British unit in the ground attack, wants to meet some Saudi ladies, so Grania gathers a group of friends; Kate plays the part to perfection by exchanging her battle fatigues for twinset and pearls.

As the air campaign develops, the resolve of the Saudi leadership to see Iraq out of Kuwait remains solid, bolstered by reports of brutal treatment of Kuwaiti citizens and by the parading on television of British and other captured aircrews who have clearly suffered maltreatment, in flagrant breach of the established rules of war. There is also impatience to get the job done before the fasting month of Ramadhan, now approaching, takes the edge off the appetites of the alliance's Muslim contingents. Public indignation is reinforced when an Iraqi force crosses the Kingdom's frontier in an ill-judged sally to capture the oil terminal of Al Khafji and is promptly driven back in a Saudi counter-attack. My regular contacts with Prince Saud include a bizarre moment when, during a call to discuss our diplomatic efforts to dissuade the Israelis from a disruptive retaliation to continuing Iraqi Scud attacks including false claims of permission to overfly the Kingdom, he seeks a quick word by telephone with Secretary Baker in Washington. It being after midnight there the call is taken by a duty officer who starts by asking the Prince who he is and to spell his name. Patiently Prince Saud complies while the letters are laboriously taken down. After a pause come the words "Well, he's not here," and the line goes dead. We exchange a wry look; I must warn Chas Freeman that the State Department needs to tighten up its out-of-hours service, particularly with a war on.

* * * * *

With the approach of a ground offensive to apply a *coup de grâce* to Iraq's eviction, we move into high diplomatic gear over the future of Iraq and of security within the Gulf's cockpit. One wild card here is revolutionary Iran who is so far keeping out of things but is in due course to play a destabilising role through support for Iraq's renascent Shi'a population. Saudi support has been invaluable in helping us towards an overdue restoration of diplomatic relations with Iran's clerical government, ever obsessed by Britain's faded imperial legacy. It is clear to us all however that if the region's tensions are to abate, there needs to be a fresh initiative to make progress towards a settlement over Palestine, particularly as the Palestinian leader,

Yasser Arafat, has put himself badly offside with declarations of support for Saddam Hussein's propaganda tactic of linking his occupation of Kuwait with Israel's presence in the West Bank and Gaza.

There is also political pressure at home for a land attack to go right through to the gates of Baghdad. To us on the ground there are strong reasons, historical as much as current, for resisting this course. Not only would it exceed the limited mandate achieved in the Security Council for action to liberate Kuwait; it would alienate Arab opinion, including the Saudis, drag us in partnership with the Americans into the morass of Iraq's intercommunal politics with little prospect of an easy exit, and could even lead to a break-up of that artificial state. Anyway there seems a fair chance that a disillusioned Iraqi army and people will themselves put an end to a defeated regime. All this forms a major ingredient in talks with Saudi and Kuwaiti leaders for which Douglas Hurd flies out in mid-February. The visit coincides with the presence of the US Defence Secretary, Dick Cheney, and Chief of Staff, General Colin Powell. A Scud strike that night on Riyadh's palatial government guest house would have achieved quite a coup for Saddam. The skies are calm however.

I find myself sought out by one of Arafat's lieutenants, Hani al-Hassan, a heavyweight figure who has come to Riyadh on a mission to retain Saudi support for the Palestine Liberation Organisation. He proves to be an interesting source of intelligence on the strains the crisis is provoking among the Palestinian leadership and the emergence of a rival and more radical faction calling itself Hamas. On one of his evening visits to the house we are interrupted by Scud alarms, obliging the two of us to retire to the sealed protection of our bedroom, where I present him with a smart Avon gas mask and we carry on our confidential talk in muffled tones while Grania finds herself turned unchivalrously into the corridor.

People are starting to become accustomed to the Scud bombardments. There are some noisy nights when the occasional explosion of a Scud warhead is offset by the more welcome din of the discharge of anti-missile rockets from nearby Patriot batteries. Disturbed in the small hours Grania takes herself off to her studio room to express in paint a wrathful crimson image of destruction. Mercifully however the missiles are doing little damage; one succeeds in striking the local offices of the British Sun Life Insurance Company. There is much ribbing of the manager when it turns out that they had neglected to insure their building. Another weapon destroys a branch of the Ministry of the Interior in which all the records of traffic offences are stored, much to the satisfaction of Saudi motorists. We find we have a private early-warning system when we get an urgent telephone call from our daughter, Emma, in London telling us to take shelter as a Scud is on its way. She has just heard it on the BBC news. Her timely call anticipates the local air-raid sirens by about a minute. In our dining room one morning Grania finds herself showered with ceiling panels as she prepares for a dinner party; they must have been dislodged by a blast from a missile that landed in the vicinity of the Sheraton Hotel about a mile away the night before. During one raid our cook, Millen, resists taking refuge in his safe room as he does not want the cake he is baking to spoil – first things first. An elderly aunt rings from rural Ireland while I happen to be wearing my gas mask, and complains she cannot make out a word I say.

The fiery trails of the Scuds and the flashes of the Patriot counter-attacks do however make for a splendid pyrotechnics display. With Mark Scrace-Dickens, who is heading up British cloak-and-dagger operations behind the lines in Kuwait and has based himself with us, we sometimes watch the show, comforting glass of cognac in hand. Some bold journalists take their chances from the vantage of rooftops. Our colleagues in the consulate in Al Khobar on the Gulf coast take the worst of the onslaught and pass some uncomfortable nights. One of Mark's undercover operations involves a radio eavesdropping operation out of a villa there with occasional clandestine forays deep behind Iraqi lines. It is manned by a most unlikely pair; the leader, who describes himself as a restorer of antique furniture, makes a hobby of collecting Victorian propelling pencils while his loyal acolyte, a Welshman inevitably known as Taff, rarely takes his headphones off. They are the very stuff of a James Bond adventure.

The onset of the ground campaign brings with it a real possibility of Iraqi use of chemical weapons on the battlefield. The Ministry of Defence in London reacts with a request to several European countries to supply medical teams. One country to respond is Sweden with the despatch of a field hospital. For the Swedish military this constitutes a significant break with their history of neutrality as it is the first occasion when a Swedish unit has operated in a war zone since Napoleon's defeat at the Battle of Leipzig in 1813. Our Swedish colleague, Lennart Alvin, hosts an enjoyable dinner to mark the event, with speeches and a sword that belonged to Sweden's ruler in that era, Marshal Bernadotte. A field hospital of the Territorial Army arrives from Scotland and establishes itself in an empty terminal at Riyadh airport. The arrival turns out to be a lively one as it coincides with a Scud raid which obliges them all to take cover. When Grania and I go out next morning to meet them we find some of the nurses a bit shaken by the Iraqis' rough welcome. One of the medical orderlies, busy setting up beds, tells me he is a driver on London's District Underground line. He had got the call-up at Earls Court station and had left his train right away. It may well still be waiting at the platform....

* * * * *

The air bombardment with its newly developed "smart" weapons is taking its toll of Iraq's installations and military formations. A dramatic report by the BBC's John Simpson of how he watched from his window in Baghdad's Al Rashid Hotel a remotely controlled Cruise missile fly along the street outside and turn the corner en route to its target brings home how technology is changing the nature of warfare. One UK paper has an amusing cartoon showing a Cruise hovering motionless above a Baghdad street while it waits for the traffic light to go green. Air Marshal Bill Wratten, the RAF's commander, has a tussle to get agreement from the pundits in London to switch his Tornadoes from low-level attacks, in which they are taking losses from Iraq's air defences, to precision bombing from higher altitude –a tactic which turns out to be well justified. His transport wing now includes a welcome detachment from the New Zealand Air Force.

The effective air campaign prompts a desperate Saddam Hussein to resort to environmental warfare, starting with the release into the shallow waters of the northern Gulf of millions of barrels of crude oil from Kuwaiti terminals. There is a real worry that the slick will drift south to affect the desalination plants near Jubail from which sweet water is piped all the way to Riyadh. Our taps start to run brackish as supply is switched as a precaution to aquifers deep under the desert. There is much concern too over the damage the oil will do to the Gulf's rare wildlife, such as turtles, cormorants, mangrove swamps and even the elusive dugong. An offer by Prince AFT to set up a rescue centre in Jubail is seized upon and a team of volunteer "bird cleaners" is formed by local expatriates. It appears that the only suitable agent for rinsing off oil from feathers is Fairy Liquid, so the RAF oblige by flying out large quantities, an untypical wartime cargo. An appeal mounted in the UK by the Royal Society for the Protection of Birds quickly collects a formidable sum to cover the rescue work – ironically rather more than is raised by a separate official appeal for funds to compensate Gulf fisherfolk who stand to lose their livelihood. The vandalism stakes are raised further when the Iraqis set fire to the oil wells themselves. Despite the five hundred miles separating us our skies in Riyadh become darkened by a grey miasma and oily smears start to stain outer walls, all adding to a growing impatience to get on with the campaign's final stage, Iraq's physical expulsion from Kuwait.

The ever-sensitive trust between the Kingdom and its main coalition partners takes another knock at this point however when the Soviet regime, now in a terminal decline, makes a last-ditch attempt to assert itself – no doubt in a forlorn hope of recovering some of the massive debt owed by Iraq for military equipment – with the proposal of a face-saving formula for Iraq's withdrawal. We hasten to reassure the Saudis that Iraq's removal must be unconditional. In the event the decision to go ahead with the attack is made easier when Saddam Hussein predictably prevaricates with his own preconditions. Even the French have at last come off the fence and belatedly committed their ground forces to the assault. Their equivocation has already prompted a sorely tried General Schwarzkopf to remonstrate that "going to war with the French is like going duck shooting with an accordion".

* * * * *

On 24 February the coalition's massive armoured force finally breaks through the Iraqi minefields into Kuwait, following a successful strategy of deception over the main point of advance. The British division's advance is preceded by what is said to be the heaviest artillery barrage since El Alamein in 1942. Saddam Hussein's riposte to the invasion takes the form of the greatest volley of Scud missiles yet. One missile strikes a US army barracks in Al Khobar with some loss of life. A British army nurse nearby finds herself pushed to the ground by a passing Saudi to escape the blast; her nerves are however calmed to hear him say imperturbably, "Hullo. I do like Victorian architecture. Do you know Harrogate?" The tanks roll forward at an unexpected pace as demoralised Iraqi units, put at around half a million strong, show little resistance. Only the crack Republican Guard tries to put up a fight. One unit even surrenders to a surprised group of journalists. By design Saudi forces are first into Kuwait City where they receive an emotional welcome. They are accompanied by Sandy Gall of ITN carrying his own dish aerial for instant TV communication to the London news studio; technology has certainly come a long way. The main sweep by American, British and French units to the north of the city and across the Iraqi frontier in order to cut off the line of retreat is swiftly completed in only four days, and with few casualties. It catches Grania and me down in Jedda on a visit to see how our community are taking the strain. Our return flight on Peter de la Billière's jet is almost scuppered when Sergeant Worrell of the protection team, who has come with us, is told to put his briefcase through the X-ray machine. "I can't, sir," comes his urgent whisper and I remember that he is in fact holding a James Bond type case whereby at a press of a button on the handle the casing falls away to reveal a loaded sub-machine gun. Fortunately a quiet word with the obliging Saudi policeman does the trick.

We return to the surprising news that President Bush, concerned at the likely negative effect on public opinion of news pictures of a routed Iraqi army, laden with booty, becoming the targets of a "turkey shoot" by coalition pilots as it attempts to flee northwards out of a pillaged Kuwait City, has ordered the suspension of hostilities at 8 a.m. next morning. The decision is not entirely welcome to the military as the cordon intended to prevent the escape of Iraqi units across the Euphrates River is not yet complete. Confusion over whether the order involves local time or Washington time eight hours later, another instance of the "fog of war", does not help, and permits elements of the Republican Guard to elude the net. Still it is a relief to us all to have secured Iraq's expulsion from Kuwait; as one cynic puts it, we have at least "kept Kuwait safe for feudalism". Michael Weston reaches us from England early next day, just in time to fly on to Kuwait, along with his US and French colleagues, to mark a prompt reopening of our battered embassy. Grania sends him on his way with copious rations to keep him going. Kuwait's refugee leadership however shows less keenness to make its return.

* * * * *

The sudden end to hostilities means a fresh burst of diplomatic activity. There are urgent arrangements to be made for a formal ceasefire as well as for international agreement through the United Nations on the political and economic conditions to be applied to Iraq to prevent any further aggression and for the reconstruction of a sabotaged Kuwait. At the same time we are inundated in Riyadh with another wave of visitors – ministers, politicians, military figures and businessfolk – all coming to see the upshot for themselves and to discuss ideas for a future relationship with the Kingdom and with Kuwait too. For all of us in the embassy a real sense of fatigue has to be put aside.

The armistice meeting with the Iraqi military, set up in haste and without clear objectives by the Americans in a tent on a desert airstrip at Safwan in southern Iraq, turns however into a mishandled affair. Not only does the location turn out to be still in the hands of a Republican Guard unit which has to be chased off the ground; significant tricks are missed when the Iraqis turn up with a second-eleven team, and then get away with permission to fly helicopters over their whole national territory, subsequently using them to suppress a civilian rising among the Shi'a community in the south which looks at one time like toppling Saddam's wounded regime. As Norman Schwarzkopf puts it later, "We were suckered." Peter de la Billière finds himself cast as a mere observer, though we do manage to secure the immediate release of captured RAF and Special Forces personnel. One airman, dazed on emerging from an abusive confinement, is unsettled to find himself handed over in a Baghdad hotel to an attractive young woman from the International Red Cross. "Who will protect us?" he asks. "This is our protection," she replies, pointing to her Red Cross insignia as she leads him out to freedom.

More significant however is the preparation of a definitive Security Council resolution, designed to set firm limits on the ability of Iraq's regime to pose a future threat to the region's security. There is a huge field to be covered here – reparations, a peacekeeping operation, border demarcation, elimination of weapons of mass destruction (including a nuclear programme which turns out to be more advanced than we had assumed), repatriation of detainees, economic and oil sanctions; no wonder the draft resolution comes to be known as "the Christmas Tree" as more and more stipulations are hung upon its branches in New York. It all involves much liaison with the Saudis. One evening I happen to be going through its ingredients on the telephone with Prince Saud when I am rung from London on another line about the sale of a painting at auction. Overhearing the subject of the London call he suggests with a characteristic touch of humour that I deal with it first and ring him back; "Your picture is more important, ambassador." A nice sense of proportion.

* * * * *

Tom King, together with the Chief of the Defence Staff, David Craig, hastens out to congratulate the victorious troops. Tom and Peter de la Billière have at times found themselves treading on each others' toes, though I have found him giving every support to our cooperation with the Saudis. We have a useful session with Prince Sultan who urges an early withdrawal of our forces' ever-sensitive presence in the Kingdom while still maintaining a watch in Kuwait. There are however worrying indications of an intention in Whitehall to pull our fighting troops out of the theatre in quick order. These are confirmed when the Prime Minister drops in on Tom King's heels. Buoyed up by an enthusiastic welcome from the troops he sees up in Kuwait and in the Kingdom, John Major is moved to announce an early withdrawal. A most friendly meeting with the King in his private villa in the Riyadh palace grounds, albeit delayed into the small hours of the morning which tries a weary prime ministerial patience more than a bit, demonstrates how in the afterglow of victory relations between our two countries are as close as they have ever been. There is much talk of future cooperation, and despite his country's depleted coffers King Fahd makes a munificent contribution of $1 billion towards Britain's campaign expenses – the prompt transfer to London of this uncovenanted deposit manages to catch the cashiers in the Old Lady of Threadneedle Street off balance. Our shared hopes are high that the unrest now emerging within Iraq will complete the job with the overthrow of Iraq's tyrannical regime, though the King asks for our help in discouraging the Iranian government from unleashing into the south the bands of vindictive Shi'a refugees to whom it has been giving shelter. Regrettably our appeal to Iran falls on deaf ears and the bloodthirsty vengeance of these irregulars plays a part in turning back the tide of revolt and enabling Saddam Hussein to restore his throttlehold over his tortured country.

John Major's aircraft gets in to Dhahran before dawn in a torrential downpour. With Peter de la Billière I take him on to the Royal guest house for an hour or so's rest before a Hercules takes him and the inevitable press contingent up to Kuwait. With the time of departure approaching and no sign of the Prime Minister I find him in his room pondering what shade of pullover to wear for his visit to troops and a call on Kuwait's Crown Prince Saad. Having helped get this point out of the way I hasten him down for a bite of breakfast. It comes as a shock two weeks later to see our personal conversation on this sartorial point lampooned almost word for word in *Private Eye*. Clearly whichever journalist has invented this piece has made a remarkably close study of their subject's sensitivity over appearance. In the back of my mind there is an uncomfortable feeling lest someone in No.10 suspects I had a hand in the story.

The Prime Minister's jumping of the gun with his assurance to the troops that they would soon be back home sets a cat among the pigeons at our end. I get an earful of appeals from Saudi leaders, including Crown Prince Abdullah, not to pull out all our force from Kuwait before any danger of renewed action by Iraq's military, still partly intact, has been removed. Moreover it is plain that to leave the field at this uncertain stage, and with American and French forces staying on to secure the ground, will mean throwing away all the goodwill we have gained in the area by our full participation in the crisis as well as the economic dividends to be gained from the task of reconstruction; it just makes no sense. We go into high gear to try to get the decision, in which I suspect the Treasury's bean counters have a hand, reversed, with telegrams to the Foreign Office and direct appeals to the stream of visiting generals, and even the House of Commons Defence Committee when they suddenly turn up, led by Michael Mates. It comes as a huge relief to hear in late March that our lobbying has worked and that a battle group will stay on until it can be relieved by a fresh battalion. Specialist troops will also remain to help clear up spent and live munitions from the battle zone – a case if ever of Lewis Carroll's "seven maids with seven mops".

* * * * *

The change of heart has its consequences however, as I find when, with Peter Sincock and one of the protection team, I fly up in the army's little Islander to see Michael Weston, reinstalled in the embassy in Kuwait. As we set out I hear that the brigadier commanding 4 Brigade, Chris Hammerbeck, wants me to stop off with his troops in order to speak to the luckless band of soldiers whose lot it is to stay behind; apparently there is considerable unhappiness about. As we fly north the desert's surface in the border area is smothered with tank tracks and dotted with the hulks of Iraqi armour. We come down on a makeshift strip where Hercules aircraft are busy loading troops for the flight home. Chris Hammerbeck takes us to a bivouac camp among the dunes where the soldiers forming the battle group are sitting in a circle – a company of the 3rd Fusiliers, mostly Tynesiders, as well as some cavalry and gunners. Their mood is clearly dejected, even resentful; apparently some of them only got the order to stay as they were embarking for home. He introduces me as the ambassador who is responsible for their having to remain. Thanks for nothing, Brigadier – well, here goes.

I stress to them that the job they have been doing so well is not yet over. Iraqi units remain not far to the north and Kuwait's security cannot be assured until a full ceasefire is in place. To leave the field now will be to throw away all they and their comrades, some of whom have not survived, have put in to the battle. They are now needed to play a part in a defensive screen, at least until other troops can be sent out to replace them. "In short," I say "we have to leave some teeth behind, and you are those teeth." There is an awkward silence, and then a diminutive fusilier gets to his feet and says, in a broad Newcastle accent, "Sir, tha says us 'as to leave some teeth be'ind. Weel," taking some object out of his mouth and chucking it down onto the sand, "ther's me teeth and I'll bide wi' 'em." His grand humour breaks the spell and we all share a friendly brew of tea. I could hug that wee Geordie.

The next stop is Kuwait airport where cratered runways are being brought back into service. On the way we fly low over the "highway of death", a graveyard where miles of military and civilian vehicles lie abandoned in the defeated Iraqis' headlong flight north. Kuwaitis are starting to pick up the pieces in their battered and looted capital. The rich treasures in the museum have been carried off to Baghdad. It is said that the occupying Iraqis ate most of the beasts in the zoo, though the elephant proved a meal too far and curiously they spared a Highland cow. Ironically in a post-war gesture of gratitude to Britain a generous and timely donation by the Kuwaiti government will save London Zoo from the threat of closure. We find Michael Weston on good form in the embassy where lunch is punctuated by explosions as engineers clear Iraqi ordnance along the nearby seafront. On the return leg the Air Corps pilot takes off through a choking cloud of black smoke rising from a veritable inferno of flaming oil wells – an experience never to be forgotten.

* * * * *

Peter de la Billière and the other commanders lose little time in departing for home, their job done. There are mutual exchanges of honours and decorations. The award to General Khaled bin Sultan of a knighthood in the Order of the Bath is well merited, though the archaic title of this honour is going to call for careful explanation in Arabic lest it gives rise to perplexity or even derision. Other key Saudis are awarded the Order of the British Empire; come to think of it here is yet another anachronism to confuse foreigners – what empire, they may well wonder?

Grania and I give a farewell dinner for our commanders, an emotional occasion with warm speeches, including one from General Schwarzkopf. Among the guests I find Jeremy Phipps, last met in Rio de Janeiro when he ran a training session for our erratic Brazilian protection team and now commanding Britain's Special Forces, to whose operations behind Iraqi lines Norman Schwarzkopf pays a generous tribute. Peter de la Billière seems surprised to learn that Grania and I are not also being relieved. "Not so," I tell him. "A war is all in the day's work for an embassy." Indeed Iraq is now in a state of turmoil. We watch with chagrin the brutal extinction of an uprising by Shi'as in the south, mindful of an earlier warning by Margaret Thatcher not to get our arms caught in Iraq's mangle, and turning a deaf ear to their appeals for support. Several thousand flee to a ready refuge in the Kingdom. In the north where a revolt by the Kurds is also being suppressed, an initiative by John Major leads to the provision of safe havens under international protection.

Saudi Arabia's military performance culminates in an unprecedented victory parade to which all her allies are convoked on a new airport near Dammam which has been providing a convenient base for US strike aircraft. The ebullient Prince Khalid bin Sultan, who has adroitly headed the Arab forces involved while successfully keeping his end up with the more experienced western generals, takes the opportunity to step down from his command. His profile has become rather too high for the Kingdom's muted political society; un-Islamic tee-shirts have appeared bearing his image in full battle kit and there are stories that he is even thinking of a Hollywood blockbuster on the crisis. An old friend from our Beirut days, the journalist Patrick Seale, has been engaged to write up his war story; he will make it a readable tale. The dynamic Prince Khalid is unlikely however to sit for long in the shadows.

Rightly the Foreign Office presses everyone to take a break. A tranquil week in Venice is our response and on to London, with batteries recharged, in time for the twins' twenty-first birthday, plus a conference in the Office to take stock of the whole crisis and connect with colleagues – Patrick Fairweather, David Gore-Booth and others – who have night and day been our trusted lifeline with Whitehall down in the depths of the old India Office. For all of us it has been an extraordinary, and exhausting, ten months.

Saudi Arabia (at peace again)
1991-1993

You can always tell a retired ambassador when he gets into the back of a car and nothing happens

Foreign Office chestnut

P redictably the war is having its impact on the Kingdom, bringing out
pressures for change from both liberal and conservative opinion. There
is unprecedented debate about wider consultation on political and social
issues with some looking to western models of an open society and others
seeking refuge in a stricter application of religious orthodoxies, a harbinger
of pockets of Islamist extremism which are starting to be exported out of
Afghanistan's violent rejection of Soviet domination. Meanwhile much of
daily life returns to its singular pattern. Social behaviour is once again being
monitored by the religious police, who have reappeared on the streets making
an officious nuisance of themselves after their enforced rustication during
the hostilities. Public executions by decapitation, which had been suspended
to take account of the sensitivities of western allies, resume for capital offences
in accordance with the Kingdom's strict application of *shari'a* law.

The King and his close family are meeting these conflicting currents with
their habitual caution. I attempt to bring the new strands together in a
despatch to the Foreign Secretary under the title "Never the same again".
When Douglas Hurd comes out a couple of months after the ceasefire, we
find King Fahd pondering over how far reform can safely be taken in a
society that has not yet emerged from a chrysalis of political infancy. To
open the door to popular democracy too precipitately risks putting the

country's destiny in the hands of a backward-looking clerical elite, a point I try to stress to the Liberal Party leader, David Steel, who is among our stream of post-war visitors. "Look at what has happened in Iran," says the King to us, making an exaggerated gesture of a lengthy beard. Yet he sagely takes advantage of his country's post-war mood to come out within a few months with a new basic law that opens the way to a National Assembly.

The end of hostilities brings no let-up in the pace of diplomacy – rather the contrary, including much unfinished business with Iraq where an unrepentant Saddam Hussein is very much back on top of his midden heap. It is a rewarding time however as our cooperation with the Saudis, infused with a warm spirit of shared endeavour, has probably never been closer; there are moreover dividends to be sought on certain business and consular fronts. Douglas Hurd and I find King Fahd in buoyant spirits and taking a well-deserved break from the pressures of the war in a secluded villa on a little island some miles up the coast from Jedda; the tidy house is dwarfed by the silhouette of the royal yacht, the size of a small liner, moored just offshore. The King has indeed played an inspired, and exhausting, role for a seventy-year-old in contriving to hold together a disparate and precarious international coalition to fight a war. We arrive a bit sore as, seeking exercise while we await the royal summons, the Foreign Secretary has insisted on passing the time with a swim off Jedda's spectacular coral reef. Disregarding a sand-filled wind and choppy water some of us feel obliged to join him; just as well as we all get caught in a current and have a struggle to get the minister and ourselves back to shore. The delicious royal carrot juice puts us right however. Palestine comes high on the agenda with discussion of how a significant shift in the Palestinian leadership towards more moderate elements, which has resulted from Iraq's defeat, can be turned to advantage, a process which will culminate in a watershed international conference in Madrid that autumn.

I fly back to Riyadh to deal with the next visitor while Ali drives the Rolls back over the long desert road at a more sedate pace. Or so I think until I am asked discreetly by someone in protocol about a report that the car has been seen parked just outside the main gate of the Grand Mosque in Mecca. This has naturally raised some Muslim eyebrows; could the British ambassador have somehow slipped into the Holy City unnoticed? Having unruffled the religious feathers, I search out Ali who admits that he did take the opportunity en route to stop off in Mecca to perform the minor pilgrimage of *'umra* around the *ka'ba* shrine in the mosque's great courtyard. A sanctuary guard, impressed by the Rolls, had invited him to park by the front door.

* * * * *

An early visitor is Michael Heseltine, the Environment Secretary, here to see for himself the operation to clean up Iraq's wanton release of oil from Kuwaiti terminals into the northern part of the Gulf. The British government has made a generous contribution to the work. As we fly up the coast in a Saudi coastguard helicopter we get a bird's eye view of the great slick that mercifully failed to drift south as far as the crucial water desalination plants at Jubail. Men are busy hosing down acres of oil-coated mangrove swamp and the crude is being pumped from the water's surface into cisterns excavated out of the desert sand, from where it will be taken off to be refined; it seems nothing is to be wasted. Cormorants are back along the shore – many have been rescued and cleaned by the expatriate team we had helped to organise. We even spot a huge turtle swimming towards a nesting beach. It is all most encouraging and a credit to the Saudis, as Michael Heseltine tells Prince Sultan when they meet back in Riyadh and renew an acquaintance formed years earlier as ministers of defence.

David Howell, an old friend from Cambridge days, is next on the carousel, leading the House of Commons Foreign Affairs Committee. They see Prince Saud and the astute Finance Minister, Mohammed Aba al-Khail, with whom they engage over some of the more querulous strands of public opinion that are emerging. Hot on their heels comes Tom King again, back to see how the withdrawal is going and to discuss future security in the region. I am still tussling with differences in Whitehall over keeping back some fighting troops in Kuwait while a formal ceasefire is still being negotiated in New York; both Saudis and Kuwaitis are pressing for this. After seeing Prince Sultan, Tom King accepts that the Royal Anglians should stay in theatre for a bit longer in the stifling summer heat. The Royal Navy's patrol in the Gulf to enforce sanctions is also to be strengthened. One morning I get a telegram out of the blue from the commander of a Japanese Navy minehunting flotilla that has found its way to the Gulf. It contains in flowery English a request to work under the supervision of the Royal Navy's mine-clearance operation – given our maritime confrontations of the not

262

too distant past this surely marks an historic turn in our naval history. In Jubail we watch British armour being back-loaded onto vessels together with an imposing haul of Iraqi trophies. Tom's visit coincides with our farewell to Ian Macfadyen and the rump of the British headquarters. It will be strange not to have them down the road – and I shall miss the handy jet.

We all remain preoccupied with future Gulf security. A defiant Saddam Hussein is becoming engaged in a prolonged and repeated game of cat and mouse with the UN inspection teams, deputed to search out Iraq's suspected stocks of mass destruction weapons including biological and chemical agents and nuclear programmes too. Despite outright attempts at concealment they are starting to uncover more Scud missiles with launchers as well as a frightening arsenal of chemical and biological weapons which could have been used in the conflict, and even an advanced nuclear enrichment programme. Time and again over the coming months Iraq's recalcitrant leader will try to defy the inspection operation by blocking access and even their flights, while holding his people to ransom through spurning United Nations proposals for limited oil exports and the import of essential goods. As 1992 opens tension rises to a point that justifies moves towards military reinforcement by the Americans and ourselves. We dust down our warning drill for the British community, now back to its pre-war strength and succeeding by and large in keeping on the right side of Saudi Arabia's puritanical code of behaviour. This time there is no tremor of alarm; the attitude is even blasé as once again the show of strength prompts the despot to climb down for a spell.

* * * * *

The return of peace affords a postponed chance to get around the Kingdom with all its variety and rich historical heritage. Down south in Najran, sandwiched between the vast sands of the Empty Quarter and the ill-defined and sensitive frontier with Yemen and with its own distinctive architecture dating from the time when it was a staging post on the important frankincense trade route to Egypt and to Rome, Grania strolls in a jasmine-scented garden with the gentle and pious wife of the governor who tells how her spare hours are fulfilled with reading the Qur'an. We have a fascinating visit to the nearby ruins of Okhdood, a rare pre-Islamic Christian settlement destroyed in the sixth century by the Jewish rulers of Yemen. Legend has it that the population were herded into a great ditch beside the walls, where the remaining stones still carry Christian symbols, and were slaughtered there. The place has an eerie feeling; even Grania's camera refuses temporarily to function while we pass by. A long drive takes us on to Abha in the Asir by a road that winds along the mountainous and porous border with Yemen. Every village has its tall watchtower and houses of stone with windows etched in white. A heavy monsoon downpour has the streams flowing in spate. It is a world away from the baked-mud dwellings of Nejd and of Qassim, the religious heartland of the austere Wahhabi creed that is the cultural hallmark of the Kingdom's devout society, and where expatriate nurses employed in the local hospitals tell us they come to Riyadh for their recreation, which is saying something. There is also the weekly bedouin market at Ramah, deep in the sands a couple of hours' drive from Riyadh, where hobbled dromedaries await buyers and the women sell bright woven rugs and water bags made from goat bellies. Weekend expeditions include forays in 4x4 vehicles into the sands west of Riyadh where one's desert-driving skills are put to the test to crest the steep red dunes. Finely worked arrowheads can be found in their wind-scoured lee by those with sharp eyes; traces of prehistoric hunter-gatherers who inhabited Arabia before the desert took over.

Other trips include the old fishing and pearling port of Qatif on the Gulf, a centre of the Kingdom's Shi'a community dominated by the tower of a fortress built by Portuguese mariners way back in the 16th century. Archaeological digs along the Gulf's coastal salt flats are starting to reveal fascinating relics of the Dilmun period, a trading civilisation that inhabited these shores as early as 2000 BC. On a trip across the causeway to the island of Bahrain to pay a post-war call on her Ruler, Sheikh Issa, we stop to visit an extensive site of intact Dilmun burial mounds which are being excavated by a team from London University. At weekends the 16-mile-long bridge carries a stream of expatriates over to the island for a thirsty break from Saudi Arabia's temperance environment. The diminutive Ruler – the Saudis have a joke that he is kitted out by Mothercare – is ever a staunch ally to Britain and has had RAF and other coalition aircraft based in Bahrain during the crisis. He expresses a concern over the future ambitions in the Gulf of Iran's Shi'a theocracy. On one visit to the Gulf coast the head of the railway company offers a ride back on the daily trans-desert express from Dammam to Riyadh – and in the comfort moreover of the royal coach, which needs the occasional run. Nick Cocking and I accept with alacrity. The coach, with its furnished lounge, double bedroom, bathroom with gold-plated brassware, and even a bar (with not a hint of a bottle), sweeps us in comfort amid a cloud of sand-blasting density through miles of oil fields and on across the desert wilderness, while an attendant plies us with glasses of sugary tea.

Shuttling between Riyadh and the villa on the Jedda compound continues to be part of the scene as Saudi personalities flit back and forth. We sometimes combine these with family breaks down on the coast including parties in the beach houses of Saudi friends and launch trips out to reefs where the colours of the coral and the shoals of tropical fish are spectacular. One does however need to keep a wary eye out for roaming sharks. It is always a pleasure, and informative, to share a *shisha* hubble-bubble pipe with Khaled al-Maeena, the editor of a major newspaper, and his wife, Samar, a champion of the emancipation of Saudi women with her own programme on the radio, and to enjoy the hospitality of the Ali Reza brothers and their families within the walls of their elegant compound. As Saudi society starts to relax post-war some good fish restaurants are appearing along Jedda's handsome seafront, now surprisingly embellished with pieces of modern sculpture. They make a welcome change from Riyadh's spartan and segregated eating houses.

There are strange encounters too. One evening when we are enjoying a family dinner in a peaceful corner of the old city the restaurant's Moroccan proprietor introduces me to a pale-faced man in full Saudi costume who has been reading *The Financial Times* at a nearby table. He produces a visiting card with the name N.F. Parker, together with an Arabic Muslim name Ali Servant of the King, and the surprising address of London's distinguished Athenaeum Club. He turns out to be a relic of the romantic military support given to Yemen's royal family by a force of former SAS irregulars raised by a buccaneering Conservative MP, "Billy" McLean, during Yemen's long civil war back in the 1960s between republican factions supported by Nasser's Egypt and royalist tribes retaining allegiance to King Badr. With the defeat of the royalists and escape of the King to a placid retirement in Kent, Parker had chosen to follow other royalist leaders into asylum in Saudi Arabia where he has remained ever since, on one of the dust heaps of history. Still he seems contented enough.

On one of our flights down to Jedda I narrowly avoid causing an airborne riot. Just as we are leaving the house in Riyadh the Pakistani housekeeper at the Jedda villa telephones asking us to bring with us some of our – illicit – bacon supply as his stock is low. I hurriedly grab a packet from the freezer and stick it in an inside pocket of my jacket. It should stay pretty well frozen for the three hours our door-to-door journey will take. From this point things start to go agley. Having boarded the Saudia Tristar it refuses to go, and we sit for what seems ages while mechanics in overalls and armed with spanners try to find the fault. Moreover it is mid-July and, without the air-conditioning system, the temperature in the cabin will soon melt an iceberg. To make the predicament worse most of the other passengers turn out to be pilgrims from Pakistan and India, and Saudis too, on their way to Mecca to make the *haj* pilgrimage which begins that very day. With the women in their white robes and the men already clad only in the ritual white *ihram* towels, they are in a high state of spiritual fervour. With their prayers and supplications reverberating around the plane, we start to feel conspicuous. As I sense the frozen packet next to my chest beginning to wilt, Grania exclaims with puzzled expression that she can smell bacon. "Impossible," I find myself saying, "surely not," while keeping my fingers firmly crossed, and adding a silent plea that the plane will hurry up into the cool sky. To be honest I do catch a whiff of forbidden pork, and can only pray that it will not reach the nostrils of our ardent fellow travellers. Grania seems by no means reassured and I button my jacket more tightly. In the nick of time, thank goodness, the fault is rectified and we trundle out to the runway. There is a crescendo of devoutness as the *hajjis* find themselves on the final leg of their journey to Mecca, accompanied by an access of relief on my part as currents of cold air start to disperse the offending aroma. To be quite safe it is only when we climb into the car that meets us in Jedda that with copious apologies I produce the now limp and fragrant packet from my pocket. It has been a narrow escape from what at one point looked like turning into the lynching of an ambassador.

The annual *haj* is producing a consular load for the office in Jedda as the numbers of British Muslim pilgrims swell year by year. This year brings its own problems when several of them are trampled to death along with hundreds of others in a stampede in one of Mecca's tunnels which connect the various stations of the pilgrimage. Ever conscious of their responsibility for managing what has become the world's largest outdoor event, the Saudis handle the aftermath of the tragedy with sensitive care. I am prompted to recommend to the Foreign Office that it would help us if in future years a

Muslim consular officer were to be attached to Jedda for the *haj* period (as had indeed been the custom of the old India Office nearly a century earlier). The suggestion is however smartly turned down – though it has since become established practice.

* * * * *

Particularly enjoyable are visits to Ha'il in the north, an historic mud-walled town that lies on the edge of the spectacular dunes of the Nefud desert with its hidden treasure of prehistoric rock carvings. Now a centre of irrigated agriculture, Ha'il was the former capital of the Al Rashid dynasty, arch-competitors of the Al Saud for control of central Arabia until they were finally subordinated during the First World War, with some assistance from Britain, by Amir Abdul Aziz, known as Ibn Saud and founder of the Kingdom. Various intrepid 19th-century British travellers in Arabia, the religious visionary Charles Doughty, the rugged explorer William Palgrave and the political radical Wilfrid Blunt with his artist wife Lady Anne Blunt, in search of Arab bloodstock to take back to their stud in Sussex, all found themselves held in semi-captivity there as infidels when they happened by.

Today the province is indulgently governed by Prince Muqrin, a half-brother of King Fahd. The prince is a considerable polymath – a former air-force pilot who returned to the cockpit to join in a few sorties during the air war, he has developed a deep interest in the breeding of desert crops in a laboratory attached to his official residence. He is also an astronomer with a complete observatory at his private farm amid the red Nefud dunes. The prince is a most hospitable host; with his family we share an Arab meal of delicacies spread out on a carpet, being careful to eat with our right hands while sitting with legs crossed, a position which tends to bring about acute attacks of cramp. The prince gets cheerful waves from passers-by as he drives us round the old town; out on the desert farm his young daughter takes the wheel. To the south of Ha'il we find the remains of one of the impressive rest stations built twelve centuries earlier by Queen Zubaida, consort of the Caliph Haroun al-Rashid of Baghdad, for the benefit of caravans on their way from Iraq to undertake the *haj* in Mecca and Medina. These waypoints with their stone-faced watering pools occur at frequent intervals along the length of the arduous pilgrim trail. We are also entertained with a bizarre fishing expedition to an artificial lake stocked with catfish. I am given a rod and a plate of fresh steak to chuck in as bait, but find there is no need to cast the line; instead a smiling oriental helper stands in the water in front of the jetty ready to grab one of the teeming shoal and impale it on my hook. To much applause I reel in fish after fish; never was there such a catch – if only all angling was like this. An evening is spent with the head of the Al Rashid clan, now a prosperous local farmer with large acres under irrigated cultivation growing wheat, and also peanuts exported to Britain. We take our repast with him and his elegant wife in sheikhly style, reclining on deep cushions in a brightly caparisoned bedouin tent. Grania turns out in what we call her Lady Anne Blunt kit – a tailored gown in the form of a Victorian lady's riding habit. It is much admired.

By happy chance I learn from Lord Lytton, a direct descendant of Lady Anne Blunt, that he has in his Sussex home a set of large paintings that she made during her epic journey on horseback to Ha'il across the northern deserts. They make a fascinating record of the age including an attack by a bedouin raiding party and scenes within the town, and deserve to be shown in the Kingdom. John Lytton agrees to lend them in a venture for which we obtain helpful sponsorship from the British Council and the Saudi-British Bank. With Clive and Ann Smith representing the Council we fly up to Ha'il for the opening of the exhibit which attracts a large crowd. An old sheikh, with beard piously dyed a deep henna red, is taken aback by the paintings with their sketches of the human form. "Did they have cameras back in those days?" he wonders to Prince Muqrin.

* * * * *

The best adventure takes a small group of us, civilian and military, for a week into the Hejaz mountain range in the far north-west to see the great rock tombs of Meda'in Saleh before proceeding by Range Rover and Toyota for some 200 miles through the sands that cover the old railbed of the derelict Hejaz Railway down to its terminus at Medina. Patrick Fairweather, who headed up the Foreign Office team during the war, has come out to join the expedition. The tomb chambers, with their monumental façades carved with a blend of classical and eastern patterns onto huge outcrops of golden sandstone, were the work of the Nabateans. This was a wealthy Semitic society that at the start of the Christian era controlled the northern section of the caravan route carrying precious cargoes of frankincense and myrrh from the shores of the Arabian Sea to the markets of the Roman Empire. Rock held a mystical significance for them and the oasis of Meda'in Saleh with its gigantic rock formations in the lee of the high Hejaz range became their second largest settlement after the fabled "rose-red" city of Petra, to the north. For the bedouin of today however the site carries a Qur'anic curse and its ruins are fenced in to protect them from zealous defacing; tourists moreover are discouraged by the powers that be with the result that only a fortunate few get to see these hidden splendours.

After camping through a clear night in a wadi bed of tamarisk trees amid the great rock boulders we explore the tombs scattered across the desert plain. As at Petra, though on a smaller scale, a narrow defile between high cliffs leads into a natural amphitheatre of rock which must have served as a centre of worship. Alongside the magnificence of its tombs Meda'in Saleh has a more modern treat in store in the shape of a derelict railway workshop within which stands a complete steam locomotive with firebox door open awaiting maintenance. It must have stood thus for over seventy years since the Arabian section of the line was closed following the series of dynamiting ambushes along its length, organised by British officers, and notably the legendary Col. TE Lawrence, who helped the tribal forces of Amir Faisal of the Hejaz to drive Ottoman Turkish forces out of western Arabia and the Levant in the final years of the First World War. The station buildings are fairly intact together with dilapidated wagons of which the timbers have long been looted by the bedouin for firewood. It amounts to a railway buff's dream. Here also stands a fort built in the 18th century by the Turks as a military garrison for the protection of the great annual caravan that, before the railway arrived, came by camel and on foot from Damascus and Turkey to celebrate the *haj* in Medina and Mecca. It was in this primitive keep that the uncompromising Christian wanderer, Charles Doughty, was held as an unwelcome guest by the garrison commander when he turned up in 1888 in the caravan in Arab disguise.

The three-day-run down the old line of rail to Medina brings us through the fertile oasis town of Al Ula, where a tidy new museum displays fascinating relics from the cliff tombs of a much earlier society, and on through spectacular mountain scenery. At times it proves a test for our sand-driving skills. At one point the carcass of a rusted locomotive lies on its side beside the railbed, precisely where it was blown off the track in an ambush by Lawrence of a Turkish military train. We find the incident described in detail in the copy of *Seven Pillars of Wisdom* which we have brought along. Indeed the whole trip is an encounter with military history. Every ten kilometres we pass stone guard-houses, their ramparts pierced by rifle slits for defence against bedouin raiders. In the ferocious heat of summer, conditions must have been infernal for the Turkish pickets within. At one halt a train still stands where it has been marooned for seventy years, blasted by wind and sand – a genuine ghost train. The terminus at Medina, now being restored, is off limits to us infidels as it sits within the *haram* precinct of the Prophet's Mosque. It is a treat however to pile into the modern Sheraton Hotel for a bath and a sleep.

✳ ✳ ✳ ✳ ✳

Riyadh has its entertainments too, though one has to look for them. The annual camel races at Janadriyah, a few miles outside the city, are an occasion for celebration with stalls offering all kinds of traditional wares, including that acme of Arabia's perfumes, the costly attar of roses that has for centuries been distilled from rose beds high on the escarpment above Mecca while the dawn dew still lies upon the petals. The races themselves can be a bit bewildering as the white racing dromedaries scuttle past the stand enveloped in clouds of sand with their diminutive jockeys clinging on for dear life. It is said the riders are young boys secured to their mounts with copious bands of Velcro tape. The Epsom Derby this year produces a win for Prince Fahd bin Salman, the Deputy Governor of the Eastern Province with whom I have had a close cooperation during the months of war. As it happens, his colt, Generous, is jockeyed to victory by one Alan Munro. The next day brings a nice personal message from London, "Thank you ambassador for winning the Derby for me." I only wish... Prince Salman, the much respected Governor of Riyadh, has talented offspring; another son, Prince Sultan, served as a crew member on an American space-shuttle flight, while a brother is a deputy to the influential Minister of Petroleum, the Kingdom's lifeblood, and another is studying for a doctorate at Oxford while also running some good horses on the British Turf. We later find ourselves sharing in a syndicate run by my trainer cousin with a greyhound at the Wimbledon dog track – no profit but fun all the same.

Saudi Arabia (at peace again)

Peter de la Billière comes out on a return visit, bringing his wife Bridget. General Khalid bin Sultan, his companion-in-arms, invites us all to his palatial estate amid the sands down on the Jedda road. This is quite a set-up. A landscaped garden which would have been the envy of Capability Brown, acres of irrigated wheat and barley, as well as a sheep station with the shearers imported from Wales and what is claimed to be the world's largest factory for quail production. The house itself is crammed with big-game trophies, stuffed into alarmingly lifelike poses among the sofas – a taxidermist's dream. The English butler who welcomes us in black tie and white gloves is a dead ringer for Jeeves. It all turns into a jolly family day. The post-war award by the British government of a knighthood in the historic Order of the Bath has clearly given the prince much pleasure, though the order's ablutionary title has taken some explaining; for an Arab it tends to conjure up images of corporal massage in steamy chambers. One evening we take our guests for a quail barbecue on the rim of the limestone Tuwaiq escarpment outside Riyadh. An old stone-flagged trail snakes down the cliff face to the desert below; it is hard to imagine that this was the roadway up which the army of the Egyptian general, Ibrahim Pasha, hauled its ordnance nearly two centuries ago on its campaign to capture and destroy Dira'iyya, the now ruined capital of the Al Saud and their legion of marauding Wahhabi tribesmen. In the gathering dusk the setting sun cloaks the dunes far below with golden shadows.

The summer following the war brings round our annual receptions to celebrate the Queen's official birthday. In Riyadh the Royal Anglians, now standing guard up in Kuwait, offer a display by their fifes and drums. We also acquire a brace of pipers from a Scots and an Irish regiment, only to find on the night that Scottish and Irish bagpipes are for some remote reason set in different keys and so cannot be played in tandem. Here is History mirrored in Music. At the reception down in Jedda a wary eye has to be kept out in case Idi Amin, Uganda's murderous ex-ruler whom the Saudis are obligingly keeping out of the world's way, should attempt to gatecrash, apparently still harbouring a fond delusion that he must pay his respects to his former sovereign.

* * * * *

Margaret Thatcher suddenly reappears on the scene when I am rung one morning by her son, Mark (he who once lost himself with a lady friend in

271

the Algerian Sahara), announcing that he will be flying in to the Kingdom with his mother in a couple of days' time for the purpose of seeing the King. He complains, none too graciously, that his long-distance contacts with officials in the Royal Diwan to set up the meeting have been getting nowhere and demands that I fix it. It turns out that the ex-Prime Minister is being jetted around the world by her son in a plane, provided by the Japanese finance house Nomura, to solicit donations to the newly established Thatcher Foundation from the wealthier of his mother's contacts during her time at the top. They are now in Brunei where the Sultan is taking good care of them. Saudi Arabia is the next stop.

What a way not to go about things. No wonder the Diwan officials feel they are being bounced. With some reluctance I agree to see what I can do at this very short notice. A call to the Foreign Office reveals that this is an entirely private venture and that they have no hand in the trip. For good order's sake however we should try to get the visit back on the rails. We contrive to rescue things, helped by the fact that King Fahd holds the former Prime Minister in a high personal esteem which has been reinforced by her forthright support over the Kuwait affair. As I am just off on a flying visit to London to join talks on the region's future which Prince Saud is to have with John Major and Douglas Hurd at 10 Downing Street, the Thatcher visit in Jedda is handled by Derek Plumbly along with Grania and his wife, Nadia. It is a relief on return to find all has gone well. When Grania takes Margaret Thatcher to pay a courtesy call on the King's senior wife and other ladies, the Saudis find themselves treated to a master class in basic economics which they follow with keen attention. The visit does however have its grubbier side. As Derek takes the party off to see King Fahd, Mark Thatcher remarks to Grania, "Time to pay up for Mumsie." Sure enough the King comes up with a generous donation to her Foundation.

* * * * *

Meanwhile a vengeful Saddam Hussein continues to be a pain to his long-suffering people, whom he holds to ransom by rejecting United Nations proposals to ease sanctions on essential supplies, and to the world at large by continually obstructing the work of the inspection teams engaged in uncovering and destroying Iraq's alarming arsenal of mass destruction weaponry, now revealed to include an advanced nuclear programme. Bouts of intensive harassment, met with renewed threats of military retaliation led by the United States, are followed by a climbdown – it is all becoming tedious. At the same time there is growing oppression of the Kurdish population in the north. A fresh crisis is created in the summer of 1992 with attacks from the air on villages in the marshes of the Euphrates delta where many from the large Shi'a community in southern Iraq have sought refuge. This violation of the ceasefire arrangements brings a proposal by the Americans with British and French support for the establishment of a "no-fly zone" across the south, to be patrolled by US and British aircraft. Suddenly we are back in war mode, negotiating with a hesitant Prince Sultan for the return of a Tornado squadron to Dhahran. As I am about to take a spell of leave the details are handled by Stuart Laing, an old Saudi hand who has taken Derek Plumbly's place. It is strange to have an RAF headquarters once again down the road but convenient to have the little jet back.

Defiant as ever the end of the year sees Saddam Hussein pushing his luck with further blocking of inspections plus violations of the newly delineated border with Kuwait, supervised by a UN observer force. Iraqi missile radars in the vicinity of the air patrols have also been activated. That our concern over where all this is leading is fully shared by the Saudis is made clear when Malcolm Rifkind, who has succeeded Tom King as Defence Secretary, comes on a visit. Patriot batteries reappear on the airfields and we go so far as to revive the warden system; once again our community takes it all in its stride. January brings a resumption of bombing raids by American and RAF aircraft on Iraqi missile emplacements with "smart" weapons. A frustrated Bush administration, now in its very last days, decides to go over the top with a major guided-missile and air attack on a suspected nuclear facility near Baghdad, a move with which neither we nor the Saudis are entirely at ease.

The show of strength does the trick with an announcement by the Iraqi leader in late January of a "ceasefire" and the unrestricted resumption, for a spell at least, of the inspection programme. The final raid however puts me on the spot when the RAF commander, Air Commodore Vaughan Morris, comes round in the evening to discuss the targets which have been allocated to his Tornadoes early next morning. Opening his aviator's map he points out an air-defence bunker that is to be destroyed. With concern I spy that this is located, no doubt deliberately, on the edge of the town of Al Najaf, one of the holiest centres of Shi'a Islam as the site of the venerated tomb of Ali bin Abu Talib, assassinated son-in-law of the Prophet Muhammad and regarded by Shi'as as the rightful caliph. The tomb with its mosque is clearly marked nearby on the map; it has already suffered damage at the hands of Saddam's army in his campaign against Shi'a insurgents. The town thus represents a highly sensitive target, particularly for Shi'a Iran; were a bomb to go astray the repercussions would be serious right across the Muslim world. Vaughan tells me no mention was made in the American briefing of the target's religious significance. This is not surprising, as this time round the US-led headquarters has no political adviser. Moreover the highly effective American ambassador, Chas Freeman, has recently been recalled and the new Clinton administration has yet to nominate a successor.

Vaughan explains how the need for the radar installation to be put out of action is crucial to the patrolling operation. He claims full confidence in his aircrews' skill. Having stressed the need for accuracy at all costs and that if in doubt the mission would be aborted, we agree it should go ahead; better perhaps not to worry the Foreign Office or High Wycombe, though we shall put the US commander, General Nelson, in the picture. When we meet again early next morning the Air Commodore is mercifully all smiles. Despite poor visibility the target was hit with precision and is out of action. A satisfied General Nelson confirms this to me from gun-camera pictures; he had been unaware of the sensitivity of the objective, "but I knew the RAF could do it." Phew, again!

* * * * *

This renewed aggressiveness on the part of the Iraqi regime leads the Saudis and their Gulf partners to consider strengthening their own defence capabilities. Discussions on the supply of a fresh batch of Tornado aircraft under the Al Yamamah programme which has proved its worth during the air war have however stalled. The aircraft order is every bit as important for Britain's defence industries as it is for the Kingdom's future security. Valuable new impetus is now provided to the negotiations by Jonathan Aitken, a junior Defence Minister who knows the Kingdom well through earlier business connections.

A late-night session he and I have with King Fahd opens the way to an impromptu visit by the Prime Minister, who interrupts a flight back to the UK from India a few days later for discussions with the King and Prince Sultan. At some point in the small hours of the night we take a break and

John Major asks where he and I can have a private word. When I suggest we retire to a cloakroom the King's head of protocol escorts us to a washroom bright with gilded plumbing where he politely stands by expecting us to perform our ablutions. Clearly the only way to avoid being overheard is for the two of us to closet ourselves in one of the WC cubicles. This the Prime Minister and I do, doubtless to our guide's surprise, and shut the door behind us. The space is a confined one. "Prime Minister," I cannot resist remarking, "this used to be called 'consenting adults in private'." I get a blank look; no point in pursuing the quip once I realise that nice Mr Major was not long out of short pants back in 1957 when the committee chaired by Lord Wolfenden produced its celebrated report leading to the decriminalising of homosexual acts between adult males (women had always been excluded from the legislation as a shocked Queen Victoria ruled that it simply didn't happen). Our busy night turns out to be a productive one however and opens an important new stage in Britain's association with the Saudi Air Force. My own considerable respect for the Prime Minister is raised yet further on witnessing the cool way in which he pauses between the King's banquet in his honour and our nocturnal talks to authorise a libel writ against a British journal over spurious allegations of an amorous affair with the female who handles the catering at No. 10. His confiding this over dinner to a sympathetic King Fahd prompts the monarch to comment with a chuckle to Jonathan Aitken that he hopes the lady in question was attractive.

* * * * *

Relations between our two countries are now as firm as they have been in a long while. There is shared concern over the chaotic situation in Afghanistan where rival *mujahideen* groups, some of which have been recipients of expedient, if ill-judged, Saudi and US subsidies, are fighting each other for supremacy. There are problems over what to do with young Saudi fighters, fired up with the extreme Islamist ideas of the renegade Osama bin Laden's emerging Al Qa'eda organisation and trained in the arts of guerrilla warfare, who are starting to return home. Many are being encouraged to move on to support their Muslim brothers in the civil war that is raging in Bosnia, a theatre in which their ill-disciplined zeal proves a thorn in the side of the United Nations Protection Force.

In early 1993 the Saudis convene a summit meeting in Jedda, chaired by King Fahd, of the Organisation of the Islamic Conference in a helpful initiative to moderate the more interventionist approach of certain Islamic states, notably Iran, to the Bosnia crisis. It is attended by David Owen and Cyrus Vance, acting as mediators on behalf of the European Union and the United Nations respectively and seeking support for the plan they have been painstakingly negotiating with the various protagonists to find a peaceful solution. As the UK happens to be holding the rotating European Union presidency I find myself a member of their delegation. Recalling the uneasy relationship I enjoyed with David Owen on African matters back in the Foreign Office fifteen years ago, it is welcome to find us in close harmony while the Saudis skilfully contrive Muslim support for the peace plan. It will be the Christian Orthodox Serbs who reject it soon after.

Meanwhile the embassy has plenty of new lines to pursue among which is the field of sports cooperation. Saudi youth has become football-mad, and Bobby Charlton comes out to do some coaching. A state-of-the-art covered stadium on the outskirts of the city resembles a galleon under full sail when seen from afar across the sands. On one big match day Grania happens to go into a pharmacy in search of Listerine, which brings the curious response that they have run out because of the football. Further enquiry reveals that young fans in pursuit of a "lift" prior to the match have discovered that the mixture contains an infinitesimal quantity of forbidden alcohol, and are prepared to drink it by the bottle in the hope of slight intoxication; at least it makes a change from Vimto.

The Saudi door is also creaking open towards political reform with a law establishing a National Assembly and regional councils as well as rules to regulate the succession. 1992 brings a celebration of the 60th anniversary of the Kingdom's foundation by King Abdul Aziz. The publicity is marked with a characteristically cryptic slogan – "Progress without change" – which just about sums it up. For the world's biggest family enterprise is starting to go public. Even the press is engaging in bolder comment on national issues. A visit from Westminster by the Minister of Agriculture, Baroness Trumpington, a lady large in size and in spirit and with her head covered at our suggestion with a stylish picture hat, gets a warm approval from Crown Prince Abdullah who brings her on television alongside himself to open the agricultural show, thereby neatly shedding another cultural taboo. Yet journalists still need to watch their step. A local English-language daily suffers official displeasure when its report on a meeting I have had with Crown Prince Abdullah is by mischance accompanied by a happy photograph of the Crown Prince with a small child sitting on his knee.

A greater break with the past is the establishment of diplomatic relations with a post-Soviet Russia and also with China, two states seen hitherto as homes of an atheist creed and as such beyond the Islamic Pale. One hopes the new Russian ambassador, Gennady Tarasov, is unaware that his only predecessor, appointed back in 1932 by a Soviet regime keen to gain influence at the heart of Islam as an extension of its rivalry with Great Britain in Asia's Great Game, was soon recalled by Stalin to face a firing squad. The ambassador and his elegant wife, Yelena, become our good friends. When she turns out to be a keen member of Robert Burns' Russian fan club we invite them along to the annual Burns Night dinner. My toast to the "immortal memory" is followed by a splendid recitation by Yelena of the bard's verses; it is a marvel to hear his Lallans dialect converted into mellifluous colloquial Russian. Our host, Don McClen, who has so skilfully led the British Aerospace team throughout the pressures of the war, wonders at how the world has changed as he finds himself presenting a Russian ambassador with a model of a British warplane.

* * * * *

The scenery is indeed changing, not least within the Kingdom itself where the shock of the Kuwait conflict has unleashed pressures for greater popular involvement in public affairs; voices seeking closer harmonisation with the ways of the outside world are offset by others calling for even stricter observance of Islamic laws and traditions. I use my valedictory despatch to the Foreign Secretary – the parting shot to which every ambassador is entitled – to point up, under the title "Islamic Revivalism; a Blighted Blessing", the risk of the intensive role played within Saudi society by a puritanical interpretation of Islam becoming a corrosive obstacle to change. As it turns out this insidious zealotry will shortly breed perpetrators of acts of terrorism, conducted under the fanatical banner of bin Laden's militant Al Qa'eda and directed not only against symbols of western influence, including the aerial attack on New York's twin towers eight years later, but striking at the authority of the Al Saud regime itself.

We have however passed four fascinating years in this ultra-pious and introverted, yet well-ordered country, making real friendships too. The war has brought us all so close. It is however time to look for a new existence outside the Service, for all the stimulus and familial embrace which it has given us over thirty-five rewarding years. Other posts are being suggested; they are bound to prove an anticlimax after the excitements of our Saudi existence. As Sir Ronald Storrs is said to have mused on transfer to become Governor of Cyprus after a turbulent tour in Britain's newly mandated Palestine following World War I, "There is no promotion after Jerusalem." Moreover there are indications that Britain's international outreach, and with it the role of the Foreign Office, is heading for another phase of self-imposed contraction and relegation. I also want to write an account of the Gulf War experience while it is still fresh in the memory; indeed Prince Saud urges me to do so, as he personally drapes a handsome green and gold ribbon around my neck to mark our tight collaboration. My warning that the story, while paying genuine tribute to the Kingdom's resolute role throughout the crisis, will contain warts as well is met with his soothing assurance that "we may ban it, but we'll buy it."

The weeks leading up to our April departure are much taken up with farewells around the Kingdom, from diplomatic colleagues, our replenished community, and many of the good Saudi friends we have both made. It being the fasting month of Ramadhan the Saudi gatherings take place in the early evening following the sunset prayers, and open with the ritual cup of coffee, with a ripe date held between the front teeth to sweeten the liquid as it passes into the mouth. Like so many Arab customs it takes a bit of practice. Prince AFT and his wife, Princess Hanna, see us off with a jolly picnic in a palm grove. My successor, David Gore-Booth, anticipates his arrival on scene with a bit of a challenge when the Foreign Office announces that he will be bringing a BBC television film crew with him to record for the British public his first weeks in office, and please will I get Saudi agreement to this course. Given the intensely private nature of Saudi culture, and not least their visceral suspicions of the British media, I put this novelty to Prince Saud with some unease. Predictably it leads him to raise an eyebrow or two, but no objection. My personal reservations however are not going to count.

As we prepare to leave, the regional scene looks unwontedly serene; islamist terror has yet to show its violent face. In a positive side-effect of the Kuwait crisis the damage to Yasser Arafat's image through his ill-judged support for Saddam Hussein and the consequential emergence of a more conciliatory leadership from inside the Palestinian territories, coupled with the fortuitous implosion of the Soviet Union, have provided new life to the Arab-Israel peace process to which both we and the Saudis are lending earnest diplomatic backing. A reflective despatch I have recently penned to the Foreign Secretary carries an optimistic label – "The Al Saud: Here Today – and Here Tomorrow". A minor flurry occurs when a call comes in the middle of one night from King Fahd's private secretary to say that his master is seeking British advice on whether Saudi troops should retaliate to an alleged incursion by Qatar into a Saudi border area on the Gulf coast. I sleepily suggest that this sounds a poor idea and go back to bed. It is a relief too to learn that I am not being summoned back to London to give an account of my part five years ago in the supply of certain components for Iraq's military arsenal to the public enquiry which a rattled government has set up under Lord Justice Scott – a case of a sledgehammer to crack a nut. I must have said the right things at the time.

It is satisfying to know that we are leaving the embassy with one helpful legacy; a concern on the part of our military during the war over the security of the compound against sabotage by agents of Iraq – a terrorist threat which will sadly become all too real with the spread of islamist fanaticism in the years to follow – has enabled us to take over and enclose a plot of waste ground adjacent to the residence. This has now been laid out as an English garden with space for the British community to hold their social events, including live music and well beyond the range of the peeled eyes and pricked ears of the custodians of virtue in the religious police.

* * * * *

Having no need to hasten back to a new appointment we opt to return home by eastabout stages, with the opportunity for a glimpse of the Orient and to visit a brother and a sister in Australia, and cousins strung across the United States some of whom I have not seen in half a century. Care needs to be taken in completing Australia's daunting visa application form. We certainly do not want to get caught up in the backwash of a recent sense of humour failure on the part of the Australian consul in Riyadh when a member of our embassy answers the question whether he had been charged with any offence with the flippant reply that he thought this was no longer a requirement. Understandably perhaps his visa is not forthcoming.

There are genuine backward glances as we fly off from Riyadh's all-too-familiar airport for the last time. First stop is nearby Bahrain whither Hugh Tunnell has moved on from Jedda to be ambassador. Together we go through old cabinets in his office to see if we can find one of those long-disused official forms for the manumission of slaves which we used to keep by when I was in Kuwait back in 1961. A dusty document eventually emerges which Hugh signs with a seal to signify our formal release from the bondage of HMG. Then it is on to Singapore (the world's cleanest public convenience as my Australian brother has dubbed it), and Hong Kong where an entertaining evening is spent at the colony's boisterous Happy Valley racecourse. Kangaroo meat and ginger in Queensland's outback are followed by winebibbing around Adelaide, ending up in stylish Sydney. Here we get a taste of the celebrated Australian disrespect for authority when a performance of *Sleeping Beauty* in the Opera House has to be danced to recorded music as the orchestra have decided to strike in protest at a curtailment of their parking facilities. The audience greets the management's apology, not with disappointment but noisy approbation of the wildcat industrial action. Hops follow to see cousins across the United States, ending up with an idyllic week in a house set deep in the woods of Cape Cod – a perfect finale.

And so it is back to the Thames, and withdrawal from diplomacy with its rich variety, its characters, intrigues, vanities, upheavals – and blunders too. Or perhaps not; new occupations beckon, involving advice on business and trade, and in higher education, plus some public speaking and a close engagement with the Red Cross and aid work overseas – yet all of them linked to places and peoples among which we have lived and worked. There is the book of the war to write too. The lands of the midday sun beyond Britain's shores are not going to release their hold.

"The dogs bark but the caravan moves on"
Al kilab tanbah, w'al qafila taseer

Index

Index